Becoming Brothertown

THE ARCHAEOLOGY OF COLONIALISM IN NATIVE NORTH AMERICA

Becoming Brothertown

Native American Ethnogenesis and Endurance in the Modern World

Craig N. Cipolla

THE UNIVERSITY OF
ARIZONA PRESS

TUCSON

The University of Arizona Press
www.uapress.arizona.edu

First paperback edition 2017

ISBN-13: 978-0-8165-3030-4 (cloth)
ISBN-13: 978-0-8165-3796-9 (paper)

Cover design by Miriam Warren
Cover image: Mrs. James Fowler (a Brothertown Indian) standing in front of her home, Brothertown, Wisconsin. Photo courtesy of the Wisconsin Historical Society.

Library of Congress Cataloging-in-Publication Data
Cipolla, Craig N., 1978–
Becoming Brothertown : native American ethnogenesis and endurance in the modern world / Craig N. Cipolla.
pages cm. — (The archaeology of colonialism in native North America)
Includes bibliographical references and index.
ISBN 978-0-8165-3030-4 (cloth : alk. paper)
1. Brotherton Indians—History 2. Brotherton Indians—Migrations 3. Brotherton Indians—Ethnic identity 4. Indians of North America—History—Colonial period, ca. 1600–1775 5. United States—History—Colonial period, ca. 1600–1775 I. Title.
E99.B7C57 2013
973.04'97344—dc23
2013007452

Publication of this book is made possible in part by a subsidy from the European Commission.

Printed in the United States of America
♾ This paper meets the requirements of ANSI/NISO Z39.48-1992 (Permanence of Paper).

For Kelly

Contents

Illustrations

Figures

Tables

Acknowledgments

AS WITH THE CONCLUSION OF ANY long-term, labor-intensive project, one naturally looks back to when it began to take stock of just how much happened in the intervening years. In the case of this project, I feel like an altogether different person than the one who began this research in 2006 and committed to writing this book in 2010. Upon the kind invitation of the series editors, I began writing this volume only a few days after defending my doctoral dissertation in the Anthropology Department of the University of Pennsylvania. I wrote while searching for a permanent job in academic archaeology. I wrote while teaching adjunct at the University of Massachusetts, Boston, and the University of Connecticut. I wrote while helping plan my wedding. I wrote in my old apartment in Somerville, Massachusetts, while teaching field archaeology in Uncasville and Montville, Connecticut, and while making the weekly commute from Somerville to Easton, Pennsylvania, after finding a job as a visiting assistant professor in the Department of Anthropology and Sociology at Lafayette College. I wrote as I moved my family across the Atlantic to take up a permanent lectureship in historical archaeology at the University of Leicester. I wrote while adjusting to UK higher education. Best of all, I wrote while my wife and I learned to be parents (admittedly a much longer-term, labor-intensive project!). Throughout this process I have had the privilege of relying on the friendship, strength, generosity, wisdom, and love of many extraordinary people. Although it is truly impossible to express what these people mean to me in a few pages, what follows is my most earnest attempt.

First, I offer my gratitude to all members of the Brothertown Indian Nation for allowing me the opportunity to work and learn with them throughout the course of this research project. Caroline Andler, who has an encyclopedic knowledge of and passion for Brothertown history, supported my work from the beginning. Pete Wilson worked in Brothertown cemeteries long before I became involved with this project, and his devotion to preserving his ancestors' grave markers was a constant source of inspiration. Courtney Cottrell's help with the initial stages of this project is also deeply appreciated. Darren Kroenke, Craig Cottrell, Dennis Gramentz, Rick Shadewald, Kathleen Brown-Pérez, and her husband, Ventura, and many others helped in a variety of ways. I thank you all and look forward to our future collaborations.

As an undergraduate and master's student at the University of Massachusetts, Boston, and as a doctoral student at the University of Pennsylvania, I had the privilege of working with a great group of mentors and advisors. I am particularly grateful to all members of my dissertation committee—Bob Preucel, Bob Schuyler, Richard Leventhal, Steve Mrozowski, and Steve Silliman—for taking an interest in this project early on and providing valuable feedback as I moved forward. Bob Preucel served as my advisor and dissertation chair. I have benefited greatly from the many conversations we had on theory and Native history. I thank him for supporting my work and for always lending a critical ear and a helping hand. Steve Mrozowski and Steve Silliman played a part in inspiring me to become an archaeologist in the first place. Steve Mrozowski gave me my first archaeological field experience at Sylvester Manor, and Steve Silliman introduced me to collaborative archaeology on the Eastern Pequot Reservation. I deeply value the advice, encouragement, and friendship that Bob, Steve, and Steve have provided over the years.

This research was funded in part by a dissertation improvement grant from the National Science Foundation (grant number 08144833) and a Marie Curie Research Fellowship from the European Commission. The University of Pennsylvania Department of Anthropology, the Penn Center for Native Studies, and the University of Pennsylvania Museum of Archaeology and Anthropology also provided financial support for this work. Any findings and conclusions or recommendations expressed in this material are those of the author and do not necessarily reflect the views of the National Science Foundation, the European Commission, or the University of Pennsylvania.

The actual fieldwork for the Brothertown Archaeology Project would have been much more difficult without the cooperation of Delmar Buechel, Courtney Cottrell, Brian Damiata, Kristen Fellows, Bill Fitts, Arleta Petty, Jordan Pickrell, John Steinberg, and Pete Wilson. I am indebted to local landowners and officials, such as Jim Bogan, Donald Burg, Robert Buschor, Nadine Damer, the Ecker family, Edward Gallagher, David Koester, Doug and Deb Marcelle, Eugene McLeod, Jim Meyer, Gib and Jerry Ortlibe, and David and Joan Petrie. For the general support and assistance at various stages of this project, thanks are also due to Jerry Burg, Julie Heuvelman, Philippa "Flip" Brown, Kevin McBride (who gave me a copy of Love's *Samson Occom and the Christian Indians of New England* before I embarked on this project), the Mashantucket Pequot Museum and Research Center, the Wisconsin

Historical Society, John Broihahn, Sherman Banker, Jennifer Kolb, the Hamilton College Archives, Katherine Collett, the New York State Archives, the Oneida County Historical Society, the Fond du Lac Historical Society, and the University of Wisconsin Green Bay Area Research Center.

I thank the University of Pennsylvania Department of Anthropology, the University of Massachusetts, Boston, Department of Anthropology, the Fiske Center for Archaeological Research, the Lafayette College Department of Sociology and Anthropology, and the University of Leicester School of Archaeology and Ancient History. My colleagues in these institutions have made conducting this research and writing this book all the more enjoyable. This work has also benefitted from my conversations and collaborations with my old friend and colleague Kat Hayes. Special thanks are due to Liam Frink, Aubrey Cannon, Allyson Carter, two anonymous reviewers, Kelly Ferguson, and Sarah Tarlow for offering useful comments on earlier drafts. Kelly Ferguson also carefully copyedited and indexed this manuscript. Of course, I am solely responsible for any shortcoming found within.

Last, I offer my gratitude to those who kept me sane throughout this experience by making me appreciate things other than archaeology: Bev, Jen, and Olive Bevilacqua; Lawrence, Rebecca, and Miles Brown; the Cipolla family; Jamie Cumming and Liz Mearkle Cumming; the Ferguson family; Dave and Claudia Leclair; Jeannie and Ray Minchack; Nate and Liz Newton; and Nick Sherman. I offer special thanks to Kelly, Maya, and Pete for the inspiration, love, and support they provide on a daily basis.

Becoming Brothertown

1

Occom's Doubts

THOUGH WITH A DIFFERENT VESSEL than many readers will envision, akin to most colonial histories of North America, the Brothertown story begins with a crossing of the Atlantic Ocean.

The ship in question, *London Packet*, arrived in Boston Harbor on May 20, 1768, after suffering eight long weeks of foul weather and stormy seas on its voyage from London. Among the sea-weary passengers rode a man named Samson Occom. He spoke fluent English, wore similar clothing, and exhibited many of the same manners and customs of his fellow seafarers, but he also stood out in several significant ways. To begin, he was a Mohegan Indian. But his reason for being aboard is what truly set him apart: Occom, an ordained Presbyterian minister, had just finished a tour of England during which he delivered hundreds of sermons and addresses and collected thousands of pounds in donations. With the encouragement of Reverend Eleazar Wheelock of Connecticut Colony and several other prominent religious officials in New England, he had set out on this journey in 1765 in hopes of raising funds to help spread the Christian message to his fellow Native American communities of southeastern Connecticut and the surrounding areas. Occom saw this project as absolutely vital for the survival of Native peoples in colonial New England (Cipolla 2010; Commuck 1855; Love 1899).

Following his return, however, the donations were put to use in ways he found wholly unacceptable. Wheelock took the funds and founded Dartmouth College in Hanover, New Hampshire, more than 300 kilometers north of the communities Occom aimed to save. In contrast to the original agreement, Wheelock also weeded out many of his Native students and came to focus largely on the education of white society. In the summer of 1771, Occom (2006g [1771]:99) voiced his unease with these changes in a letter to Wheelock:

> We told them [European donors], that we were Beging for poor Miserable Indians,—as for my part I went, purely for the poor Indians, and I Should be as ready as ever to promote your School according to my poor Abilities ^if^ I Coud be Convinced by ocular Demonstration, that your pure Intention is to help the poor helpless Indians, but as long as you have no Indians, I am full of Doubts.

A microcosm of the deep-seated tensions between Indigenous peoples and European colonists and settlers in the area, these doubts led Occom to further question his trust of white society and eventually scrutinize the place of Native peoples in New England. These deliberations brought Occom and other local Native leaders to seek a new strategy for the survival of their Native brethren.

They set to work reformulating a plan that Wheelock himself had suggested over a decade earlier, this time with an underlying theme of Native revitalization (Jarvis 2010). It involved heavy emphasis on the practice of sustainable, European-style agriculture, and—most important—physical removal from white colonists and settlers on the East Coast. During the early 1770s, Occom and his collaborators traveled between reservations and spoke with other communal leaders as they refined this plan, all the while garnering support (Belknap and Morse 1955 [1796]; Brooks 2006; Cipolla 2010; Cipolla and Andler 2007; Love 1899; Murray 1998a; Silverman 2010).

Although the American Revolution seriously hindered their progress, this new group began putting the plan into action in the mid-1770s. At that time, Narragansett, Eastern Pequot, Mashantucket Pequot, Mohegan, Montaukett, Niantic, and Tunxis peoples began to break away from their home settlements in Rhode Island, Connecticut, and coastal New York for a chance at starting over. These peoples embarked on a slow emigration approximately 400 kilometers northwest to Oneida Country in central New York, where they founded a new multitribal Christian settlement known as Brothertown (figure 1.1). Later, in the nineteenth century, the community relocated to the Fox River Valley of what is now Wisconsin, where the Brothertown Indian Nation remains centered today.

This book follows the Brothertown Indians and their predecessors across New England, New York, and Wisconsin, from the community's inception in the eighteenth century to the present day. Drawing on archival and archaeological data sets, it explores the ways Brothertown Indians negotiated their places in colonial society through the use of language, material culture, and space. In pursuing this goal, I develop a pragmatic approach to the archaeology of colonialism in Native North America. This perspective

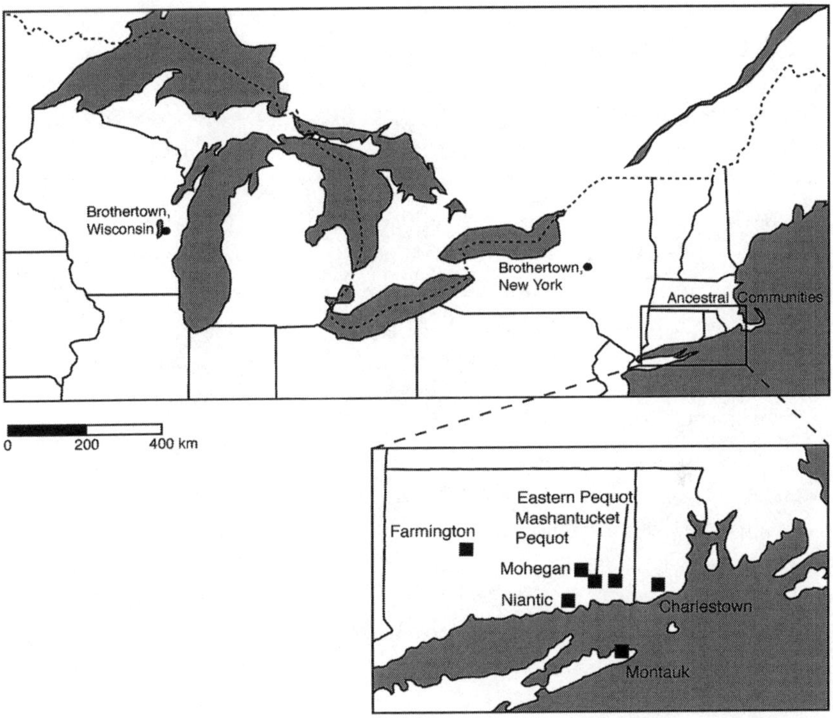

FIGURE 1.1. Locations of the ancestral communities and both Brothertown settlements.

functions both as a theoretical framework that complements and critiques existing interpretive models of colonial interactions and as a philosophy for archaeological practice. It works toward a deeper engagement with colonial culture of the past without losing sight of the interconnections between archaeological practice, identity politics, and descendant communities in the present. This framework tests certain limitations of archaeological studies of colonialism, challenging practitioners to reassess their understandings of the colonial past, Native American identities, the modern world, and archaeology in general.

Becoming Brothertown

The social, political, and economic backdrop that framed the ethnogenesis of the Brothertown Indian community ties directly to the reservation system, an epitome of the injustices and challenges faced by Native peoples in colonial New England. The English established the first reservations of Connecticut Colony in the mid- to late seventeenth century (Den Ouden 2005; McBride 1990a, 1993). By setting aside small tracts of the least arable land for local Native communities, colonists opened up additional lands for their own use while buttressing their control over Native populations (Cipolla 2008; Cipolla, Silliman, and Landon 2007; Den Ouden 2005:16–17). Although reservations were homelands—safe havens that Native communities continually fought to maintain—they came with many restrictions. The reservation system seriously limited tribal groups' subsistence practices, consequently transforming family and communal social structures. The forced sedentary nature of reservation life prevented regular access to seasonal fishing, gathering, and hunting grounds, and reservation soils were neither fertile nor ample enough to sustain entire communities. These conditions frequently led able-bodied men to leave their reservations in search of employment (Bragdon and Simmons 1998; Silliman and Witt 2010; see also Silverman 2001). They found jobs as laborers, soldiers, and sailors, most of which took them away from their families and tribes for months and years at a time. Reservation life and the constant struggles for land, resources, and community entailed within also fueled alcoholism within Native populations, only adding to these difficulties.

By the eighteenth century, the hardships of life in colonial New England had begun to open the hearts and minds of many Native peoples to Christianity. Influenced by this willingness to accept the Christian message, local white missionaries increased their efforts to spread the word of God to Native communities (Love 1899). Native converts found comfort in New Light Evangelism for several reasons. In the most basic sense, its denial of earthly possessions and promise of justice for the faithful made sense to those struggling for survival on reservations (Jarvis 2010:62–64). There were also many parallels between New Light Evangelical preachers and powwows, or shamans (Silverman 2010:46–53). Christian sects thus materialized on many reservations at this time, in some instances factionalizing tribal groups. During this general time period—often referred to as the Great Awakening—a young Samson Occom devoted his life to spreading Christianity to his Native brethren. For him, Christianity was the only viable option for revitalizing his people and surviving colonization.

Shared hopes of escaping the land politics and corrupting influences of colonial culture on the East Coast fused with Christian beliefs to create the seed of the Brothertown movement. Nurtured and energized by individuals like Occom and Joseph Johnson—another community leader highlighted in the next chapter—this seed grew into a new Native community, which eventually combined Algonquian, European, and, to a lesser extent, Iroquoian cultural traditions. The Narragansetts, Eastern Pequots, Mashantucket Pequots, Mohegans, Montauketts, Niantics, and Tunxis, whose descendants eventually identified as Brothertown Indians, chose to sacrifice the world they knew on the reservations of New England—often leaving behind family and friends—in pursuit of a brighter future and a new way of life in Oneida country.

Unfortunately, many of the nascent community's land concerns followed them out west (Cipolla and Andler 2007; Commuck 1855; Love 1899). The state of New York sold off large tracts of tribal lands in the early nineteenth century, further restricting Native communities and ushering in Euro-American settlers who repeatedly ignored property boundaries and encroached on Brothertown lands. Driven by these developments, the Brothertown Indians sought out new lands once again, relocating to current-day Brothertown, Wisconsin. Although this second move freed them from land troubles for a while, it was only a brief respite. Within a few years, the federal government passed the Indian Removal Act, which was an effort to force all eastern Native peoples farther west into Indian Territory, now Kansas. In an effort to hold on to their new lands, the Brothertown Indians petitioned for US citizenship and associated land rights (Brothertown Indians 1838). In 1839, they became the first Native American community officially recognized as US citizens (Loew 2001, 2003).

With citizenship came the allotment of Brothertown, Wisconsin, so the Brothertown Indians were required to divide their settlement into individually owned lots. Soon after allotment, there was an influx of German farmers looking to purchase land in the area. Combined with high property taxes and internal changes in the Brothertown Indian community, these new opportunities to sell their properties led some individuals and family groups to begin moving away from the community with which they and their ancestors had lived for eight decades in some cases. This dispersal rapidly increased as the nineteenth century drew to a close, spreading Brothertown Indians across the greater Midwest and beyond.

Largely based on the community's decision to become US citizens 170 years prior, the Bureau of Indian Affairs recently denied the Brothertown Indian Nation federal acknowledgment as an Indian tribe (US Department of Interior, Indian Affairs 2009). In contrast to the Bureau of Indian Affairs' findings, the Brothertown Indians continually maintained their community since its creation in the 1780s. Today, the Brothertown Indians have a tribal meetinghouse in Fond du Lac, Wisconsin, just over twenty minutes south of

Brothertown. The community continues to hold regular council meetings and communal events, elect officials, and participate in the ongoing archaeological research on their cultural heritage.

Pragmatism and the Archaeology of Colonialism

This book explores cultural entanglements of several kinds. First, it focuses on the theories used to reconstruct and interpret past colonial interactions in Native North America. It attempts to move beyond the standard set of dichotomies often lurking at the heart of such studies. Earlier generations of anthropologists and archaeologists conceptualized Indigenous and European practices and materials as rigid opposites. At the time, archaeologists primarily "read" European-manufactured material culture recovered from Native American sites as evidence for cultural change. More recent approaches are influenced by the recursive nature of practice theory (Bourdieu 1977; Certeau 1984; Giddens 1984; Ortner 1984; Sahlins 1985; see also Cipolla 2012b), recognizing the fluidity of social identities and asking deeper questions of the archaeological and historical records. The pragmatic approach developed in this book serves to further eradicate the dichotomous tropes that continue to haunt the archaeology of colonialism, such as those between Native American and European cultural essences, accommodation and resistance, and—of course—cultural continuity and change (Ferris 2009; Silliman 2009).

Some concept of culture undergirds all studies of colonialism in anthropological archaeology, no matter how vague or covert. Anthropologists initially conceived of cultures as relatively static and stable, uniformly distributed across their "bearers," physically bounded by land, and derived largely from isolation and adaptation to certain environments. Such unyielding models of culture are less than adequate for studying the modern, globally connected world. As European colonialism brought together peoples, practices, and materials once separated by vast distances of geographical and cultural space, colonial subjects—European, Indigenous, or otherwise—forged a shared colonial culture as they continually reproduced and transformed their respective cultural milieus in each others' presence (Gosden 2004; Hayes 2013; Loren 2008; Silliman 2009; Thomas 1991; see also Horning 2007). Rather than concentrating solely on the maintenance or decay of monolithic cultural essences in such contexts, I choose to focus on the emergence and endurance of a distinct communal identity *despite* the increasingly connected world (Gupta and Ferguson 1992, 1997) the Brothertown Indians shared with other groups. In the spirit of pragmatism, I explore the practical outcomes of these interconnections, considering the difference that shifts in Brothertown writing, commemorating, and settlement made for different members of the community and the larger colonial society of which it was a part.

Second, this book extends these themes to the present day, examining the continuities between the past and the present, between archaeological knowledge and archaeological practice, and between archaeologists and other stakeholders. I specifically target the interconnections between archaeological inquiry, the data it produces, and the broader social relations surrounding these practices and materials. The troubled history of archaeology in Native North America serves as evidence for the pragmatic effects the discipline has on communities typically situated beyond the walls of academia, many times intentionally. Over the decades, these effects forged deep, seemingly untraversable rifts between archaeologists and the communities whose ancestors they study (Thomas 2000). Yet there is hope. Seen in the burgeoning interest in decolonizing methodologies (Smith 1999) and in the emergence of Indigenous, collaborative, and postcolonial archaeologies over the past few decades (Colwell-Chanthaphohn and Ferguson 2008; Preucel and Cipolla 2008; Silliman 2008; Watkins 2000), archaeologists and Native communities have begun to repair these broken relationships. The resulting research is often dual in the sense that it takes influence from two or more stakeholders, typically archaeologists and descendant communities (Cipolla 2010, 2011, 2012c, 2013b).

I designed and carried out this research in collaboration with the Brothertown Indian Nation and members of other related groups, thus the methodologies and data sets discussed and analyzed in this volume are not those of a standard "below-the-ground" archaeology. The project originated as a standard archaeological survey of Brothertown, Wisconsin, but soon took an alternative form as I continued to interact with tribal members and integrate their perspectives. For these reasons (discussed further in chapters 3 and 8), all of the data presented and analyzed in this book come from above the ground, from either archival collections or cemeteries. In terms of the former, I collected data from archives in New England, New York, and Wisconsin, concentrating specifically on documents written by Brothertown Indians and maps depicting the two settlements. In terms of the latter, I located, mapped, and cataloged nearly all known Brothertown cemeteries. In total, this survey yielded data from thirteen cemeteries, five in the former

Brothertown, New York; four in or near Brothertown, Wisconsin; and four scattered throughout Wisconsin, ranging between 25 and 240 kilometers away from Brothertown. These data represent 344 Brothertown grave markers, which mark at least 394 graves dating between 1780 and 1910. For comparative purposes, I also collected data from other Native, European, and Euro-American cemeteries in New England, New York, and Wisconsin.

On the Negotiation of Brothertown History

Cultural formations such as the Brothertown Indian community are neither wholly Native nor wholly European but mixed responses to the cultural and social pluralities of colonialism. In such contexts there is always some degree of give and take between once-distinct cultural repertoires. In New England, individuals and groups often knowingly accepted certain changes to persevere in the new social and physical settings of colonialism. This frequently involved the admixture of the "traditional" with the "foreign," and the redefinition of each in the process. The Brothertown Indians clearly challenged and altered traditional Algonquian schemes of social and cultural organization as they appropriated European-introduced materials and practices, but they often did so to maintain their communal boundaries and *endure* the challenges of European and Euro-American encroachment. This process was contingent on different forms of discourse—in the form of words, things, and spaces, which they used to negotiate colonial politics (Cipolla 2010).

Culturally ambiguous names, practices, and materials were particularly important in these negotiations. As I discuss in subsequent chapters, the name "Brothertown" and the grave markers used in nineteenth-century Brothertown cemeteries were interpretable from several distinct cultural perspectives, allowing the Brothertown Indians to socially align their community with a number of disparate groups. In certain cases, the ways the Brothertown Indians constructed and communicated their identities helped maintain communal boundaries. However, these choices sometimes had unforeseen consequences. For instance, the commemoration practices and grave markers considered in this volume challenged dominant schemes of social classification, helping Brothertown Indians achieve certain goals, but they also played a part in the emergence of new understandings of personhood, individuality, and social identity within the community. These changes had pragmatic effects on the ways Brothertown Indians remembered their collective history and related to one another, likely influencing the choices of individuals and family groups who began selling their lots in Wisconsin and moving away from the community during the late nineteenth and early twentieth centuries.

Because the Brothertown Indians moved to foreign lands three times between the late eighteenth and early twentieth centuries, the negotiation of Brothertown history also involved landscape changes. As conceived in the broadest sense, landscape is the way actors experience their surroundings at any particular point in time; these surroundings are imbued with memory and therefore weigh heavily on the ways actors construct their identities (Basso 1996a; Ingold 1993). As groups dwell in new landscapes, their self-understandings and relationships with one another are subject to change. Once divorced from yesterday's landscape, they remember, they forget, and they sometimes choose to represent their histories and identities in a new light (see also Hayes 2011). Brothertown history provides the opportunity to explore the practical effects that continually starting "anew" in foreign landscapes has on communities. The archival analyses point to the importance of the first Brothertown settlement in forging the community, and also suggest that the community was no longer dependent on a shared landscape after the mid-nineteenth century. The cemetery patterns tell a slightly different story, speaking to the power of starting anew and reforging the materiality of a new settlement within the racial politics of nineteenth-century North America.

Social categories such as gender, race, religion, and class also played important parts in the negotiation of Brothertown history. They added texture to everyday life, determined communal boundaries, and at times cleaved the community into factions. As found in other studies of colonial communities, the difference between Brothertown Indians and outsiders depended on a confluence of gender and race politics (see also Silverman 2010). Building on a strong body of colonial identity studies in archaeology, this work explores these interconnections between social identification, colonial politics, and cultural reproduction. Given the subject matter of this book, particular emphasis is placed on ethnic categories and ethnogenesis.

Organization of the Book

Chapter 2 elaborates on this work's pragmatic perspective. It situates this approach in relation to three major themes in the archaeology of colonialism: acculturation, identity, and decolonization. Pragmatism's foci on the practicalities of social action and the deep continuities inherent in social life build on and integrate components of each of these themes. As an interpretive framework, this perspective considers the linguistic, material culture, and spatial discourses analyzed here in terms of the differences that they made for Brothertown Indians and for the groups who interacted with them in the past. As a philosophy of archaeological practice, pragmatism also concerns itself with the relationship between archaeological research and descendant communities in the present. After introducing these dimensions of pragmatism, I consider other studies of ethnicity and ethnogenesis, outlining a pragmatic approach to these social phenomena, particularly as they pertain to Brothertown history.

Chapter 3 provides an historical overview of the Brothertown Indians from the eighteenth century to present. Drawing largely on historical and ethnohistorical accounts and syntheses, it establishes the general backdrop for this particular study of Brothertown history. In this chapter, I also discuss the ways the Brothertown Archaeology Project took shape as I interacted with different stakeholders.

Chapter 4 focuses on documentary analysis. Although the tribal groups who formed the Brothertown community originally communicated via Algonquian dialects, they eventually came to speak and write in English, leaving behind a rich documentary record (Brooks 2006; Cipolla 2012a, 2012d; Murray 1998; Schneider 2003). From a purely methodological standpoint, this allows a rare insider perspective on Brothertown history that can be used to complement and challenge extant ethnohistorical and archaeological records. From a more theoretical standpoint, however, it offers glimpses of appropriated (English) language from the pens of Native authors writing as early as the eighteenth century, sometimes directly in regard to their identities as Native peoples.

The chapter begins with a theoretical discussion of textual artifacts, situating the present approach within historical archaeology and anthropology. This pragmatic approach treats historical documents as past speech acts, analyzable not only in terms of what they say but also how they say it. I analyze a collection of documents written by, to, and about the Brothertown Indians in the eighteenth and nineteenth centuries, focusing on modes of referencing the community, particularly the genesis and negotiation of the name *Brothertown* as it occurred in written dialogue between Brothertown Indians and outsiders. I also examine instances in which Brothertown Indians intentionally manipulated texts to align their community to different addressees, navigate colonial politics, and achieve certain goals. Altogether these documents demonstrate the fluidity and dialogic aspects of social identification while offering unique perspectives on the agency of a group of Native American authors in the eighteenth and nineteenth centuries.

In addition to these linguistic changes, the Brothertown Indians also rapidly incorporated a breadth of European-introduced practices and materials as they negotiated their identities and made their places in the modern world. The next two chapters focus on these changes as observed in Brothertown cemeteries. Chapter 5 begins with seventeenth-century commemoration practices in Native New England and goes on to examine the cemeteries and grave markers of eighteenth- and nineteenth-century Brothertown, New York. Chapter 6 analyzes nineteenth- and early twentieth-century cemeteries in and around Brothertown, Wisconsin.

Between the eighteenth and twentieth centuries, the Brothertown Indians dramatically transformed their commemoration practices, replacing blank, handmade grave markers with text-bearing gravestones purchased from professional stonemasons. Given current disciplinary concerns over the agency of objects, such a shift in materiality presents an opportunity to assess the social, cultural, and political effects of these appropriations, both intended and unforeseen. I explore these pragmatic repercussions in terms of both intra- and intercommunal dynamics.

Chapter 7 analyzes historic maps to interpret Brothertown settlement patterns. Taking a reflexive approach, I recognize these patterns as the result of short-term or momentary decisions structured by personal preferences for certain landscapes features and neighbors, the results of which indexically link to intracommunal social relations. In particular, I examine spatial relations between families descended from different tribal groups through time as a means of gauging the shifting importance of ancestral tribal affiliations within the Brothertown community. I also juxtapose these patterns with uses of space in Brothertown cemeteries, investigating the link between social relations in everyday life (i.e., residential patterns) and representations of social life (i.e., in Brothertown cemeteries).

Chapter 8 concludes by tying together the linguistic, material culture, and spatial patterns uncovered in each of the preceding chapters, discussing the broader implications of the Brothertown Archaeology Project.

2

Pragmatism and the Archaeology of Colonial Ethnogenesis

> I am, kind friend, an Indian of the Mohegan tribe, known by the name of *Joseph Johnson*, and at present I am Employd by the Honorable Board of Commissionaries at Boston, in teaching Children. I keep a School at Farmington amongst my Indian Brethren, and it is to be hoped that I maintain a good Character both among the English and also, among my brethren, as perhaps, kind friend, you might easily be Satisfied, if you Enquired a little of my Character, where I am known.
>
> —Joseph Johnson (1998a [1772–73]:178)

IN WRITING THE LETTER EXCERPTED in the epigraph, Joseph Johnson—then a nascent leader in the Brothertown movement—aspired to raise funds for his school among the Tunxis Indians of Farmington, Connecticut. Like all people enmeshed in colonial contexts, Johnson continually refashioned his identity in relation to the "foreign" peoples, ideas, and regimes of power that surrounded him in eighteenth-century Connecticut Colony. Explicit statements on identity combined with other, more nuanced signs to shape the ways society categorized Johnson. Conversely, Johnson adjusted the ways he presented himself to different addressees depending on his particular goals in addressing them and his understanding of their respective cultural backgrounds and social positions. A master of several social registers, Johnson danced between white and Indian worlds as he wrote, constructed his identity, struggled to help his "Indian brethren," and played a part in reproducing the complex culture of colonial New England.

There are a number of contrasting positions from which to interpret the excerpt from Johnson's letter. Polarizing approaches focus on the cultural origins of practices and materials in such contexts, yet pay little attention to long-view perspectives on colonial histories. Common in early archaeologies of culture contact and colonialism, these views divided colonial worlds in terms of cultural essences or different pieces of evidence supporting either cultural change or cultural continuity. In this narrow light, Johnson's explicit claim of Indian-ness is somewhat negated by the fact that he made it by writing in English. Among the many interpretive hazards associated with this general stance is the risk of reducing the complexities of colonialism in favor of reified cultural stereotypes. There is no reason to assume that—after more than two and a half centuries of colonial entanglement in North America—people like Johnson and his contemporaries simply conceived of their surroundings as partitioned into stable, neatly bounded categories of "Indian" and "European."

A more contextual approach considers the fact that Johnson, born in 1751, always lived in a world consisting of English colonists, reservation lands, and Christian Indians. In that world, the boundaries between Native American and European culture were quite blurry compared to early colonial encounters and situations of culture contact (Silliman 2005). Practitioners taking this approach acknowledge that colonial interaction always involved cultural continuities and cultural transformations of some sort. Instead of fixating on the European or Native origins of certain practices and materials, they might focus on the politics of difference within the shared culture of colonialism. For instance, as groups like the Mohegan and the English interacted, how did individuals negotiate social categories (e.g., Indian-ness) and communal boundaries, such as those created by the ethnogenesis of the Brothertown Indians? These questions transcend cultural essentialism to engage with the complexities of colonial culture and social identification in the modern world. In so doing, however, these approaches sometimes overlook or downplay the limitations of Native agency, resistance, and social navigation in the oppressive contexts of colonialism (Orser 2006).

This chapter outlines the contributions that pragmatism offers these various perspectives within the archaeology of colonialism, as both a theoretical framework for interpreting archaeological and archival patterns and a philosophy for archaeological practice. Combined, these facets advance efforts to decolonize the archaeology of colonialism by further articulating interpretations of the past with the contemporary peoples and the politics that surround them. In regard to Joseph Johnson, such a perspective focuses on the differences his actions made for the people around him (both Native American and European). Even a cursory reading of his letter shows that, like Samson Occom, Johnson adopted European-introduced practices and ideas in hopes of improving the conditions of life for his Indian brethren in colonial New England. A pragmatic perspective examines the ways Johnson's intentions compare to the results of his actions. It also considers the practical effects of Johnson's identity as a Christian Indian, assessing his influence on others' understandings of Native peoples, Christianity, and social categories in general.

This book concentrates on the differences that the Brothertown Indians as a whole made in the culture of colonial North America by constructing their identities and negotiating their communal boundaries as they did. The actions and identity discourses reconstructed and analyzed here had profound effects on the community, some of which continue to reverberate today. In addition to considering the practicalities of past actions and identity discourses, pragmatism also focuses archaeologists' attention on the differences that their own actions make in the world, particularly those that affect the descendants whose ancestors they study.

Historical Context: Acculturation, Identity, Decolonization

The pragmatic framework of this book builds on and interconnects three major themes in the history of archaeological studies of colonialism.

Acculturation and Archaeology

The first theme, *acculturation,* is perhaps the most influential concept in the history of archaeological studies of colonialism in Native North America. Although responsible for a majority of the polarizing approaches previously mentioned, this concept motivated much of the early research on culture contact and colonialism and has since inspired many important critiques. First used in nineteenth-century debates over citizenship and immigration in the United States, *acculturation* originally referred to the process that new citizens went through in the "melting pot," as they potentially lost touch with their cultural traditions (Cusick 1998a, 1998b; Rubertone 2000). These early uses framed cultural interaction as rigid, deterministic, and one-sided; they presumed that the erasure of previous cultural identities was inherent in the process of becoming American.

Anthropologists incorporated the acculturation concept during the second quarter of the twentieth century. In their "Memorandum for the Study of Acculturation," Robert Redfield, Ralph Linton, and Melville Herskovits

(1936) defined the term broadly as any type of cultural change that results from the interaction of different cultural groups. At the same time, Meyer Fortes also argued for the dynamism and creativity inherent in situations of culture contact. Although he did not use the term *acculturation* specifically, he framed culture contact "not as a transference of elements of one culture to another, but as a continuous process of interaction between groups of different culture" (Fortes 1936:53). In this light, Fortes focused on the maintenance of cultural differences in such interactions *despite* the exchange of ideas, practices, and materials that occurred therein. Notwithstanding the flexibility of these early anthropological definitions and applications, most studies of the time treated cultures and societies as homogeneous, discretely bounded entities, assuming that sustained contact between previously distinct cultural groups would always lead to a reduction in cultural differences (Jones 1997:53–54).

By mid-century, cultural anthropologists such as George Foster (1960) and Edward Spicer (1961, 1962) iterated the complexities of acculturative change through their research in Native North America. Spicer's work touched on the capricious relationships between material culture and Indigenous beliefs and practices. In some instances, he found that Native American communities had changed the types of material culture they used while maintaining traditional practices and beliefs. In other instances, however, he observed the opposite: communities that had dramatically transformed social structures and religious practices while retaining their traditional artifacts (Spicer 1961:542).

In spite of these observations on contemporary societies, early archaeological studies of acculturation reverted back to the roots of acculturation theory and leaned heavily on simplistic material essences to interpret past cultural interactions. Such studies took influence from George Quimby and Alexander Spoehr's (1951) article "Acculturation and Material Culture," which outlined a typology of historic-period Indigenous material culture housed at the Chicago Natural History Museum. The authors classified Indigenous artifacts based on the origins of their various components (e.g., form, raw material, technology, intended function). For example, a Chippewa rattle made with a tin baking soda can instead of the traditional gourd combined the form and function of a "Native artifact" with an "imported material" (Quimby and Spoehr 1951:136). The classificatory and quantitative nature of this work appealed to archaeologists, many of whom applied the typology uncritically (e.g., White 1974). They assumed that observed changes in material culture directly reflected the types of social and culture change that took place in the past and that Native American cultures simply transformed into close replicas of European culture(s) in and around the colonies of North America (Rubertone 2000). These studies embody the polarizing perspectives already discussed, cleaving various archaeological assemblages into one of a finite number of permutations of European and Native American cultural essences.

By privileging the origins of materials and ideas over their local uses and meanings, archaeologists fell prey to a general pattern that literary theorist Roland Barthes (1977) critiqued in his influential essay "The Death of the Author." He argued that a text should be understood in terms of the multiple and contrasting meanings inscribed on it by its readers, rather than the meanings intended by the author. The heart of this critique applies to archaeology in the sense that meanings of material culture—the text in this analogy—are not fixed and determined solely by its designers and producers. Once material culture crosses social and cultural boundaries, this "text" is divorced from its original use contexts and meanings and is thus subject to redefinition. As anthropological archaeology matured, practitioners came to focus more on context and local meanings of material culture, effectively "killing" (or at least deemphasizing) the "author" in the spirit of Barthes.

For instance, archaeologist Constance Crosby (2003 [1988]) argued for the importance of Algonquian cosmology in dictating the rapid incorporation of European-manufactured material culture into Algonquian societies of New England from the sixteenth century onward. Crosby found that the amount and variety of European-manufactured goods placed into Native graves increased in proportion to European–Native interaction between the sixteenth and mid-eighteenth centuries. Rather than interpreting this profusion as evidence for complete and utter cultural transformation, Crosby saw the concept of *manit*—for Algonquians, a form of spiritual power—as central to the observed changes in Native grave goods from the seventeenth century onwards. She explained, "To the Indians, the more powerful technology of the English and their resistance to disease meant that the English and their gods possessed greater *manit* than the Indians and their gods" (Crosby 2003 [1988]:193). Native peoples thus extended this spiritual power to European-manufactured goods, making such items highly sought after. Ethnohistorical accounts also document the incorporation of European-manufactured items into Algonquian religious and curing rituals, further demonstrating their redefinition in Native contexts. In other words, these items were not harbingers of cultural and religious transformation as much as vehicles for new iterations of deep-seated spiritual traditions. The Brothertown grave markers analyzed in this volume offer novel perspectives on the long-term outcomes of cultural entanglements like those described by Crosby.

Social Categories, Power Structures, and Colonial Interaction

The second theme, *social identity,* examines the interconnections between material culture, discourse, and social classification to investigate the roles that different individuals and groups played in negotiating their places in colonial worlds. Archaeologists started to move away from polarizing models of colonialism by complementing and challenging the archaeological record with other data sets (Brown 1978; Ferris 2009) and by incorporating less rigid interpretive models. Written and oral records of colonial encounters added new depth to archaeological interpretations and mitigated the reliance on material essences in such research. Beginning in the 1980s, the recursiveness of postprocessual archaeology and practice theory influenced archaeologists to accept the complex part that the "stuff" of archaeology—material culture—played in past colonial interactions. These trends turned attention toward issues of identity, leading archaeologists to acknowledge the significance of social categories such as personhood, gender, and ethnicity in processes of colonial entanglement and cultural reproduction (e.g., Deagan 1983; Deetz 1978 [1963]; Lightfoot 2004; Lightfoot, Martinez, and Schiff 1998; Silliman 2001, 2004).

Such studies vary in regard to the types of power they attribute to different individuals and groups in the past. In the contexts of North American colonialism, Indigenous peoples were obviously constrained by overarching colonial power structures—such as the reservation system—established by European encroachers and their descendants. The types of *agency* ascribed to Native peoples in such situations depend upon the particular researcher's theoretical stance. Some studies (e.g., Deetz 1978 [1963]) treat power as a top-down phenomenon, explaining most patterns in the archaeological record as directly connected to the agency of European colonists. Practice-based approaches of the 1970s and 1980s began to challenge these top-heavy models of power (Bourdieu 1977; Certeau 1984; Giddens 1979, 1984; Hodder 1982). Practice theory is a body of thought developed in the social sciences that builds on Marxist notions of praxis—putting theories into action. It generally focuses on the recursive ties between individuals and their surroundings, which include other people, collectivities, and material culture. These recursive ties shape a person's choices and actions. Because they are recursively entangled, however, there is a "duality of structure" (Giddens 1979): social contexts influence practices, just as practices influence the social contexts in which they occur. Practice approaches thus strive to locate the individual or agent within processes of cultural reproduction and social change. Rather than simply categorizing social entities as either powerful or powerless, practice approaches recognized the diffuse nature of power. Following poststructuralist thinkers such as Michel Foucault (1990), archaeologists considered the agency of subaltern groups in situations of extreme power differentials.

These theoretical shifts entailed rethinking the influences and choices that Indigenous peoples had in colonial contexts, whether in the form of outright resistance to colonial power structures (Liebmann and Murphy 2011) or through the seemingly mundane aspects of everyday life (Silliman 2004). In contrast to earlier perspectives, practice-based approaches noted that subaltern peoples always had some form of agency. The difficulty lies in interpreting just how this agency took shape from—and reflexively influenced—colonial power structures. Returning to Barthes, these works look past the "authors" of the material culture that they study to focus on the multiple meanings inscribed on it by its "readers."

The pragmatic framework developed in this chapter offers new means for sorting out the various forms of agency and structure at Brothertown while also drawing attention to the actual differences that Brothertown agency made in the world. Ranging from the extraordinary to the mundane, *becoming Brothertown* involved a variety of choices and actions on the part of community members. I focus specifically on the ways Brothertown Indians communicated in various forms, commemorated their deceased loved ones, consumed material culture, and settled in relation to one another and outsiders. These choices and actions resulted in understandings of personhood, gender relations, individuality, and community that were simultaneously new and old. Although some of these changes were intentionally orchestrated, others were unforeseen by their authors.

Decolonizing Archaeological Practice

The third and most recent theme emanates from outside of archaeology and academia but represents a major force of change in the field. Over the past twenty years, Indigenous issues and Indigenous rights movements have emerged as powerful critiques of Western thought (Preucel and Cipolla 2008). For some archaeologists, these forces first manifested themselves in the form of NAGPRA (Native American Graves Protection and Repatriation Act) legislation, which necessitated interaction between scholars and federally recognized tribes in regard to issues of repatriation and cultural heritage. For others, these forces are evident in the advent and evolution of new ways of conducting archaeological research with, for, and by Indigenous communities (Atalay 2006, 2012; Nicholas and Andrews 1997). The many labels applied to this type of research (e.g., Indigenous, tribal, collaborative, covenantal) demonstrate the variety of forms it takes across North America and beyond. In the general spirit of postcolonial critique, these new forms of archaeology and collaboration share a common interest in decolonizing research (Smith 1999). For the purposes of this book, I define this variety of archaeology (referred to hereafter as "postcolonial archaeology") in contrast to other forms in its respect for Indigenous sensitivities, interests, and needs. By incorporating Native American perspectives into archaeology in this way, postcolonial archaeologies concern themselves with the effects that research has for stakeholders typically situated outside of academia.

A Pragmatic Framework

In the most fundamental sense, pragmatism concerns itself with the effects that knowledge has in the world (e.g., James 1907; Peirce Edition Project 1998; Rorty 1991; see also Preucel 2006; Preucel and Mrozowski 2010; Saitta 2003, 2007). American philosopher Charles Sander Peirce first developed this perspective in his late-nineteenth-century writings, arguing that the significance of an idea was contingent on its effect on the general populace (Preucel 2006:50). In other words, Peirce assessed the clarity and utility of ideas based not on what they meant to the individual thinker but what they did for the community situated around that thinker (Peirce Edition Project 1998). Pragmatism is thus practical to its very core! It considers the differences that particular ideas or actions make in the world. This general premise is applicable to all ideas and actions, both past and present. It emphasizes communities over individuals and actual results over intentions. Also folded into this perspective is a tacit acknowledgment of the deep connections and continuities inherent in social life. These practicalities and continuities are crucial for archaeologies of colonialism as they complement, advance, and critique various components of archaeological notions of acculturation, social identity, and decolonization.

Working in the Present

First and foremost, pragmatism resonates with researchers engaged in various forms of postcolonial archaeology. Although rarely framed explicitly in terms of pragmatism, all questions concerning the social relevance of archaeological research (e.g., Leone 2010; Leone, Potter, and Shackel 1987) embody the pragmatic spirit in one way or another. As practitioners begin to consider how archaeological research and the knowledges of the past that it produces shape the world that lies beyond professional conferences, academic journals, and tenure-review boards, archaeology becomes increasingly pragmatic. This trend is what Robert Preucel and Stephen Mrozowski (2010) refer to as the "new pragmatism." It encompasses all varieties of postcolonial archaeology along with many applied and public archaeologies.

The Brothertown Archaeology Project is certainly pragmatic in this regard. The fieldwork involved a number of different stakeholders, including members of the Brothertown Indian Nation, local (non-Native) landowners and residents, students, and archaeologists. As we collaborated, we forged new and important connections between different groups of people, humans and things, the past and the present. From this perspective, our work at Brothertown was much more than the "controlled destruction" of a standard archaeology project. As they systematically dismantle their respective archaeological records, many postcolonial and public archaeologies simultaneously generate new learning communities. They typically do so in pursuit of multiple goals. For example, participants in the Brothertown project studied Brothertown history while revitalizing connections between younger generations of Brothertown Indians and their cultural heritage, creating a public venue that highlighted local history, collecting and preserving information from Brothertown cemeteries, and working toward protecting sacred sites (discussed further in chapters 3 and 8).

Wrought in relation to multiple stakeholders' sensitivities, interests, and needs, this variety of archaeology typically yields novel forms of research design and data acquisition. Yet these innovations also extend to the interpretive process. With various stakeholders come alternative and sometimes starkly contrasting understandings of the past. Here, pragmatism's underlying theme of continuity comes into play. As articulated by philosopher Richard Rorty (1991:23), "For pragmatists, the desire for objectivity is not the desire to escape the limitations of one's community, but simply the desire for as much intersubjective agreement as possible, the desire to extend the reference of 'us' as far as we can." A truly pragmatic approach thus refrains from simply pitting competing claims about the past against one another and relying on empirical data to discredit all other models in favor of one perspective on the past (i.e., what "really" happened). Instead, pragmatism avoids dichotomizing scientific knowledge from other epistemological modes, recognizing alternative perspectives on the past. This facet of pragmatism challenges positivist science by stipulating that practitioners "test the ideas of other cultures and descendant communities by weaving them together with ones we already have" (Saitta 2007:11; see also Rorty 1991). This process of weaving is present in all forms of postcolonial archaeology to some degree. For example, participants in the Brothertown project engaged in dialogue with each other as they conducted the fieldwork, exchanging and comparing their respective understandings of Brothertown history as they collected data. Although these interactions often led to revisions in their respective understandings of the past—sometimes in direct reference to the material record we were collectively studying—we did not seek to endorse a monolithic version of Brothertown history. Thus, although I am the sole author of this work, the pragmatic interpretations of the history presented herein take influence from my interactions with members of the Brothertown Indian Nation and other stakeholders (chapter 8).

Reconstructing the Past

In addition to its most prominent influences on archaeological research design, data collection, and interpretive processes in the present, pragmatism also sheds light on colonial interactions and cultural identities of the past. I see pragmatism as complementing the general practice-based approaches that pervade contemporary studies of identity and colonialism (e.g., Cipolla 2008; Ferris 2009; Silliman 2009, 2010; Voss 2008a, 2008b, 2008c). Most notable among practice theorists are Pierre Bourdieu (1977, 1990), Anthony Giddens (1979, 1984), and, to a lesser extent, Michel de Certeau (1984). Although each theorist positions agency within processes of cultural reproduction in a distinct manner from the next, all emphasize the simultaneity of structure and agency. Rosemary Joyce and Jeanne Lopiparo (2005:365) point out the interpretive dangers of treating agency and structure as intermittent, "as an alternation of moments of the exercise of agency in an otherwise continuous flow of structure," rather than as constant and seamless. I advocate an integrated pragmatic approach to avoid this pitfall. For me, pragmatism embodies and strengthens the reflexive frameworks of practice theory through its underlying emphasis on the deep continuities inherent in social interaction. However, it also controls for the seamlessness of structure and agency through its focus on the practicalities of social action. Peirce wrote of the continuities and reflexivity of social life well before practice theorists. For instance, Bourdieu's habitus replicates many of the same qualities as Peirce's "habit" (Peirce Edition Project 1998). Peirce's grand theory of synechism also treated the universe as a continuous whole, constantly increasing in complexity and connectedness via social interaction, which hinged on the production and use of signs.

Peircean signs are much more than the cultural conventions of language highlighted in the work of linguist Ferdinand de Saussure (2005 [1972]) and his followers; in fact, they are any phenomena—linguistic or otherwise—that are interpreted. Peirce divided all forms of signification into three modes that often overlap: symbolism, iconicity, and indexicality (Cipolla 2010; Peirce Edition Project 1998; Preucel 2006; Preucel and Bauer 2001). The symbolic mode links the sign or signifier to its "meaning" or signified via conventional knowledge. The readers of these types of signs can only do so by drawing on their respective cultural milieus. Most linguistic signs work within the symbolic mode of signification, the main focus of Saussurian and other structural approaches to semiotics. The iconic mode links the signifier to the signified via physical resemblance. For example, a map iconically represents a locale via some form of physical similarity. The last sign mode, indexicality, links the signifier to the signified via spatiotemporal contiguity. For example, the direction that a weathervane points indexically marks the direction of the wind in that particular area. The contextual nature of the indexical sign mode is important for practice approaches, which, again, view practices (potential signs) as reflexively tethered to the particular contexts in which they arise. It is important to emphasize that most instances of semiosis draw on more than one sign mode: for example, many of the grave markers analyzed here convey meaning via cultural convention (e.g., text inscriptions), iconicity (e.g., gravestone imagery depicting willow trees), and indexicality (e.g., stones marking burial locations). These modes of signification shifted as the Brothertown Indians incorporated new forms of grave marker (chapters 5 and 6) that made differences in the ways individuals and families within the community remembered their respective pasts and related to one another and outsiders.

Most significant for this study is the fact that Peirce viewed signs as processual and ever changing, continually generating new meanings and new types of sign as they are put to use and interpreted in new social contexts (Parmentier 1994; Peirce Edition Project 1998). For instance, Joseph Johnson's understanding and use of Christianity (a set of signs) was somewhat distinct from that of white missionaries in New England. A close reading of his diary and letters shows that Johnson truly believed in Christianity as a religion but also saw it as a means of revitalizing Native American communities in colonial New England (Jarvis 2010; Murray 1998a). This, of course, was not true of the white missionary community, whose members played a part in introducing Christianity to Johnson. On the contrary, many members of the white missionary community saw Christian conversion as a tool for assimilating Native peoples. In this particular case, Christianity served a dual purpose. The signifiers (e.g., the term *Christian*, Bibles, crosses, practices such as prayer and church attendance) remained relatively stable, while their meanings fluctuated between different communities of users (or "readers" in Barthes' sense). As European colonists brought this set of Christian "signs" into foreign social and political contexts, they created new connections and continuities that transformed these signs and led to unforeseen social and cultural consequences, such as the ethnogenesis of the Brothertown Indians.

These continuities are what made personhood and identity so fluid and dialogic for Peirce and his followers. In a paper published in 1893, he explained that "carnal consciousness is but a small part of a man. There is, in the second place, the *social consciousness*, by which a man's spirit is embodied in others, and which continues to live and breathe and have its being very much longer than superficial observers think" (Peirce Edition Project 1998:3, emphasis added). Nearly a century later, cultural anthropologist E. Valentine Daniel (1984) described culture as the emergent set of signs that exist between an ethnographer and his or her informants. In the spirit of Peirce's social consciousness, this process is also fluid and dialogic. On one hand, informants formulate answers to the ethnographer's queries in relation to their understanding of what and how the ethnographer will make sense of their responses. On the other hand, the ethnographer decodes the responses in regard to his or her understanding of how the informant made sense of the original question. "The creation or invention that the native presents as culture and the anthropologist interprets as a culture is precisely this area of admixture, this area of significant intercourse, this area brought together into mutual interpretation in the communicative act, an act that is . . . a creative one, in which both anthropologist and informant(s) are involved" (Daniel 1984:48–49).

The interstitial positioning of culture in each of these models is again dual; it depends on both senders and receivers. In the case of Daniel's ethnography, neither sender nor receiver is wholly responsible for the emergent understanding of culture or cultures that result. Rather, it is a weaving together of different points of reference between informant and ethnographer that ultimately defines the other. This model also applies to colonial interactions. Although in many ways distinct from an ethnographer's interaction with an informant, Native–European entanglements in colonial New England certainly consisted of similar kinds of cultural negotiation and interpretation.

As European and Native peoples interacted in the landscapes of North America, they each drew on their accumulated knowledge of the other—their "addressees" from a communicative standpoint. As they did so, they sometimes negotiated colonial politics by creating, enhancing, erasing, or downplaying social and cultural distinctions between them and other groups. Johnson's writings clearly demonstrate his adroit manipulations of social registers and cultural conventions, which he used to navigate between European and Native American worlds. Negotiations like this took place within an environment filled with a diversity of ideas, practices, and materials operating on dual (or even multiple) registers, such as those of Christianity. Rather than characterizing these practices and materials ("signs" for Peirce) based only on their origins—as either Native American or European, in the vein of many acculturation approaches—this book examines the complexities of these potentially discursive acts in constructing a communal identity, namely, that of the Brothertown Indians. These identity discourses had pragmatic effects on the Brothertown Indians, other Native groups, and Euro-Americans who "read" them. In the chapters that follow, I explore the practical outcomes of Brothertown identity construction for these different groups.

This practical dimension is what sets the pragmatic approach apart from other practice-based frameworks. I accept the Foucauldian premise that power is diffuse rather than top-down, but I add to it a pragmatic twist to explore the different restraints and limitations of subaltern agency, particularly that of Native peoples negotiating and enduring colonial encroachment. Though all individuals have agency, the types of results they can produce in the world are limited by their particular surroundings. Returning to the basis of pragmatism, I shift focus from the intentions and beliefs of the individual agent or sender to consider how agentive action makes a difference for the receiving community around that agent or sender. This focus on social consciousness and the practical implications of discursive action provides a means for interpreting the intended and unintended consequences of practice and agency. I explore these dimensions in terms of both intra- and intercommunal transformations, or the pragmatic differences that the Brothertown Indians' actions and identities made for insiders and outsiders. As I discuss next, this general pragmatic approach articulates closely with other contemporary studies of ethnicity and ethnogenesis, particularly those taking influence from the work of Fredrik Barth.

Approaching Brothertown Ethnogenesis

Ethnogenesis is the process by which new ethnic identities emerge (Hill 1996; Sider 1994; Sturtevant 1971; Voss 2008a, 2008c). As with the Brothertown Indians, subaltern groups sometimes reinvented themselves. This is particularly true in situations of colonialism, where individuals and groups created new identities and modes of social classification as they incorporated once-foreign ideas, materials, and practices and responded to colonial power structures. Within the contexts of North American colonialism specifically, new identities also resulted from the consolidation of once-distinct Indigenous groups—often reeling from the aftermaths of colonial encroachment—into larger multitribal and pan-Indian communities (Merrell 1989; Smoak 2007; Wallace 1956).

The concept of ethnicity first made its way into archaeology in the nineteenth century. At the time, culture history archaeologists focused specifically on identifying ethnic groups in terms of their respective archaeological "signatures" and on tracing their distinct histories (Trigger 2006). Later in the same century, archaeologists incorporated the concept of culture to describe the phenomena they studied (Díaz Andreu and Lucy 2005; Jones 1997; Shennan 1989). Archaeological cultures were defined by the unique characteristics of artifacts and sites found within a particular spatiotemporal context. Archaeologists assumed that continuities in the archaeological record equated to cultural and ethnic continuities, and they attributed changes in the archaeological record to diffusion (the movement of ideas) or migration (the movement of people). Like the early acculturation studies, these approaches operated on the assumption that ethnic and cultural identities were stable, objective, and inherent, effectively equating pots with people.

The past fifty years mark a sea change in the ways archaeologists and anthropologists conceive of ethnicity. Most contemporary studies draw on the seminal work of ethnographer Fredrik Barth and his colleagues. He published an edited volume, *Ethnic Groups and Boundaries: The Social Organization of Cultural Difference* (Barth 1998b [1969]), in which he conceptualized ethnic identities as social phenomena. In opposition to standard views of the time, which treated ethnic groups as pregiven, normative, and stable, Barth argued that ethnic identities were fluid and contingent on social interaction. Instead of focusing on the cultural traits exhibited by various ethnic groups, he innovated a new approach by directing his attention toward the creation or maintenance of ethnic boundaries. He saw such boundaries as negotiated between insiders and outsiders rather than as stable and unchanging (Barth

1998a [1969]:15). In contrast to the diffusionist assumptions already mentioned, Barth conceptualized ethnic boundaries as rooted in culture contact, interaction, and entanglement; he saw societies as inherently polyethnic (Voss 2008c:26). Furthermore, he took multiple perspectives of ethnic classifications into account, recognizing the importance of self-ascription in defining group boundaries rather than relying solely on outsiders' (etic) perspectives of ethnic groups. According to this approach, identities are rooted both in the ways we classify our social world and in the ways the social world classifies us (Cipolla 2008).

To varying degrees, contemporary approaches to ethnicity define it as subjective, multivalent, and fluid. Although these approaches agree that ethnicity is a form of social classification that cleaves the world into groups based on certain criteria shared by its members, the precise criterion for ethnic group membership varies among definitions. Depending on the researcher, emphasis is placed on shared histories and experiences, similar origins and genealogies, collective opposition to other social entities, and/or shared economic and political goals.

These distinctions stem from primordialist and instrumentalist understandings of ethnicity (Barth 1994; Roosens 1994; Vermeulen and Govers 1994). On one hand, primordialists conceptualize ethnicity as a connection between individuals, ascribed to them since birth and continually reemphasized though shared experiences (Voss 2008c:27). From this perspective, the deep emotional connections assumed to be inherent in ethnic ties set them apart from other types of social relations and dimensions of identity (Geertz 1963; Jones 1997). Such an approach treats ethnicity as rigid, deterministic, and immutable vector of identity, emphasizing the influences of an ambiguous but universal human nature over the specific social and historical contexts surrounding ethnic groups. On the other hand, instrumentalists strictly conceptualize the formation and maintenance of ethnic groups as strategic means of social negotiation designed to assist members in meeting certain economic and political ends. Such an approach pays little attention to the distinctions between ethnic groups and other collectivities, such as religious groups or social classes, and places minimal emphasis on the emotions at play in ethnic ties (Jones 1997; Voss 2008c). At the extreme, this view operates on the assumption that human behavior is inherently rational and economic.

Because neither of these approaches accounts solely for all instances of ethnic group formation and maintenance throughout history, they should be treated as differences of degree (rather than kind) and used in conjunction with (rather than in opposition to) one another. Ethnic boundaries result from intentional politicking, emotional connections related to common origins and shared histories, and combinations of the two reflexively interwoven. The Brothertown case speaks to the mutual importance of each of these perspectives. Brothertown Indians shared origins, histories, and spiritual outlooks to some extent, but also left their home reservations for a chance at starting over on arable lands and with hopes of surviving the hardships of colonial encroachment.

Archaeologies of Ethnogenesis

Archaeological studies of ethnogenesis are few and far between. This is due both to the definition of the term and to the types of data available to researchers. Because *ethnogenesis* refers to the forging of new ethnic identities, one criterion used by researchers to differentiate it from other types of identity negotiation is the replacement of old communal names (ethnonyms) with new ones. The emergence of a new communal name, like "Brothertown Indians," marks a distinct type of identity transformation and signals a conscious shift in schemes of social classification (discussed further in chapter 4). Unfortunately, evidence for past practices of ethnonymy is limited to oral and written records, which are scant for most periods of human history, thus reducing the number of archaeological studies specifically focusing on ethnogenesis (see Cordell and Yannie 1991:97). Moreover, ethnogenesis is just one form of identity negotiation, sharing similarities with acculturation, creolization (Ferguson 1992), and hybridity (Gosden 2001; Liebmann 2008a, 2008b).

Although most social scientists approach ethnogenesis primarily using documentary evidence, Barbara Voss' innovative work at El Presidio de San Francisco (Voss 2008a, 2008c) illustrates the merits of historical archaeological perspectives. The Presidio was an eighteenth- and nineteenth-century Spanish military outpost that housed a diverse group of mixed Mexican-, Indian-, African-, and European-descended peoples recruited from various parts of present-day Mexico. Rather than simply accepting their places within the Spanish colonial system of racial classification (*sistema de castas*), members of this community constructed new identities as "Californios." Voss interweaves archival and archaeological sources, reconstructing transformations in landscape, architecture, ceramics, foodways, and dress that speak to the nuances and limitations of identity construction in colonial California.

Like Voss' study, this work draws on a diverse set of data, focusing primarily on grave markers and cemetery spaces to explore Brothertown ethnogenesis. As demonstrated in the chapters that follow, historical archaeology offers new perspectives on the types and methods of social distinction that emerge in such contexts. For instance, in the earliest Brothertown cemeteries of New York, Brothertown Indians combined their East Coast traditions of commemoration with those of their Iroquoian neighbors. Later-period Brothertown cemeteries in New York and Wisconsin sit in stark contrast, however, exhibiting major differences from other contemporaneous Native American cemeteries in New England, New York, and Wisconsin and bearing close resemblance to those of Euro-Americans. The following analysis also illustrates that ethnogenesis is much more than a reduction of intracommunal differences in favor of intercommunal ones. For example, Brothertown Indians practiced not one form of Christianity but several. Separate cemetery spaces, distinct stone forms, and disparate uses of words and images to represent spirituality and the afterlife speak directly to the religious factions that existed within the community. Subtle distinctions between grave markers in the Brothertown assemblage also affirm that certain gender relations were contested within the community.

Voss (2008c) concludes her study of the Presidio by warning against the limits of ethnogenesis. Although Californios challenged and rejected Spanish racial classifications by forging new ethnic identities, in the end they were still subject to "stigmatization, discrimination, and subordination by Europeans and Anglo-Americans who followed the 'one-drop' rule of hypodescent" (Voss 2008c:304). Researchers must remember that although agency is diffuse à la Foucault, individuals and communities will never fully control the ways outsiders view and make sense of them. Following a general pragmatic approach, discursive interactions rely on much more than the perspectives and goals of the senders of messages (e.g., I am *this* type of person, and not *that* type!), and must take into account the larger "receiving community," particularly those with the power to substantially constrain others' potential to make differences in the world. Returning to the definitions already discussed, ethnicity is not wholly contingent on insiders' views but is entangled within a network of social constraints in which boundaries are negotiated via discursive interactions between insiders and outsiders.

Summary

Exemplified by Joseph Johnson, the identity discourses analyzed in this book played key roles in the emergence, evolution, and endurance of the Brothertown community and in the reproduction of colonial culture of New

England and beyond. The theoretical framework developed in this chapter builds on archaeological studies of acculturation and identity and is influenced by recent efforts to decolonize archaeological practice. Pragmatism ties these themes together. It melds with practice-based approaches as a means of exploring the dialogic and shared dimensions of colonial interaction, identity formation, and agency in the past. Yet as a philosophy of archaeological practice, pragmatism also considers the practical outcomes of the work that archaeologists do, specifically the effects that research has on descendant communities and other stakeholding publics in the present. I apply this pragmatic framework to analyze the complexities of Brothertown ethnogenesis and assess the differences that this study makes in the present.

3

Brothertown Histories

> Here, then, are the Brothertown Indians on the east side of Winnebago Lake, in Calumet County, trying to imitate our white brethren in all things except their vices. Here we have taken our last stand, as it were, and are resolved to meet manfully, that overwhelming tide of fate, which seems destined, in a few short years, to sweep the Red Man from the face of existence.
>
> —Thomas Commuck (1855)

SO WROTE THOMAS COMMUCK FROM mid-nineteenth-century Brothertown, Wisconsin. Only three decades before, Commuck—a Narragansett Indian—first joined the Brothertown community in their New York settlement just as they were preparing for their next move west. He remained with his new community for the next thirty-one years, writing two syntheses of local history before meeting a tragic end in the winter of 1856 by falling through the ice on Lake Winnebago. The quotation above comes from a letter submitted by Commuck to Lyman Draper, correspondent for the Wisconsin Historical Society, and published in the Wisconsin Historical Collections shortly after. In it, Commuck wrestles with many of the tensions highlighted in this volume. Although he used different terms and wrote on the subject in a far more nuanced manner than I do, Commuck addressed the complexities of Native American endurance and cultural negotiation more than a century and a half before I sat down to write this book. In contrast to the ostensible pessimism of the quotation, as a whole, his work speaks to the injustices of colonial North America, the perpetual struggle between cultural continuity and change, the Brothertown Indian community's successes in navigating the tides of colonialism, and—most important—to survival.

Commuck (1855:291) began his essay with a brief description of the Native people of the Atlantic coast "at the time of the landing of the Pilgrim

Fathers," framing the remainder of his discussion as a response to his own queries concerning the state and whereabouts of those Native communities in the mid-nineteenth century. He saw such issues as grossly misunderstood: "even at the present time, it is perhaps thought by thousands of American born citizens, that some, if not all, of the aforesaid tribes, have become now entirely extinct" (Commuck 1855:292). Commuck thus wrote to correct such assumptions. Of course, cultural change constituted a large part of his discussion. For instance, at one point in his narrative he provided a list of several "Indian words of the Narragansett Tribe," all that he knew of his ancestors' language (Commuck 1855:297). He also emphasized the physical distance traveled by the Brothertown community, to its members becoming US citizens, and to their intermarriage with white society.

Yet the act of writing such a history speaks to the group's endurance in the face of adversity. At several points in his historical synthesis, Commuck noted where most nineteenth-century Americans would end Native history. For example, after describing the founding of the first Brothertown settlement in New York, he wrote, "Here sir, I might leave them [the Brothertown Indians], and let it be again supposed that they had become extinct; but the fact that the writer hereof (who is a Narragansett), united [with] them in 1825, and has continued with them until present time, he trusts will be deemed a sufficient apology, if he feels inclined to continue their history" (Commuck 1855:293–94). When considered in context, the gravity of the Brothertown Indians' "last stand" parallels other colonial challenges they and their ancestors faced since the seventeenth century. With a close reading, Commuck's history not only emphasizes Native endurance in the mid-nineteenth century but also predicts that the Brothertown community would overcome such challenges and continue to survive, all while adapting to its new place in the modern world.

In this chapter, I elaborate on the histories of the Brothertown community and the Brothertown Archaeology Project presented thus far, establishing additional context for the analyses and interpretations that follow. I return to the stories of Samson Occom, Joseph Johnson, and the seven East Coast communities that eventually contributed to the Brothertown Indian movement. I focus on the ethnogenesis and evolution of the Brothertown Indians before discussing the contemporary community and its connections to the archaeological project on which I base this volume. In the later part of this chapter I pick up Brothertown history where Commuck left off, extending the story into the present. Indeed, the latter components of this chapter—specifically the description of the contemporary Brothertown community's active involvement and participation in the production of this particular iteration of Brothertown history—confirm that Commuck's veiled prediction was absolutely correct.

Samson Occom

Samson Occom (1723–92) was born on Mohegan lands in the area of current-day Uncasville and Montville, Connecticut (Love 1899; Occom 2006e [1768]; Ottery and Ottery 1989). His mother, Sarah Sampson, was Mashantucket or Groton Pequot, and his father, Joshua Okham, was Mohegan. Although Occom (2006d [1765]) later described his parents and his upbringing as "heathenish," his mother encouraged his path toward Christianity. She converted early in his life and likely encouraged her son to begin attending Christian sermons when he was a teenager. As he discussed in his diary, Samson often sought out religious sermons at local churches rather than waiting for missionaries to come to him. He also studied with white schoolteachers at Mohegan (Silverman 2010:53), learning the English language so he could read the Bible for himself.

By his seventeenth year, Occom had found his calling in life: to spread Christianity to his Native brethren in southeastern Connecticut and the surrounding areas. As described in the introductory chapter, this mission tied in directly to his plans for Native revitalization and survival in colonial New England. Together these twin goals constituted his life's work, a fact that he seemed aware of at an impressively early age (Occom 2006e [1768]). Following these ambitions, he first looked to the local white missionary community for assistance.

When he was twenty years old, Occom's mother asked Reverend Eleazar Wheelock of Lebanon, Connecticut, to train her son as a missionary. Wheelock agreed, allowing Occom to live with him in Lebanon. Under Wheelock's tutelage, Occom learned to read several languages, including Latin, Greek, French, and Hebrew. He also began keeping a diary, which he maintained regularly until the last few days of his life (Brooks 2006). In the winter of 1749, bad eyesight forced Occom to cease his studies with Wheelock and begin work as a missionary.

In November of the same year, Occom moved among the Montaukett Indians on the south fork of Long Island, New York, to serve as their schoolmaster, preacher, judge, and general community leader (Love 1899; Occom 2006a [1752]). He remained there for a total of twelve years, during which time he forged important relationships with the Montaukett and became increasingly well known among the white missionary communities of the Northeast (Occom 2006a [1752]). For example, in 1751 he married Mary Fowler, a Montaukett Indian, and in 1759 he was officially ordained as a Presbyterian minister after receiving approval from Wheelock and the Society for Propagating Christian Knowledge (SPCK) in Scotland.

At the same time, inspired by Occom's missionary success in Montauk, Wheelock decided to seek out other Native pupils to train in Lebanon. Using funds from the SPCK and the Society for Propagating the Gospel (SPG), he established a school that—unbeknownst to him—later trained many future Brothertown community leaders. Originally known as Moor's Indian Charity School (after the land donor), the school was officially established in 1755. In addition to spreading the Christian message, Wheelock also sought to teach European-style agriculture and craft production to Indians. Therefore, in addition to their more traditional studies, Wheelock required his male students to labor on neighboring farms several days a week and expected his female students to learn sewing, knitting, and other domestic skills (Murray 1998c:53). He used this labor as a source of revenue for his operation. His first official students came from Brotherton, Reverend David Brainerd's missionary town in New Jersey (Flemming 2005; Murray 1998b: 170), and were thus likely Lenape in descent. Also among the first group of students were Samson Wauby (Mashantucket Pequot), Joseph Johnson (Mohegan), and Occom's new brother-in-law David Fowler (Montaukett), each of whom went on to play major parts in the Brothertown movement.

It was not until the 1760s that Occom began to travel across the Northeast and beyond to spread the Christian message. During this time he forged new and important ties with other Native communities, began fighting for Native rights, and started to question the motivations of the white missionary communities of the Northeast. He first left Montauk to work as a missionary in central and upstate New York, where he established friendly relations with the Oneida that later proved integral for the founding of Brothertown, New York (Occom 2006b [1761], 2006c [1761]).

Following his missionary efforts to the west, Occom finally returned to Mohegan lands in 1764. There he became embroiled in controversy almost immediately due to his involvement in the Mohegan land case, a longstanding land struggle between the Mohegan tribe and Connecticut Colony (Jarvis 2010; Love 1899; Silverman 2010). Occom supported his people, arguing that colonial officials had wrongfully appropriated Mohegan lands. Moreover, he openly critiqued Robert Clelland, the Anglo schoolteacher at Mohegan, and lured away many congregation members of Reverend David

Jewett, the local preacher. These tensions culminated in a meeting of the Connecticut Board of Correspondents in which Occom was accused of misconduct against Connecticut Colony. Under pressure from Wheelock and other members of the white religious community, Occom apologized for his involvement in the land struggle and his open critiques of Clelland and Jewett, begging the pardon of the board. Although the board granted him forgiveness in this instance, it was short-lived.

Occom exacerbated his increasingly tumultuous relationship with the white religious communities of New England by going against the wishes of many and traveling to England in the mid-1760s. Some saw this trip as a covert effort on his part to appeal directly to the Crown in regard to the Mohegan land case (Silverman 2010:80). In contrast to these accusations, it appears that Occom went primarily in hope of raising funds to help spread Christianity to Native communities via institutions such as Wheelock's Indian Charity School. While overseas, one of his biggest supporters was the Earl of Dartmouth (from whom Dartmouth College takes its name). The earl contributed greatly to Occom's cause and even commissioned two paintings of him. In 1768, Occom returned from England, bringing with him approximately £12,000 in donations to aid his mission.

Upon his return to Connecticut, however, tensions quickly arose between Occom and his former mentor, Wheelock, for both personal and professional reasons (Love 1899:152–55). To begin, Occom, who found his wife in poor health and his children "undisciplined" (Occom 2006f [1768]), blamed Wheelock for going against his word to properly attend to the family in Occom's absence. Additionally, he strongly disagreed with the changes that Wheelock implemented at his school, using the funds collected in England to found Dartmouth College (see chapter 1).

To add to these difficulties, the Connecticut Board of Correspondents prevented Occom from working as a missionary during this time because he had defied their wishes by traveling to England. Unemployed and impoverished, he struggled to eke out a living. Amplifying these challenges even further, Wheelock accused Occom of turning to alcohol during this period of his life (Silverman 2010:86). Investigations by several religious institutions such as the SPCK found Occom innocent. Despite these rulings, however, the word of his brushes with alcohol added fuel to a long-burning fire: the negative feelings that white residents of Connecticut had harbored for him ever since his involvement in the Mohegan land case.

During these difficult and uncomfortable times, Occom began formulating plans that led to the Brothertown movement. After delivering a now-famous sermon at the execution of Moses Paul, a Native man from Cape Cod who had been found guilty of murder due to a state of drunkenness, Occom began to focus on the issue of alcoholism for Native communities (Love 1899:175). He thought it necessary to separate Native people from such temptations. Due to popular demand, he published his sermon for Moses Paul, which went through eighteen subsequent editions. He also published a book of hymns and spiritual songs. William DeLoss Love (1899:179) argued that Occom used these publications to unify the several tribes that eventually joined the Brothertown movement, effectively creating an imagined community (see Anderson 1983).

Joseph Johnson

While Occom began his work among the Montaukett on Long Island, back home in Connecticut, Joseph Johnson (1751–76) was born to parents Joseph and Betty Johnson, both Christian Mohegans (Murray 1998a). Although they did not cross paths for some time, Johnson's life was clearly influenced by Occom's work and accomplishments. For instance, Johnson became a student at Wheelock's Indian Charity School when he was only seven years old. After studying there for eight years, he moved west to serve as a schoolmaster among the Oneida. During this time, he worked with David Fowler, Occom's brother-in-law, and Samuel Kirkland, a white student of Wheelock's (Murray 1998d). In only a few years, however, Johnson ceased his work due to charges of drunkenness and misbehavior, which were probably a function of his young age. These events marked the beginning of a vague period in his life, during which he strayed away from the path of Christianity. Right around the time that Occom returned from his trip abroad, Johnson was back east in Providence, Rhode Island. There he first worked as a schoolteacher, and later took a job on a whaling ship, traveling all across the Atlantic.

In 1771, just as Occom began to question the integrity of the white missionary community and the future of his brethren in coastal New England, Johnson returned home to Mohegan. The thriving religious community there inspired him to renew his efforts to spread Christianity. He described this period of his life as a metamorphosis of sorts: "I was 21 years in this World, before I was born, and Soon as I was born, I had my Eyes Opened" (Johnson 1998a [1772–73]). Following this personal revelation, in 1772, Johnson moved to Farmington, Connecticut, to work as a schoolteacher and general community leader among the Tunxis Indians.

During this crucial time he began to interact and work closely with Occom and other future Brothertown leaders. In fact, Johnson married Tabitha

Occom in 1773, making him Samson's son-in-law (Johnson 1998b [1773]). As these community leaders began considering the possibility of moving west and starting anew, Johnson's connections with the Oneida made him a valuable asset for the nascent Brothertown community. His charisma, public speaking skills, and youth played major roles in securing a tract of land in Oneida country on which to found the first Brothertown settlement. The last years of Johnson's life were spent traveling back and forth between Connecticut and New York to negotiate with the Oneida and secure new lands. Unfortunately he never had the opportunity to see the fruits of his labor. His life was cut short during the American Revolution, when he mysteriously disappeared among the chaos at the youthful age of twenty-five.

The Seven East Coast Settlements

In this section I provide a brief sketch of each of the seven East Coast communities that contributed to the Brothertown movement (refer to figure 1.1). For each settlement, I pay particular attention to the population size, general living conditions, tribal affiliation, and degree of exposure to Christianity. Although there was clear interest in spreading Christianity to such communities as early the seventeenth century, major efforts did not commence until the early to mid-eighteenth century. These "awakenings" reached their apex around 1740; by the second half of the eighteenth century, Native schoolteachers and ministers like Occom and Johnson had supplanted white ones in each of the settlements discussed here.

Charlestown

We begin with the easternmost of the settlements. Charlestown or Misquamicut sat in southern Rhode Island and housed both Narragansett and Eastern Niantic peoples. At the very beginning of the Brothertown movement in the 1770s, Charlestown's population was 528 (Mandell 2008; see also Wonderley 1999). It subsequently fell to 429 by 1815 and 300 by 1825 (Mandell 2008). The Brothertown movement thus drew away about 18 percent of Charlestown's population during the late eighteenth century.

Like the other settlements discussed in this section, Christianity was prevalent in the Charlestown community. This trend began in 1721, when the SPG sent a minister to work there. The sachem at the time, Charles

Ninigret, allowed the missionaries to build a church. In the 1740s, a Native minister, Samuel Niles, took over the role as preacher and schoolmaster for the community. The "awakenings" that took place in Charlestown during the eighteenth century affected the internal coherence of the community. For instance, a portion of the Charlestown Indians became Separate Baptists in the mid-1740s, creating a religious rift between them and other members of the community who were Presbyterian (Love 1899:192–95). As seen in the cemeteries analyzed in chapters 5 and 6, these religious distinctions were present in both Brothertown settlements.

The Eastern (Stonington) Pequot Reservation

The Eastern and Mashantucket Pequot split in the seventeenth century when Connecticut Colony established two different reservations: the Mashantucket Reservation, established in 1666 (discussed next), and the Eastern or Lantern Hill Reservation, established in 1683 (Bragdon and Simmons 1998; Cave 1996; DeForest 1964 [1851]; see also Cipolla 2008; Cipolla, Silliman, and Landon 2007). The Eastern Pequot Reservation, located in North Stonington, Connecticut, spanned approximately 115 hectares at the time of the Brothertown movement (Bragdon and Simmons 1998; Silliman 2009). Reservation soils were notoriously rocky and intractable, making life there difficult. Anglo missionaries such as Reverends Nathaniel Eells and Joseph Fish began working with the Eastern Pequot community in the early to mid-eighteenth century, but were replaced in 1758 by Edward Nedson, a Native teacher.

Historian Daniel Mandell (2008) estimates that the Eastern Pequot Reservation's population dropped from 237 in 1780 to just 30 by 1815 (see also DeForest 1964 [1851]; Den Ouden 2005). This drastic population decline was due largely to the fact that Eastern Pequot men were forced to move away from the reservation to work as soldiers and seamen (Bragdon and Simmons 1988), and others worked seasonal jobs to establish credit with local merchant farmers (Silliman and Witt 2010; Witt 2007; see also Silverman 2001). Others joined the Brothertown movement, sometimes leaving friends and family behind in hopes of a better life in Oneida country. Of note, the settlement patterns analyzed in chapter 7 demonstrate that a sizable Pequot population did not actually arrive in Brothertown until the mid-nineteenth century, skipping over Brothertown, New York, and moving directly to Wisconsin Territory.

The Mashantucket (Groton) Pequot Reservation

Located in Groton, Connecticut, the Mashantucket Pequot Reservation originally covered approximately 800 hectares (Jarvis 2010; Love 1899). Like the Stonington Reservation to its immediate east, Mashantucket had rocky soils that were difficult to farm. Beginning in the 1720s, several Anglo ministers began working on the reservation and established a school. By the 1750s, Native schoolmasters and preachers had taken over; these included Samuel Ashbow, Samson Wauby, Hugh Sweetingham, and David Fowler (Occom's brother-in-law).

In 1725, there were approximately 321 Pequot people living on the reservation (Den Ouden 2005), but the population dropped drastically in the decades to come. By 1766, records show only 164 individuals living on the reservation, the majority of which were children no more than sixteen years old, and by 1815 the population had dropped to only 35 (Mandell 2008). This general pattern mirrored that of the Eastern Pequot Reservation, with many able-bodied men leaving the reservation to find work. Archaeologist Kevin McBride (1990a) notes evidence for a sizable population dispersal from this reservation during the late eighteenth century. Although he associates these departures with the Brothertown Indian movement, again, the Brothertown settlement patterns analyzed in chapter 7 suggest that significant numbers of Pequots did not join the Brothertown community until the founding of the second settlement in Wisconsin Territory during the second quarter of the nineteenth century. Where these Pequots went in the late eighteenth century remains unclear; however, their presence in mid-nineteenth-century Brothertown, Wisconsin, was so strong that a neighborhood therein was known as Pequot (chapter 7).

The Mohegan Reservation

The Mohegan Reservation sits on the western side of the Thames River in current-day Uncasville and Montville, Connecticut. As previously discussed, Occom was born at Mohegan in 1723 and returned to live there in the mid-1760s. The Mohegan settlement was both literally and figuratively at the center of the Brothertown movement. In 1725, colonial officials estimated the Mohegan population at 351, the largest of the Connecticut reservations of the time (Den Ouden 2005). By 1800, however, only eighty-four individuals were reported as living on the reservation (Mandell 2008). As demonstrated by the settlement data in chapter 7, a significant portion of this population decline was tied directly to the Brothertown Indian movement.

The Niantic Reservation

A small community of Western Niantic people lived on this 120-hectare reservation, located in Lyme, Connecticut. As of 1725, 163 individuals lived there (Den Ouden 2005:248). The population declined fairly rapidly, however, with only sixty people reported as living on the reservation by 1800 (Mandell 2008). Anglo missionaries began working on the Niantic Reservation as early as 1736, establishing a small school there.

The Farmington Reservation

Farmington is located along the Farmington River in west-central Connecticut. The Farmington Reservation was about 100 hectares in size and housed mostly Tunxis peoples—also known as the Sepous, along with some Quinnipiac and Mattabeeset, or Wangunck, peoples (DeForest 1964 [1851]; Love 1899; Wonderley 1999). In 1761, about twenty-five families called the Farmington Reservation their home. At the time of the Brothertown emigration, historians estimate a population of approximately fifty persons, most of whom relocated to Brothertown (Mandell 2008; Wonderley 1999). Among the Farmington Indians who became members of the Brothertown community were Elijah Wampey and Solomon Mossuck. These men went on to play important roles within the community. In fact, they requested a copy of colony laws from the Connecticut General Assembly, and the Brothertown community later used this document as a model for their own form of governance. In the 1730s, a Native minister named John Mattawan began working at Farmington. Joseph Johnson replaced him in 1772, becoming a key representative for the community and an important player in the early phases of the Brothertown movement.

Montaukett Reservation

The southernmost of the seven settlements was Montauk, located on the southern fork of Long Island. In 1741, thirty-four families, or approximately

160 people, lived there, and many of them joined the Brothertown movement (Ales 1993; Wonderley 1999). As already discussed, Occom served as minister, teacher, and judge among the Montaukett beginning in the 1750s. Later his brother-in-law, David Fowler, performed these duties for this community.

Brothertown Ethnogenesis

Formulating the Plan

During the early 1770s, Occom, Johnson, Fowler, and other local Native leaders associated with the seven ancestral communities spent much of their time hashing out plans for removal. They saw the move as a means of improving their living conditions. Not only would it allow them access to arable land and sustainable living, it also gave them the opportunity to distance their people from the corrupting influences of colonial culture, namely, alcohol, or "fire water" in the words of Thomas Commuck (1855). Moreover, such a community would serve as an example for neighboring Native communities of New York, in turn helping spread Christianity and European-introduced methods of agriculture—two central tenets of Occom's plan for Native survival. Finally it offered them the chance to escape the "tyranny" of living under the rule of one all-powerful sachem or family, as they had on their respective reservations for generations. In opposition to traditional Algonquian schemes of governance, Occom and his followers were interested in instituting a democratic form of government in which community members would vote.

A key step toward removal, taken in March 1773, was a meeting at Mohegan of members of the seven communities (Love 1899:210–11). At that time, the group decided to send representatives to Oneida and officially ask for land. By fall 1773, the Oneida had granted the group a modest parcel. The New England Indians deliberated and decided to ask for additional land to sustain their entire group (Occom 2006h [1774]). They sent a subsequent group of representatives in winter 1774 to ask for the additional land, which was eventually granted to them. In summer 1774, Occom, Fowler, and Johnson traveled to Oneida country to examine the land and decide on boundaries. Finally, in October 1774, the Oneida officially deeded the land to the "New England Indians" (Murray 1998a; Venables 1993).

The next major hurdle to overcome was the actual move. The plan was to send the able-bodied men early in the spring so they would have ample time to build houses and plant fields before the harsh winter months. The first group, including Joseph Johnson, David Fowler, Elijah Waumpy, John Skeesuck, John Shattocks, and Samuel Tallman, set out during the spring of 1775. They had reached their new land safely and had begun putting their plan into action when they were interrupted by the outbreak of the American Revolution.

The Oneida and the New England Indians were loyal to the Colonies. In fact, during the revolution, many Brothertown men enlisted as soldiers. Those who remained were isolated and surrounded by the dangers of warfare, including raids by pro-British Iroquois and Loyalists (Venables 1993). These dangers likely led to the disappearance of Joseph Johnson. Because it would have been perilous for the remaining Brothertown Indians to journey back to the East Coast, they retreated east to Stockbridge, Massachusetts, the home of a Christian Mohican community known as the Stockbridge Indians (see Silverman 2010).

At the time, the Stockbridge Indians were also dissatisfied with their situation. During their stay with the Stockbridge, the Brothertown refugees influenced them to attempt a move west as they had. In 1783 the Brothertown began moving back to Oneida country, bringing with them several Stockbridge Indians. The Stockbridge eventually met with the Oneida and asked for land, receiving nearly ten square kilometers to the north of what became Brothertown. From this moment onward, the Brothertown and Stockbridge shared a close connection. The groups remained neighbors for many decades and often intermarried.

Founding Brothertown

After 1783, increasing numbers of New England Indians embarked on the journey to Brothertown. Occom described (2006j [1785]) the official founding of the settlement in his journal entry dated November 7, 1785 (discussed further in chapter 4). He continued to play an important role in the emigration process and did not settle in Brothertown until 1789; before that, he continually moved back and forth between New England and New York (Love 1899; Occom 2006i [1784]). In the early years of the Brothertown settlement, Occom served as minister to both Brothertown and New Stockbridge and was widely accepted by both communities.

Soon, however, Occom's relationship with the Brothertown community became stressed for several reasons. A large schism developed within the Brothertown community over two major land issues (Love 1899; Occom

2006k [1786]; Silverman 2001). It began in 1786 when the Oneida attempted to renege on their land agreement with the Brothertown Indians. They claimed that the New England Indians had not met certain conditions of their agreement, which therefore voided the deed in the Oneida's opinion (Brothertown Indians 1791). They wished to restrict Brothertown lands to as little as one and a half square kilometers (Venables 1993). Occom vehemently opposed the Oneida on this matter, arguing that the New England Indians had rights to the tract originally agreed on. At this time, some of the Brothertown Indians began to oppose Occom in fear that they would lose their land altogether if he challenged the Oneida too strongly.

The disagreements with the Oneida stemmed from two distinct understandings of the original land negotiations. While the Brothertown Indians saw the new land as strictly their property, the Oneida saw it only as set aside for Brothertown use (Wonderley 1997, 1999). These tensions were amplified as Oneida lands became inundated with other "refugee" Native groups after the revolution. According to historian Anthony Wonderley (1999), the Oneida wanted to distribute lands evenly in relation to the size of each group. In 1785, the Stockbridge Indians numbered more than 400 and were restricted to ten square kilometers (compared to only 200 Brothertown Indians then living in New York), so the Oneida likely felt justified in trying to redistribute some of the Brothertown lands.

These tensions came to a close in 1788 with the Treaty of Fort Schuyler, in which the Oneida ceded all of their lands to New York except their reservation and the lands set aside for the Stockbridge and Brothertown Indians. The treaty reduced Brothertown lands to a three-by-five-kilometer tract (New York State 1788). Again, Occom fought for the tract size originally agreed on, petitioning the General Assembly of New York, which eventually complied. This decision was a pivotal event in Brothertown history because it officially transferred ownership of the reservation to the Brothertown Indians.

The next major land issue concerned leasing (Brothertown Indians 1791; Love 1899; Occom 2006g [1771]). One of the main problems with leasing was its connection to alcoholism in Native communities. Indians would sometimes lease or even sell their lands to get money to buy alcohol, or settlers would offer alcohol to Natives before negotiating for land in hopes of cheating them while they were inebriated (Belknap and Morse 1955 [1796]). The short-term appeal of quick cash or goods in such leasing agreements often trumped the long-term consequences of dispossession for Native peoples. Knowing these things, Occom forcefully opposed leasing and strove to seriously restrict the leasing rights of Brothertown Indians.

Elijah Waumpy, a Brothertown Indian originally from Farmington, disagreed with Occom on this issue and convinced a majority of the community to allow leasing in Brothertown (Occom 2006n [1792]). After gaining support, Waumpy's faction immediately began leasing their new lands to Euro-American settlers for periods of ten years. In fear of what may have happened next, Occom appealed to the New York state government to regulate leasing in Brothertown, which led to the passing of "An Act for the Relief of the Indians residing in Brothertown and New Stockbridge" (February 21, 1791). This act regulated and restricted leasing while also recognizing and describing the Brothertown system of governance. Occom's actions against leasing made him unpopular among many of the Brothertown Indians (Occom 2006l [1791], 2006m [1791]), to the point that he moved to New Stockbridge in the winter of 1791. Before he died in June 1791, Occom predicted that ongoing land struggles would eventually necessitate another move for the Brothertown Indians.

Brothertown After Occom

Ironically, once the leasing problem was under control, most Brothertown Indians—including Waumpy himself—came to agree with Occom's stance against leasing. The community banded together to oppose Euro-American trespassing. In 1792, they wrote to the New York state government and complained about continued Euro-American encroachment on their lands, which resulted in the passing of "An Act Relative to Lands in Brothertown" (New York State 1795). The law divided the original Brothertown tract of just under 10,000 hectares in two, allowing the Brothertown Indians to remain on a parcel of approximately 3,600 hectares. The remainder of the land was sold off to Euro-American settlers. Funds from these sales went into an account for the Brothertown community that later helped in their move west (Brothertown Indians n.d.; Commuck 1855:294; Love 1899:292; New York State 1795). The interest from the account also went toward financing a school at Brothertown (Jarvis 2010:136). Despite these positive aspects, the state government used this intervention as an opportunity to increase their control over the community. They appointed three non-Native superintendents to oversee the Brothertown community, approve communal decisions, and monitor land use. As part of this change, the superintendents divided Brothertown into 149 individual lots, assigning 59 of them to Brothertown individuals and families by 1796 (Jarvis 2010:137; see also Belknap and Morse 1955 [1796]; New York State 1791, 1795, 1796; chapter 7).

Religious factions continued to thrive within the Brothertown community after Occom's death (Love 1899:309–15). Visitors to Brothertown, such as Euro-American missionary Samuel Kirkland, noted the presence of Methodists, Separatists, Baptists, and Presbyterians within the community. The Baptist faction eventually fragmented once again, this time into Freewill Baptists, ministered by elders Isaac Wauby and Benjamin Garrett Fowler, and Communion Baptists, ministered by elder Thomas Dick. To complicate matters further, in 1798 the Brothertown superintendents hired a white Quaker schoolmaster named John Dean. His son Thomas succeeded him in 1801 and soon became well trusted by the Brothertown community. Thomas Dean served as much more than a schoolteacher, advising the tribe on legal matters and eventually assisting them with their move to Michigan Territory. This is where current-day Deansboro, New York (part of the former Brothertown settlement) gets its name.

The Next Emigration

During the early nineteenth century, the state of New York began buying up large tracts of land surrounding Native settlements, isolating the various Indian communities and seriously limiting their respective land bases (Cipolla and Andler 2007). This trend coupled with continuing land conflicts with encroaching Euro-Americans and growing population pressure, forcing the Brothertown Indians and several other groups to look for new lands (Commuck 1855; Love 1899). Following their neighbors, the Stockbridge, the Brothertown Indians first looked toward Indiana Territory among the Miami and Delaware Indians. Unfortunately, the War of 1812 delayed their efforts to relocate to Indiana, and by 1818 the lands they wished to claim had been purchased from the Delaware by the federal government (Brothertown Indians 1825).

During this time, a number of the neighboring Six Nations groups began looking for land in the Green Bay area of Michigan Territory (Bread 2006 [1820]; Jarvis 2010:183). Following this lead, the Brothertown Indians also turned their gaze farther westward. They subsequently reached an agreement with the Oneida and Stockbridge; the Brothertown group would join the movement and receive a new tract of land in Michigan Territory in exchange for making the final payment of $950 in goods to the Menominee Indians (Jarvis 2010:179). These groups originally agreed on an enormous tract of land—approximately thirteen by fifty kilometers in size—on which the Brothertown would settle (Brothertown Indians 1827a, 1827b) and the

Brothertown paid the $950 in goods using funds from their account in New York. Frustratingly, the Menominee quickly reneged on the agreement, leading to a major conflict between them, the various groups of New York Indians, and the federal government (Jarvis 2010; United States 1832a, 1832b). In the end, the Stambaugh Treaty of 1832 reduced the new Brothertown tract from the originally agreed-on 60,000+ hectares to just under 10,000 hectares (approximately 6.5 by 13 kilometers in size) and relocated the settlement farther south of Green Bay to the eastern shore of Lake Winnebago.

Brothertown, Wisconsin

Despite all the difficulties and setbacks, the Brothertown Indians finally began moving away from New York in 1831. Because their new settlement was thickly wooded, they spent considerable effort clearing the land, building homes, and setting up other infrastructure (Heller n.d.; Titus 1938). Once cleared, the land turned out to be optimal for planting and remains so today. The Brothertown first cultivated corn, beans, squash, and other vegetables as they had in New York (Jarvis 2010:218). As time passed, however, they came to focus increasingly on wheat production. In 1836 the federal government funded the construction of both a gristmill and a sawmill at Brothertown. These mills processed Brothertown grains as well as those from other surrounding farms and produced lumber for construction. In 1840, a Methodist church was also constructed in Brothertown—the first erected in Wisconsin Territory.

As of 1837, the tribe had about 360 members, 250 of whom then lived in the new Brothertown (Love 1899). Although the new land was held communally at first, the Brothertown soon divided the land into four-hectare lots to be held in fee simple. This important change occurred in 1839, when the tribe's membership was granted US citizenship with land rights (Brothertown Indians 1838; Jarvis 2010; United States 1839; see also chapter 4). Their motivation for seeking citizenship was to avoid being dispossessed of their lands once again. Just as the Brothertown group had begun to develop their new settlement, the United States passed the Indian Removal Act, which attempted to push all local Native groups to Indian Territory west of the Mississippi (Loew 2001). By becoming citizens, the Brothertown Indians exempted themselves from the Indian Removal Act and temporarily secured their new Wisconsin land base.

The new land rights that came with citizenship certainly influenced emergent conceptions of personhood and individuality at Brothertown (discussed later in this volume). Their new legal status meant that Brothertown Indians could pass down ownership of their properties to new generations of Brothertown landowners. This change placed even more emphasis on individuality and specific genealogical histories within the community. Kathleen Bragdon (1997:3) found a similar pattern among the seventeenth- and eighteenth-century Massachusett. As they, too, gained legal ownership of individual properties, their kinship terminology shifted to emphasize the nuclear family. Of course, these new rights also meant that Brothertown Indians could sell their individual properties if they chose. They began doing so in the second half of the nineteenth century, forever changing the internal makeup of the community. Although these shifts were clearly tied to economic factors, in subsequent chapters I make the case that they were part of a much longer-term process of social and cultural transformation related to colonial entanglement and modernity. As I argue later, this process was in motion well before the Brothertown Indians made their way to Michigan Territory, and it is evident in the cemetery data explored in chapters 5 and 6.

The Civil War only augmented these communal changes. Consistent with their ancestors—large numbers of whom fought in the French and Indian War, the American Revolution, and the War of 1812—many Brothertown boys and men served in the army between 1861 and 1865 (Brucker and Andler 2011). Most fought in Wisconsin's regiment cavalry (1st, 2nd, 3rd, and 4th) or regiment infantry (1st, 3rd, 5th, 6th, 16th, 17th, 18th, 19th, 21st, 22nd, 32nd, 35th, 36th, and 38th). Brothertown Indians living in Kansas, Ohio, and New York also served. Less than a decade before the war, the Bureau of Indian Affairs (Schoolcraft 1853) listed the Brothertown Indian population at 600. During the Civil War, more than 100 Brothertown Indians enlisted, and many of them never returned home to Wisconsin. Thus, similar to the social effects that the reservations had on the East Coast (chapter 1), the Civil War created a sizable tear in the social fabric of the Brothertown community just after its members had been bestowed with new land rights. In many instances, these two factors, combined with new opportunities for land sales and ongoing changes within the community, influenced Brothertown Indians to begin moving away from Brothertown.

Financial hardships associated with population pressure, property shortages, and exorbitant land taxes in Wisconsin also influenced Brothertown Indians to begin selling their properties in search of brighter prospects elsewhere. In the 1870s, Euro-Americans were able to purchase large amounts of Brothertown land due to the fact that many Indians could not pay their land taxes (Loew 2003). Although the Brothertown Indians initially held on to their Wisconsin land by becoming citizens, this decision ultimately had negative repercussions. By becoming the first Native American citizens of the United States, they unintentionally forfeited the dual citizenship (sovereign nation status and US citizenship) that the federal government eventually granted other Native communities. Although some interpret the Brothertown Indians' decision to become citizens as a dismissal of their Indian identities or a forfeiture of rights to govern their land, after gaining citizenship they continued to function as a tribe and continue to do so today.

Nineteenth-Century Departures, Twentieth-Century Connections

Despite the far-reaching dispersal of Brothertown Indians across the United States by the late nineteenth and early twentieth centuries, the tribe kept track of many of its members. In 1904, a special agent for the Office of Indian Affairs named Guion Miller approved a roll of the Brothertown community (Miller 1904). This document lists the names and addresses of 570 Brothertown Indians and thus offers a valuable perspective on late-nineteenth-century departures from Brothertown, Wisconsin (chapter 7). By the turn of the century, 121 Brothertown Indians (21 percent of the tribe) remained in Brothertown, Wisconsin, with an additional 84 members (15 percent) in seven different towns located within thirty kilometers. According to this document, just over half of the Brothertown community lived within 160 kilometers of Brothertown, Wisconsin; the rest lived farther away. Of the latter group, John F. Dick was the most distantly located, living over 3,000 kilometers to the southwest of Brothertown, in Stockton, California. Out of the eighty-one towns and cities listed on the roll, sixty-six were home to ten Brothertown Indians or fewer, usually representing nuclear families. Other members of the community opted to remain together. For instance, large numbers remained in Brothertown, Wisconsin (121), whereas other clusters emerged in Long Prairie, Minnesota (53), over 640 kilometers to the west, and in Fond du Lac, Wisconsin (21), approximately 30 kilometers to the south of Brothertown.

The emergence of the new Brothertown community in Long Prairie, Minnesota, demonstrates that departures from Brothertown, Wisconsin, did not always entail physical separation from fellow Brothertown Indians. However, this story also speaks to the entangled nature of Brothertown histories. The town listed as Long Prairie in the 1901 tribal roll started out as the settlement of Whiteville. It sat near the Long Prairie River Valley of northern central Minnesota and took its name from George White, who founded the settlement in 1865 with members of his extended family, including the families of his three sisters (Sheets, Henderickson, and DeLaurier 1935). A Euro-American born in Vermont, George White moved to Brothertown, Wisconsin, as an adult. While there he married Lettie Shelley, a Brothertown woman. The couple had three children together, the first two born in Brothertown and the last born in Minnesota. Another founding member of Whiteville was Albert Madison, who was first married to George White's sister. After his wife's untimely death in Minnesota, Albert married Wealthy Dick, a Brothertown women. Similarly, Lester Hoadley—yet another founding member of Whiteville—had a daughter who went on to marry Elmer D. Johnson, a Brothertown man. In the decades that followed, approximately eight more Brothertown families relocated from Brothertown, Wisconsin, to Long Prairie, adding to the Brothertown presence in Minnesota.

Like many members of the Brothertown community of Wisconsin, the Brothertown Indians of Long Prairie were Methodists. A local newspaper article printed in the 1930s described the community as follows: "It might be stated here that these Indians were 'praying Indians,' belonging to the Methodist church and their religion was the kind that did not rub off with hard usage" (Sheets, Henderickson, and DeLaurier 1936:147). Up to the second half of the nineteenth century, the Brothertown Indian community was multidenominational in nature, with factions of Methodists, Baptists, and other groups (chapters 5 and 6). When Brothertown Indians began selling their Wisconsin properties and seeking new lands, however, these religious differences seem to have shaped decisions on where to go and with whom to live. In this case, spiritual boundaries were more important than tribal or racial differences in shaping the new community (see discussion of ethnicity in chapter 2). Despite these changes, the contemporary descendants of this initial Long Prairie community of Brothertown Indians continue to play an important role in the Brothertown Indian Nation today.

During the early twentieth century, Brothertown community ties remained strong. The diary of Belva Mosher, a Brothertown Indian born in 1890, offers an invaluable perspective on these interconnections in Brothertown, Wisconsin. Diary entries recorded the rhythms of Mosher's everyday life between 1917 and 1923 (Mosher n.d.). Most striking is the role that community and family played in Belva's life. On a daily basis, she mentioned her interactions with other Brothertown Indians—both kin and nonkin. The diary mentions shared meals, social activities—such as day trips and dances—and correspondence, including letters written and received. As reflected in Belva's diary, the births, birthdays, sicknesses, struggles, and deaths of her fellow community members figured prominently in her life. Along with the mundane aspects of her daily routines, the reader gains a picture of a close-knit community. Like the Long Prairie Brothertown Indians, church and spirituality played an important role in Belva's community. Fitting for this study are the commemoration practices that Belva recorded. For example, she described her preparation for Mother's Day 1917 with the following: "sent up to Fond du Lac by J. L. Fowler and got me a dozen carnations for Mother's Grave." Interconnections between Brothertown Indians, past and present, were thus important in Belva's world. Furthermore, her writing hints at the maintenance of ties to Brothertown Indians living elsewhere. Her diary is the first to document a Brothertown Homecoming celebration. Her entries for July 1 and 2, 1917, note that a large crowd attended Homecoming, suggesting that this celebration was already an annual occurrence at the time. As implied by the event's name, Belva's description, and knowledge of contemporary Brothertown Homecomings, this celebration likely entailed a gathering of Indians in or nearby Brothertown, Wisconsin—some of whom presumably no longer lived in the area.

The Brothertown Indian Nation Today

As documented in more recent tribal records, the Brothertown Indians continue to maintain ties to one another and their shared histories. Records from meetings in Minnesota and Wisconsin demonstrate the significance of these ties. As described in the records, the Brothertown Indian Nation organizes regular meetings to create opportunities for tribal members "to get together, get acquainted, share information, and ask questions about what is happening in our tribe" (Brothertown Indian Nation n.d.). For over three decades, a central component of these meetings concerned the tribe's petition for federal recognition and quest for tribal sovereignty (chapter 8). However, their unique tribal history and cultural heritage occupies a prominent place in such meetings. For example, invitations to these gatherings often note that "fellowship and sharing of pictures, articles, books and other information is encouraged" (Brothertown Indian Nation n.d.). In addition to regular monthly meetings, the Brothertown Indian Nation holds annual Homecoming celebrations (mentioned by Belva Mosher in 1917) and annual tribal picnics. Both events take place in or nearby Brothertown, Wisconsin, and focus on maintaining connections to the landscapes that their ancestors created and inhabited.

In the late 1990s, the Brothertown Indian Nation took special steps to reconnect with their ancestral homelands by organizing a communal trip back east (Brothertown Indian Nation n.d.; Pickering 1999). On June 11,

1999, nearly fifty travelers embarked on a bus journey that brought them to the former Brothertown, New York; Stockbridge, Massachusetts; and a number of sites in Connecticut. The group included Brothertown Indians from several families, ranging from teenagers to eighty-year-olds. In Brothertown, New York, tribal members met with local townspeople and historians, attended a special service at a local church where the choir performed hymns written by Samson Occom, examined Brothertown archival materials housed in the Hamilton College archives, and visited sacred sites. The latter included three of the cemeteries discussed in chapter 5: Fowler, Skeesuck, and Niles Occom cemeteries. Some tribal members took away rocks and dirt from these cemeteries, while leaving flowers or tobacco for their ancestors (Pickering 1999). After departing from Brothertown, New York, the group stopped briefly in Stockbridge, Massachusetts, where they examined archival materials and visited several historical Stockbridge Indian sites. In Connecticut, they visited Tunxis sites in Farmington, Mashantucket Pequot sites in Ledyard, and Mohegan sites in Uncasville and Montville. In Farmington, they visited the Day-Lewis Museum to see artifacts related to various facets of local Indian history, had lunch at a local church, and toured a number of Tunxis sites—including several burial grounds as well as more ancient sites, such as rock shelters and a soapstone quarry. The travelers met with members of the Pequot tribe at the Mashantucket Pequot Museum, sharing a meal and exchanging small gifts as well as touring the museum. The next day, tribal members visited the Mohegan tribe's Tantaquidgeon Indian Museum and several other important Mohegan sites. Upon their return to Wisconsin and before going their separate ways, many opted to visit the local Brothertown cemeteries together.

Though US citizenship, land sales, and physical separation certainly challenged and changed the Brothertown community during the late nineteenth century, the contemporary meetings and events described here speak directly to the endurance that Commuck predicted. These meetings and events also demonstrate the importance that the contemporary community places on its unique history and cultural heritage. These factors each fed directly into the successes of the archaeology project situated at the heart of this study.

Genesis of the Brothertown Archaeology Project

Discussion of a potential archaeology project began in fall 2006 when I contacted Brothertown tribal genealogist Caroline Andler. The Brothertown Indian Nation soon invited me to one of their tribal council meetings to discuss the idea in person. I attended a council meeting in February 2007 at their meetinghouse in Fond du Lac, Wisconsin. After I presented a short proposal explaining my interests in such a project and outlining my understandings of how it would operate, we spent the remainder of our time together discussing possibilities for the project. As expressed during this conversation, tribal interests in the archaeology project centered on getting the younger generations of Brothertown Indians further involved in community history. In the end, the council voted to support the project, which was to commence as a field survey of Brothertown, Wisconsin—involving both archaeologists and Brothertown Indians—the next summer. Tribal member and University of Wisconsin, Madison, anthropology student Courtney Cottrell was appointed the tribal cultural preservation officer for the project.

In spring 2007 we began a standard archaeological survey of the settlement. During this time a few of the tribal elders broached the topic of their historic cemeteries with me. They mentioned their concern with the current state of many of the grave markers. Several of the stones were missing—they had probably toppled over and were covered by the heavy spring mud—and many were severely weathered and crumbling. Based on the elders' interest, I began researching Brothertown cemeteries that summer, even visiting Brothertown, New York, to see the earliest Brothertown gravesites—including Fowler and Niles Occom cemeteries (chapter 5).

It became apparent that locating Brothertown cemeteries, collecting gravestone data, searching for lost stones, and mapping the precise locations of grave markers would serve a breadth of tribal and academic interests and needs. Such a project would preserve the information contained on gravestones while identifying those stones most in need of protection. Similarly, the Brothertown Indians could recommemorate "lost" graves detected with remote sensing and locate specific gravestones using the database, and the fieldwork would be relatively friendly to all ages of Brothertown volunteers—particularly tribal elders. In addition, such a project would provide an invaluable and unique perspective of Brothertown history and on the complexities of colonial endurance.

In the fall of 2007, the cemetery project received funding from the National Science Foundation. The grant would support the mapping and cataloging of all known Brothertown cemeteries in New York and Wisconsin along with a limited amount of remote sensing to look for unmarked graves and fallen headstones. I visited the tribal council again in winter 2008 to discuss plans for the upcoming summer. The tribe helped greatly by providing information on the locations of historic Brothertown gravestones throughout the Midwest. At the meeting I was introduced to Pete Wilson,

FIGURE 3.1. Pete Wilson cleaning a grave marker in Union Cemetery, Brothertown, Wisconsin. (Photograph by author)

a Brothertown Indian who was already deeply involved in caring for and preserving cemeteries in the Brothertown, Wisconsin, area (figure 3.1).

We began working in the Wisconsin cemeteries in summer 2008. Pete Wilson took time off from work to volunteer, acting as the main tribal representative on site. During that time the team mapped and cataloged all known Brothertown cemeteries in or nearby Brothertown, Wisconsin. In the fall, we moved the survey to Brothertown, New York. Unfortunately, the distance separating the New York cemeteries from Wisconsin prevented tribal members from volunteering for this portion of the research. During this time, my team mapped and cataloged all known (extant) Brothertown cemeteries in New York except one (chapter 5). We returned for a third field season in Brothertown, Wisconsin, in June 2009. This time we performed a ground-penetrating radar survey in the Indian half of Union cemetery, locating several unmarked graves—and we cataloged other isolated Brothertown grave markers located well outside of Brothertown, Wisconsin (chapter 6).

4

Brothertown Writing

PEOPLING THE PLACE, PLACING THE PEOPLE

ON NOVEMBER 7, 1785, SAMSON OCCOM described the founding of Brothertown, New York, in his journal:

> But ^now^ we proceeded to form in^to^ a Body Politick—We Named our Town by the Name of Brotherton, in Indian Eeyawquittoowauconnuck. . . . Concluded to have a center near David Fowlers House the main Street is to run North and South and East and West, to Cross at the Centre Concluded to live in Peace, and in Friendship and to go on in all their ^Public^ Concerns in Harmony both in their Religious and Temporal Concerns, and everyone to bear his ~~Public~~ part of Public Charges in Town,—They desired me to be a Teacher amongst them, I Consented to Spend Some of my remaining [time] with them, and make this Town my Home and Center. (Occom 2006j [1785]:308)

As described, Occom saw Brotherton, or "Brothertown" as it came to be known, simply as place rather than as an identity. For him, the newly formed body politic was exactly that—a community linked by shared religious views and approaches to the politics of colonial North America—rather than an emergent ethnic group. In the decades that followed, however, individuals and families living at Brothertown formed senses of place and identity distinct from those of Occom, and they came to see one another as more than neighbors. Reflections of this social transformation show through in the documentary record, specifically in uses of the name "Brothertown" and other modes of reference to the community and its members. For example, in a letter sent to state officials forty-two years after Occom's journal entry, a group of Brothertown community leaders typified themselves as "the chiefs, head men and peacemakers of the Brothertown Indians, a nation or Tribe of

Indians residing in the County of Oneida—state of New York" (Brothertown Indians 1827a). Shifting uses of the name "Brothertown" such as these offer valuable insights into the complexities of colonial entanglements, revealing the processes by which Brothertown Indians negotiated their identities in dialogue with outsiders.

Similar to all cases of ethnogenesis, the emergence of the Brothertown Indian community involved new social and cultural markers. I begin my analysis of Brothertown history with the most conspicuous of these markers—their new communal name, or *ethnonym*. It supplanted the ethnonyms used previously by its members and their ancestors, signaling a clear and conscious change for Brothertown Indians who previously identified as Narragansetts, Eastern Pequots, Mashantucket Pequots, Mohegans, Montauketts, Niantics, or Tunxis. I examine these transformations in detail along with other patterns found in eighteenth- and nineteenth-century documents written by, to, or about the Brothertown Indians. Using the pragmatic framework outlined earlier, I consider the differences that observed changes in writing (and communication in general) made for the Brothertown Indians and for the larger colonial society of which they were part. The Brothertown community adopted the English language by the late eighteenth century, so the documents under analysis offer unique perspectives on both sides of such negotiations, detailing the gives and takes of identity formation described in chapter 2. Returning to Fredrik Barth's work, ethnonymy represents a key form of boundary maintenance, and Brothertown texts provide an ideal opportunity to explore its negotiated nature. The archaeology of Brothertown discourse presented in this chapter, therefore, speaks to the role of written language in constituting places, peoples, and colonial interactions (Cipolla 2012a, 2012d).

Approaching Brothertown Documents

Before turning to the archival data, I first contextualize the approach taken in this chapter by comparing it to other methods of documentary analysis in historical archaeology. This requires a brief discussion of how historical archaeologists typically think about and analyze the texts they uncover and encounter in archival and archaeological contexts. Most notably manifested in debates over the weight of the written word in relation to "mute" material culture, features, and spatial patterns uncovered from archaeological sites, this issue is nothing new to historical archaeology (Beaudry 1988a; Hall 1999; Leone and Potter 2003 [1988]; Schuyler 1978 [1977]). It points to the complexities and strengths of working with multiple data sets, some of which speak in the void left by other's apparent silences (Deetz 1996 [1977]; Orser 1996; Wilkie 2006). For the most part, however, these debates have been confined to the study of documents produced primarily by European colonists and settlers rather than those written by Native Americans. In this regard, the study at hand covers new ground that will only benefit from broader engagements with other forms of text-aided archaeology (e.g., Moreland 2001).

Many practitioners agree on the need to treat documents as material culture, deprivileging the written word in relation to artifacts and archaeological features lacking texts. Often inspired by the recursive frameworks of practice theory, these archaeologists recognize that archaeological and archival records are equally partial, albeit in distinct and interesting ways. This is because all forms of material culture—including documents—were subject to social manipulation as past actors situated and represented themselves in relation to others (Voss 2007). For instance, I discuss the ways in which Brothertown authors adjusted their styles of writing depending on their addressees and goals at the time. The same general pattern holds true for the ways Brothertown Indians represented themselves (and their ancestors) with material culture, such as the grave markers analyzed in chapters 5 and 6. The key concept here is that neither linguistic nor artifactual traces alone represent who the Brothertown Indians "really" were any more than the other. From a pragmatic perspective, the intentions behind such representations must always be considered in terms of the actual differences they made in the world (see chapter 2). In other words, whether successful in the eyes of their senders or not, these "messages" (linguistic or otherwise) partially constituted reality when they shaped social interactions and influenced historical trajectories. Rather than treating text-bearing artifacts as fundamentally distinct from their "mute" counterparts, I seek to reconstruct precisely how these potentially discursive fragments shaped—and took shape from—past social relations at Brothertown.

Despite these acknowledgments in the broader field of historical archaeology, there is still a tendency to engage primarily with the "surface meanings" or "dictionary definitions" of the words and phrases encountered in archives and uncovered at archaeological sites. When compared with the seemingly taciturn nature of many of the artifacts and patterns drawn on in archaeological interpretation, historical texts "speak" out, often tempting archaeologists away from deeper engagements with the linguistic patterns contained therein. These disparities set the stage for asymmetrical approaches, constituted by superficial readings of historical texts and unending quests to squeeze new types of information from archaeological materials lacking texts. Although the perspectives on archaeological data gleaned from new analytical techniques should be applauded, with few exceptions, historical archaeologists have yet to approach historical documents and other text-bearing artifacts in parallel manners. Given archaeology's history of adopting analytical techniques developed outside of the discipline (e.g., carbon dating, Geographic Information Systems), historical archaeology's lack of engagement with linguistics is surprising in many regards. With the exception of Mary Beaudry's (1988a, 1988b, 1988c) edited volume, *Documentary Archaeology in the New World*, in practice, the utility of linguistic analysis in historical archaeology remains grossly underexplored. The linguistic approach taken in this chapter is thus novel in several ways.

Taking inspiration from the work of Michael Silverstein (1976) and other pragmatists studying language and signs (Agha 2007; Hanks 1987; Keane 2003; Silverstein and Urban 1996; Singer 1978), I approach Brothertown documents not only in terms of semantics (i.e., what they say) but also in terms of their pragmatic implications (i.e., what they did). Beyond the pure referential function of words and phrases contained within, speech acts (Agha 2007; Fairclough 1992)—in this case represented as historical documents—contain subtle, pragmatic clues into the dynamics of past social realities. For example, in "The Secret Life of Texts," Silverstein (1996) constructed new understandings of anthropologist Edward Sapir's interactions with a Native informant in the early twentieth century. He detected shifts in the voicing of a narrative concerning traditional practices that revealed the personal biases and orientations of both Sapir and his informant. Similar to Daniel's pragmatic description of ethnography discussed in chapter 2, Silverstein demonstrated how Sapir's field notes represent an amalgamation of the cultural repertoires of both ethnographer and informant. Treating instances of ethnonymy and other related modes of reference as miniature texts, I explore their "secret lives" via the pragmatic continuities of written discourse.

Peopling the Place, Placing the People

In the first few decades of its existence, there were several names for Brothertown. In the journal entry quoted above, Occom offered the "Indian" (i.e., Mohegan-Pequot-Montaukett) gloss "Eeyawquittoowauconnuck" (Brooks 2006:25). The precise meaning of this term is unclear, though some argue that it roughly translates to "a place of eternal respect for each other," "town or plantation of equals or brothers," or "many eat from one dish" (Cipolla

2010:95). Because Occom's journal is the only known historical document in which the Native version of the name appears, its use may be a reflection of his personal views of the settlement rather than those of his fellow community members; it might also represent a primarily spoken version of the name. Regardless of the precise reasons for the near omission of this Indian gloss from the historical record, authors writing in the eighteenth and nineteenth centuries—both Indian and Euro-American—primarily referred to the settlement using the English versions of the name, "Brotherton," or "Brothertown." Shifting uses of these names through time and between different social groups offer insights into processes of identity change and negotiation. A close consideration of the larger discursive contexts of the time also suggests that these names played a significant role in the unfolding of Brothertown history, allowing a number of distinct cultural readings. In this case, the name created a neutral ground on which Euro-Americans and Native peoples could relate (Merrell 1999; White 1991), reading "Brothertown" as the name of a community of Christian and/or Indian brothers.

As discussed previously, the name of their new domicile eventually replaced the ancestral tribal names—Narragansett, Eastern Pequot, Mashantucket Pequot, Mohegan, Montaukett, Niantic, and Tunxis—of those living at Brothertown. That is, Brothertown's inhabitants eventually came to identify as "Brothertown Indians" rather than as Narragansetts, Pequots, or otherwise. By necessity, this change coincided with new uses (and meanings) of the name "Brothertown." As evinced by the excerpt from Occom's journal, the name first appeared as a toponym, or place name, in the late eighteenth century. This changed as Brothertown's inhabitants and their interlocutors began gradually transforming the toponym into an ethnonym. In fact, this change was conventionalized to such a degree by the time of the Brothertowns' next emigration to current-day Wisconsin in the 1830s, that they "took" the toponym with them; subsequent to their departure for Wisconsin, Brothertown, New York, became known as the towns of Waterville and Deansboro. These transformations attest to the mutual constitution of place and people (Ingold 1993), revealing the importance of a shared space (e.g., the Brothertown settlement) in forging communal identities (e.g., the Brothertown Indians) and the role the actual people played in constituting the place they inhabited, bestowing on it certain attributes, or "senses" (Feld and Basso 1996).

This transformation warrants further attention because it speaks to the processes by which the place became a people via written discourse between insiders and outsiders. As they interacted, authors—both inside and out—used the name in a variety of manners. To study the nature of this transformation in the archival record, all uses of the name "Brothertown" and other forms of communal reference were cataloged from a total of eighty-six documents written by, to, or about the Brothertown Indians (table 4.1). The documents range in date between 1788 and 1842, providing glimpses of a wide swath of Brothertown history that complement those provided by

Table 4.1. Analyzed Documents

Year	Author(s)	Number of Documents
1788	State official	1
1789	State official	1
1790	State official	1
1791	State official	1
1795	State official	2
1796	Brothertown commissioners	3
1796	State official	4
1796	Brothertown Indians	2
1796	Brothertown superintendents	4
1797	Brothertown commissioners	2
1797	State official	1
1797	Brothertown superintendents	9
1798	Brothertown superintendents	6
1799	Brothertown superintendents	8
1800	Brothertown Indians	1
1801	Brothertown superintendents	12
1801	State official	1
1802	Brothertown superintendents	4
1802	State official	1
1804	Brothertown superintendents	2
1811	Brothertown Indians	1
1825	Brothertown Indians	1
1827	Brothertown Indians	3
1827	Brothertown superintendents	1
1827	Oneida Indians	1
1832	Brothertown Indians	1
1832	Oneida Indians	1
1832	Federal official	2
1832	New York Indians	1
1838	Brothertown Indians	1
1839	Federal officials	1
1842	Federal official	1
Total		86

Table 4.2. Typology of Ethnonymic Noun Phrases

Type	Example	Relation of toponym to ethnonym	Implied relationship between people
Locational adjunct to group designation	"the Indians residing at Brothertown"	Adjunct	Weakest
Adjective modifying group designation	"the Brothertown Indians"	Modifier	Intermediate
Independent group designator	"the Brothertowns"	Identical (no distinction)	Tight

the gravestone analysis discussed in chapters 5 and 6. To be precise, the name appears 306 times in the analyzed documents, 136 times as an independent toponym and 170 times as part of ethnonymic nouns or noun phrases. I sort the latter group into three basic types (table 4.2). First are examples where "Brothertown" appears as a locational adjunct to group designation (e.g., "Indians residing at Brother Town"); second are examples where "Brothertown" appears as an adjective modifying group designation (e.g., "the Brothertown Indians"); and third are examples where "Brothertown" appears as an independent group designator (e.g., "the Brothertowns"). The differences among these types are crucial for this project, as they typify the community in distinct manners, emphasizing varying criteria for group membership. Similar to the reflexive links between toponymy and senses of place (Basso 1996a, 1996b; Feld and Basso 1996), ethnonymy and other modes of reference also reflect and contribute to schemes of social understanding and classification.

The three types link the place with the people in a hierarchical order. Within the first category, phrases such as "Indians residing at Brother Town" use the term as a toponym, emphasizing shared residence as the sole criterion for group membership and creating the weakest link between members of the group. Examples in the second category, such as "the Brothertown Indians," use the term as an ethnonym but as a modifier of another term, "Indians" in this case, formulating a more coherent bond between members of the group (i.e., as sharers of Indian-ness). Finally, examples in the third category laminate toponym and ethnonym so that there is virtually no distinction between the two, such as in "the Brothertowns." More so than the other types of reference, examples in this category portray the group as a coherent, bounded social entity. Thus, following Barth (1998b [1969]), these three categories represent semi-distinct degrees of group boundary.

As time passed and the Brothertown identity congealed, authors shifted between the first and second categories. In documents dating to the late eighteenth century (1788–1800), the name "Brothertown" appears as a locational adjunct to group designation 65.5 percent of the time, as an adjective modifying group designation 33.3 percent of the time, and as an independent group designator only once (table 4.3). During this early period, most authors referred to the new community as "the Indians residing at Brothertown," "the Brothertown Indians," "Inhabitance of Brothertown," or "the Indians at/in Brothertown." Nearly all of these examples emphasized shared place as the sole criterion for group membership, representing ties between individuals and families at Brothertown as loose and boundaries between insiders and outsiders as fairly fluid.

This pattern changed by the early nineteenth century (1801–1842), during which time authors used "Brothertown" as a locational adjunct to group designation only 5.8 percent of the time, as an adjective modifying group designation 90.7 percent of the time, and as an independent group designator only 3.5 percent of the time (table 4.4). The most frequently occurring noun phrases during this period were: "the Brothertown Indians," "the Brothertown Tribe of Indians," and "the Brothertown tribe." Each of these

Table 4.3. Uses of the Name "Brothertown," 1780–1800

		Occurrences	Percentage
Location adjunct to group designation			
Indians residing at Brothertown		25	29.8
Inhabitance of Brothertown		8	9.5
Indians at/in Brothertown		8	9.5
White inhabitants of Brothertown		2	2.4
Person residing in Brothertown		1	1.2
Indians and Indian families living in Brothertown		1	1.2
New England Indians now settled in Brothertown		1	1.2
Persons in Brothertown		1	1.2
Indians as may be in law in Brothertown		1	1.2
	Subtotal	55	65.5
Adjectives modifying group designation			
Brothertown Indian(s)		27	32.1
Brotherton or Brothertown Indians		1	1.2
	Subtotal	28	33.3
Independent group designator			
Brothertons/Brothertowns		1	1.2
	Subtotal	1	1.2
Total ethnonymic noun phrases		84	100
Total uses as independent toponym		96	

Table 4.4. Uses of the Name "Brothertown," 1801–1842

	Occurrences	Percentage
Locational adjunct to group designation		
Inhabitance of Brothertown	1	1.2
Indian(s) entitled to land in Brothertown	1	1.2
Seven tribes . . . now inhabiting the Town of Brothertown	1	1.2
Indians at Brothertown	2	2.3
Subtotal	5	5.8
Adjective modifying group designation		
Brothertown Indians	51	59.3
Brothertown Tribe of Indians	8	9.3
Brothertown Tribe	6	7.0
Brotherton or Brothertown Indians	4	4.7
Brothertown people	2	2.3
Tribe of Brothertown Indians	1	2.3
Brotherton Indians	1	1.2
Brothertown Indian Nation	1	1.2
The Tribe of Indians . . . the Brothertown Indians	1	1.2
Tribe of Indians known as the Brothertown tribe	1	1.2
Subtotal	78	90.7
Independent group designator		
Our Brothertown	2	2.3
Brothertowns	1	1.2
Subtotal	3	3.5
Total ethnonymic noun phrases	86	100
Total uses as independent toponym	40	

forms defines the group's coherence as based in shared Indian ancestry and/or political organization. Although the word *tribe* primarily referred to political organization, it also carried connotations of shared ancestry and cultural identity, thus representing the ties between individuals and families at Brothertown as much deeper compared to the prevalent modes of reference in the eighteenth century.

This change speaks to the reclassification of those groups living at Brothertown into a unified tribal entity, "the Brothertown Indians." The transition took place in the early nineteenth century, approximately three to five decades after the Brothertown Indians' initial move from the East Coast. This period correlates loosely with the second and third generations of Brothertown Indians. As reflected in the changes already outlined, the new generations seemingly viewed themselves, their community, and their history in manners distinct from how their parents and grandparents did. Notably, authors rarely referred to the Brothertown community as they did other Native groups, that is, using ethnonyms as independent group designators (third type from above), such as "the Oneidas," or "the Pequot."

Table 4.5 quantifies these distinctions, comparing references to the Brothertown community with references to other Native groups. In contrast to the ways they made reference to the Brothertown community in the eighteenth and nineteenth centuries, authors referring to other Native groups used proper names as locational adjuncts to group designation only 1.4 percent of the time, as adjectives modifying group designation 66.4 percent of the time, and as independent group designators 32.2 percent of the time. As mentioned, the most popular means of making reference to other Native groups were independent ethnonyms, such as "the Oneidas." During this time, authors emphasized shared space as the central criterion for group membership much more with the Brothertown community than with other Native groups. As discussed next, I partially attribute these patterns to the

Table 4.5. References to Other Native Groups, 1788–1842

		Occurrences	Percentage
Locational adjunct to group designation			
The Indians residing in New Stockbridge		2	1.0
The inhabitants of New Stockbridge		1	0.4
	Subtotal	3	1.4
Adjective modifying group designation			
(Proper Name) Indians		44	20.1
(Proper Name) Tribe of Indians		38	17.4
(Proper Name) Tribes		33	15.1
(Proper Name) Nation		15	6.8
(Proper Name) Nation of Indians		11	5.0
Indians called the (Proper Name)		1	0.4
Nations of Indians		1	0.4
(Proper Name) Tribe or Nation		1	0.4
Tribe or Nation of Indians called the (Proper Name)		1	0.4
Tribes of (regional designation) Indians		1	0.4
	Subtotal	146	66.4
Independent group designator			
The (Proper Name)s		62	28.4
The (Proper Name)		8	3.8
	Subtotal	70	32.2
Total ethnonymic noun phrases		219	100

English roots of the name "Brothertown," which clearly limited the ways certain authors used and read the name.

In most cases, Brothertown authors used the name as an adjective modifying group designation, whereas Euro-American authors used the name in a variety of ways, most frequently as an independent toponym (table 4.6). Distinct spellings of the name used by each group offer one possible explanation for these disparities. For example, Brothertown authors spelled the name consistently, using the standard spelling ("Brothertown") 94 percent of the time, while Euro-American authors used a number of different spellings, several of which emphasized the *town* in *Brothertown*. Approximately 25 percent of the time, Euro-American authors spelled the name "Brother-Town," or "Brother Town," demonstrating the significance of the root *town* in the name for Euro-American authors and suggesting that the name simply denoted a domicile for Euro-Americans, whereas it meant something more for Brothertown Indians.

Between the late eighteenth and mid-nineteenth centuries, Brothertown authors consistently used "Brothertown" as part of ethnonymic noun phrases marking shared ethnic and racial identities, such as in "the Brothertown Indians," and/or political organization, such as in "the Brothertown tribe." These uses stressed unified qualities of the group that ran much deeper than shared residential space, portraying those living at Brothertown as an ethnic group not only united in terms of shared Indian ancestry but also organized as a politically coherent unit. These patterns complement the silences observed in the gravestone inscriptions discussed in the next two chapters; together these two distinct forms of discourse suggest that members of the

Table 4.6. Uses of the Name "Brothertown" by Authorship

	Occurrences	Percentage
Brothertown authors		
Locational adjunct to group designation	2	3.8
Adjective modifying group designation	36	69.2
Independent group designator	3	5.8
Independent toponym	11	21.2
Euroamerican authors		
Locational adjunct to group designation	58	22.8
Adjective modifying group designation	70	27.6
Independent group designator	1	0.4
Independent toponym	125	49.2

Brothertown community saw themselves as part of a unified tribal entity rather than as a conglomerate of tribal groups simply sharing residence.

In comparison, Euro-American authors clearly changed the ways they used the name through time. During the late eighteenth century, the most frequent means by which Euro-American authors referred to the Brothertown community were: "the Indians residing in Brothertown," "the Brothertown Indians," "the Indians at Brothertown," and "the Indians entitled to land in Brothertown." In contrast to those of Brothertown authors just discussed, most of these examples emphasize shared residential space as the sole criterion for group membership, portraying those living at Brothertown as a mishmash of displaced Native peoples from various tribes. For example, in an act passed in the state of New York in 1789, the authors wrote, "[The] tract of land so laid out shall be called Brother-Town and shall remain for the cultivation, improvement and use of the said New England Indians and their Brethren, consisting of the tribes calleth Mohegan, Montague, Stonington and Narragansett Indians, and the Pequots of Groton and Nihantics of Farmington and their Prosperity" (Brothertown Indians n.d.). In contrast to the patterns of the late eighteenth century, Euro-American authors writing only a few decades later (early to mid-nineteenth century) mainly referred to the community as "the Brothertown Indians." Compared to the mode of reference used in the foregoing quotation, later forms of reference such as this portrayed the group as a discrete and unified social entity.

These patterns indicate disparate internal and external conceptions of the name and the community in the eighteenth century, followed by a marked shift in the ways in which Euro-American authors referred to—and presumably conceived of—the community in the early to mid-nineteenth century. On one hand, Brothertown authors consistently represented their community as unified in terms of ethnicity, race, and/or political organization, referring to their community as "the Brothertown Indians," "the Brothertown Tribe of Indians," "the Brothertown Tribe," and "the Brothertown people." As discussed in subsequent chapters, the nearly complete omission of ancestral tribal ethnonyms in Brothertown cemeteries and the subtle wording of several grave marker inscriptions complement this pattern. On the other hand, Euro-American authors first referred to the community as a collection of various peoples (usually, but not always typified as "Indians") sharing coresidence at the place known as Brothertown, but later came to refer to the community as a cohesive entity. From this perspective it appears that Brothertown authors influenced their Euro-American addressees in certain ways. More important than this, however, is the fact that both insiders and outsiders played a role in shaping this particular instance of ethnonymy and ethnogenesis. Although the name was clearly English in origin, the Brothertown Indians used it in slightly distinct ways than did their Euro-American interlocutors, presumably influencing them to refer to (and think of) the inhabitants of Brothertown as a unified tribal entity by the nineteenth century.

The Ambiguity of Colonial Texts: What Kind of Brotherhood?

As with other cases of ethnogenesis, such as Voss' (2008a, 2008c) study of Californio identities at El Presidio de San Francisco, the emergent identity (and ethnonym in this case) challenged the dominant social hierarchy by rendering the community difficult to classify in relation to contemporaneous Euro-American and Native communities. This ambiguity—tied to the non-Native roots of the name and its inclusion of the root word *brother*—assisted the Brothertown Indians in their negotiations of colonial politics. The *brother* in the name *Brothertown* allowed multiple, competing interpretations depending on the reader or receiver, an ambiguity that helped the Brothertown Indians align their community with a diversity of addressees, both Indian and Euro-American. Terms of fictive kinship—specifically fictive brotherhood—sat on the boundary of at least two discursive conventions (one Christian and the other Native). The meaning one ascribed to "brother" in such instances depended on the classification of the overall work in which it appeared and on the orientation of the reader (Hanks 1987; Morson 1981).

When read from the perspective of a Christian community, references to fictive kinship primarily denoted Christian brotherhood, although the same terms likely carried alternative meanings when read by a Native community. Native groups regularly used kinship terms to fictively align nonkin. For example, Lewis Henry Morgan noted relations of fictive brotherhood between Iroquoian tribes. "In the eyes of an Iroquois, every member of his own tribe, in whatever nation, was as much his brother or his sister as if children of the same mother" (Morgan 1962 [1851]:81–82). Similarly, in the Massachusett language, *netomp* denoted both "my friend" and "sibling of opposite sex," a pattern found in other Algonquian languages such as Unami and Munsee (Bragdon 1997:9–10). As Native communities converted to Christianity, these two traditional uses of fictive kinship fused in certain instances. For example, Bragdon (1997:5) notes the use of terms such as *nemattog* ("my brothers," or "my same-sex siblings") and *nettahtueog* ("my sisters," or "my siblings of opposite sex") in a letter written by a Native minister of Martha's Vineyard to address fellow church members (i.e., Christian siblings). In cases such as this, speakers and writers used Native kinship terms to denote Christian brotherhood, a subtle transformation.

The pattern also holds for Native uses of the English language, where terms such as *father* and *brother* were used to align various social entities in terms of power relations. For example, Joseph Johnson addressed the Oneida as "brethren" or "older brothers" when inquiring about land in Oneida country on which to found Brothertown in the mid-1770s (Murray 1998a; Oneida Headmen 2006 [1775]; Venables 1993). The Oneida also used fictive kinship terms in their responses to Johnson, at times explicitly discussing fictive kinship relations: "Brethren, we look upon you, as upon a Sixth Brother. We will tell you, of all your elder Brothers, the Onoidas, Kiyougas, Nanticuks, Tuskaroras, Todelehonas, these five are your Elder Brothers. But as for the Mohawks, Onondaugas, and the Senecas they are our fathers, and they are your fathers" (Murray 1998a:219). Native groups also used these terms to describe their relations to non-Natives. For instance, Native authors commonly used the phrase "Great Father" to refer to the president of the United States (e.g., Decora 2006 [1829]; Potawatomi 2006 [1836]). The ambiguity of the name "Brothertown" parallels that of the purchased gravestones described in chapters 5 and 6. In both cases, the words and things associated with the Brothertown Indians allowed community members to easily situate themselves in relation to a breadth of audiences, both Native and non-Native.

Fictive kinship terms likely took on even more weight in contexts of multitribal and pan-Indian communities. In North America, such settlements emerged in response to colonialism and its legacies, consolidating small Native communities whose populations had been decimated by disease and warfare (Merrell 1989) and/or uniting disparate Native communities against a common adversary (Smoak 2007). A letter written by the Brothertown Indians (1811) addressed to another multitribal community in White River, Indiana, contains several uses of kinship terminology to align the authors with their addressees. The writers addressed certain members of the Indiana group as "Fathers Brothers and friends," "Fathers and Brothers," and "Grand Fathers and Brothers" on several occasions. Since the Indiana group was largely non-Christian, such kinship terms were used (and read) as a gloss for Indian kinship. Within the same letter, however, the authors also refer to the Mohiconuck (Stockbridge) as "our Brother," which may have denoted Native and/or Christian brotherhood for the authors, since the Stockbridge were a fellow Native Christian community (Frazier 1992; Silverman 2010). Despite this double meaning, their addressees probably read the latter example as denoting Indian brotherhood given their particular orientation.

In another letter written by Brothertown community members to President John Quincy Adams in 1827 (Brothertown Indians 1827b), several uses of fictive kinship terms hint at the nuanced meanings behind "brother" in such contexts. The letter concerns the land conflicts between local Wisconsin Indigenous groups and the "New York Indians"—the Brothertown, Stockbridge, Oneida, Tuscarora, and St. Regis communities—who were planning a move west to current-day Wisconsin at the time. In the letter, the authors referred to several different Indigenous groups, including the Stockbridge, Oneida, Tuscarora, St. Regis, and Menominee communities. Every time the authors referred to one of the New York groups, they aligned their respective communities as "brothers." Yet the authors never used kinship terminology to align themselves with the Menominee (a Wisconsin group). In this particular context, the authors used fictive kinship terms to denote both shared Indigenous descent and shared settlement area (New York State), regardless of religious affiliations.

Uses of fictive kinship in the letter to President Adams parallel the shifts that occurred with the name "Brothertown" as it transformed from a toponym to an ethnonym. As members of distinct Native communities came together to form the Brothertown community and began sharing a residential space, they were transformed into a unified tribe. Similarly, the spatial proximity of the Brothertown, Stockbridge, and other New York tribes' settlements translated into a fictive kinship alignment as seen in the letter to President Adams. In these cases, the emergence of in-group unity relied on strikingly similar tropes. As members of distinct groups came to share residence, they became fictive kin, albeit on different scales. In the case of the Brothertown Indians, this occurred as members of the seven East Coast tribes came to live together at Brothertown, whereas for the New York Indians, it occurred as various tribal entities came to live near one another in New York State. As colonial encroachment pushed various coastal groups westward, forming new multitribal communities, it seems likely that shared spaces came to supersede deep kinship ties and cultural memories as criteria for in-group membership.

Manipulated Texts

Because language is reflexively tethered to social life, authors and speakers often use their knowledge of accepted norms of communication to manipulate meanings in ways that help them achieve their goals. Among other methods, speakers and authors choose words and phrases to align with—or create distance from—other social entities via the pragmatics of communication (Agha 2005, 2007). As mentioned previously, the English roots of the name "Brothertown" set it apart from the Brothertown Indians' ancestral tribal names, such as "Mohegan," and from the names of other tribal groups such as the Oneida or the Menominee, which were typically read as "Indian" names. Although the name "Brothertown" generally supplanted the names of the ancestral tribes from whence the Brothertown Indians came, there are a few notable exceptions where Brothertown authors purposefully used the ancestral names in place of the ethnonym "Brothertown." In these cases, the broader contexts of the documents shed light on the reasons for the intentional shifts.

In the 1811 letter written to the confederacy of Native groups in Indiana discussed previously, the authors typified their community as "the seven tribes to wit Mohegan Farmington Montock Pequot Stonington Narraganset and Nihanticks now inhabiting the Town of Brothertown" (Brothertown Indians 1811). The letter mainly concerns a land inquiry, as the Brothertown Indians anticipated the necessity of a move from their New York settlement due to Euro-American crowding and a scarcity of land at that time. In this context, it was advantageous for the Brothertown Indians to tie themselves to their ancestral communities as a means of aligning with their addressees. In this sense, they accented the similarities (as Indian people) between them and their addressees and downplayed potential distinctions (e.g., the fact that they were a Christian community who practiced European-style agriculture and spoke English). The authors also used nature metaphors (e.g., "the clouds of misunderstanding") and references to traditional Algonquian practices (e.g., "to smoke the pipe of Peace with you"), further demonstrating efforts to align their community with their addressees by emphasizing shared Native roots.

In an 1825 letter written by Brothertown community leaders to President James Monroe, the authors referred to their community as, "Inhabitance of Brothertown in the County of Oneida and State of New York . . . the *remnants* of the Six tribes or Nations of Indians formerly residing in Connecticut Rhode Island and on the East end of Long Island known by the name of Mohegan Montauk Stonington and Narragansett Pequot of Groton and Nihanticks of Farmington" (Brothertown Indians 1825, emphasis added). The letter concerns the federal government's appropriation of the land the Brothertown Indians had reserved in White River, Indiana, mentioned in the previous example. The Brothertown Indians argued their case by emphasizing their history of displacement and struggle, in which it was necessary to accent their community's multitribal composition and East Coast origins.

Their use of the term *remnants* added a tone to the letter that reinforced the seriousness of its subject matter (i.e., the group's current state and their need for new lands). The authors used subtle distinctions in modes of reference to further emphasize their needs, portraying their community as incoherent and fragmented compared to other Native groups in the area; in addition to "inhabitants" and "remnants," they also refer to their community as "tribes." Compared to their references to other Native groups as "Nations," "Tribes of Indians," and "Tribes or Nations," the latter modes of references set the Brothertown community apart from other groups in this particular instance.

In other cases, Brothertown authors clearly wished to distance themselves from their traditional East Coast roots, particularly when addressing federal representatives with the power to grant land rights. For instance, when petitioning for US citizenship and associated land rights in the 1830s, Brothertown authors appropriated a rhetoric of social evolution, emphasizing distinctions between their community and other Native groups, past and present. The petition reads: "your petitioners have *long since laid aside the ancient manners and customs of our forefathers* and have *adopted those of our white neighbors* and have made considerable improvements in almost all the useful arts and sciences of a civilised people and are still making valuable improvements by building mills school Houses etc." (Brothertown Indians 1838, emphasis added). In this document, the authors use "the Brothertown Indians" once, and "the Brothertown Tribe" three times, with four additional uses of the word *tribe* to refer to the community. The authors mention their recent move from New York, but omitted other details of their past, such as their East Coast origins.

In each of these examples, the authors portrayed their community in distinct ways depending on their objectives. In the letter written to tribes in Indiana inquiring about land, the authors highlighted the Brothertown community's traditional tribal roots, portraying Brothertown simply as a refuge for tribes from the East Coast. In the letter written to President Monroe concerning their need for a new land base, the authors portray their community as incoherent, marginal, and distinct from other Native groups (perhaps because of the latter groups' comparatively ample land bases). In the petition for citizenship, the authors portrayed their community as a single tribe, with no recognition of their multitribal origins on the East Coast. Unlike the other examples, however, this petition explicitly depicts the community as neo-Indian, a tribe that practiced Euro-American style agriculture and "improved" their Wisconsin land base, yet had no laws to protect the fruits of their labor, as did their white neighbors. In each of these cases, the forms of the texts overtly contributed to the authors' overarching arguments in subtle if not wholly transparent manners.

A federal report filed on the Brothertown Indians' 1838 petition demonstrates the success of their arguments. "Your Committee are further informed that the said Brothertown Indians having laid aside the habits and customs of their ancestors have abandoned the chase, and have devoted themselves to the cultivation of the Soil and have become both civilized and Christianized to a higher degree than perhaps any other tribe of Indians on this continent" (United States 1839). At another point in the report, the author refers to the Brothertown Indians as "this *community* of Indians—(for *tribe* they ought no longer be called)" (United States 1839, emphasis added). Following this report, the Brothertown Indians became the first Native American tribe granted US citizenship, and their Wisconsin settlement was subsequently parceled out to individuals and families within the community (Cipolla and Andler 2007; Loew 2001, 2003). The ways they represented themselves in writing—both semantically and pragmatically—certainly played a role in their successful petition.

Discussion and Conclusion

"Peopling the place, placing the people" refers to several historic processes. On one hand, *peopling the place* refers to the process of physically populating a geographic locale with bodies. In this case it refers to the peopling of the place known as "Brothertown." On the other hand, *placing the people* refers to the processes by which the name of a place—"Brothertown"—transformed into the name of a people, "the Brothertown Indians." It also refers to the process of socially situating the Brothertown community in relation to other Euro-American and Indigenous communities in the eighteenth and nineteenth centuries. Both of the latter processes took place partially in the form of written discourse.

Using documents written by, to, or about the Brothertown Indians dating from the late eighteenth through mid-nineteenth centuries, I tracked subtle shifts in naming and other related modes of reference that speak to processes of ethnogenesis and the negotiation of colonial politics via the pragmatics of written discourse. Similar to other studies of ethnogenesis, this analysis demonstrates the centrality of a shared place in constructing new identities (Basso 1996a, 1996b; Feld and Basso 1996). As portions of seven tribal groups came to share residential space in Brothertown, New York, they also began sharing a new cultural moniker, which supplanted their ancestral tribal designations. Nuanced uses of kinship terminology to align groups sharing both Native roots and residential space further support this notion. For example, when the Brothertown Indians wrote to President Adams in 1827, they referred to their Native neighbors in New York as "brothers," while they offered no such gloss for the other groups discussed, Native or otherwise. James Merrell (1989) found a similar pattern in his study of the Catawbas of South Carolina, a conglomerate of several Native communities sharing land around the Catawba River Valley. In each of these cases, new communal identities were contingent on shared places.

In many instances of ethnogenesis, new groups created new places (Feld and Basso 1996; Ingold 1993), which in turn gave their inhabitants new communal names and, to some extent, new identities (Larson 1996). This was clearly the case with the Brothertown Indians as it was for the Californios (Voss 2008a, 2008c) and the Catawbas (Merrell 1989). In such cases ethnonyms contributed to the internal cohesion among the new group (i.e., a common name to rally under), while also providing a means for outsiders to classify group members within their social milieu. In the case of the Brothertown Indians, the creation of a new ethnonym was important in several regards. Instead of remaining Mohegans, Pequots, Narragansetts, Montauketts, Tunxis, and Niantics, those individuals and families living at Brothertown became "Brothertown Indians." This transformation forged ties to their new home and to each other. The new ethnonym represented the community as a coherent social entity to outsiders, rather than an admixture of various groups simply sharing residence, a particularly important detail when negotiating with other politically cohesive units (e.g., the Oneida Nation, the United States).

As nearly four decades of anthropological and historical research show, social identities often result from the interaction of insiders with outsiders. I used the unique qualities of the Brothertown context to explore the give and take of identity as seen in the emergence and negotiation of the ethnonym "Brothertown"—an ethnic boundary of sorts (Barth 1998b [1969]). The Brothertown Indians' comparatively early adoption of the English language allows a unique glimpse of Native authors and the roles they played in negotiating their identities by way of pen and paper.

Samson Occom's journal entry in 1785 represents a baptismal event (Agha 2007:65–68) for the place and the people now known as Brothertown, at least in terms of written discourse. It is true that Occom used a slightly different spelling of the name, "Brotherton," along with an Indian gloss *Eeyawquittoowauconnuck* to refer to the new settlement. Yet as various individuals and groups discussed the new community, the name quickly changed to its current spelling, "Brothertown." This subtle transformation seems to relate to Euro-American readings of the name. Since it began strictly as a toponym, it was natural that they read and subsequently wrote the name with the English spelling, t-o-w-n. The ways in which Euro-American authors used and spelled the name in the late eighteenth century support this hypothesis. Despite Euro-American modes of reference to the community, Brothertown authors used the name in their own ways, in most cases as part of ethnonymic noun phrases (as adjectives modifying group designation), such as "the Brothertown Indians" or "the Brothertown Tribe." By the early to mid-nineteenth century, Euro-American authors began using the name in ways similar to their Brothertown interlocutors. These negotiated forms and uses of the name resulted only from the confluence of insider and outsider perspectives of the community. Neither group was solely responsible for the transformations the name went through as they communicated across their respective group boundaries.

Because it held salience for several different groups in the eighteenth and nineteenth centuries, the name "Brothertown" allowed a certain degree of cultural ambiguity. Tropes of fictive kinship were traditionally used in both Euro-American (specifically Christian) and Native societies (Bragdon 1997; Morgan 1962 [1851]; Murray 1998a). This ambiguity assisted the Brothertown Indians in aligning themselves with Euro-Americans who read the name as that of a society of "progressive" Christian Indians and Native communities who read the name as that of a multitribal and/or pan-Indian community. The interstitial space that the Brothertown community occupied between Euro-American and Native American worlds aided them in accomplishing certain goals such as gaining US citizenship and land rights as early as 1839.

The Brothertown Indians also used patterns of ethnonymy and other modes of reference to construct subtle (and pragmatic) arguments, which reinforced the direct messages sent in their letters. Taking influence from pragmatic anthropology (Agha 2007; Silverstein 1976, 1996; Singer 1978) I approached the documents as past speech acts, analyzable not only in terms of what they said but how they said it. In the broadest sense, this chapter demonstrates the need for practitioners of historical anthropology and archaeology to develop similar means of analyzing documentary artifacts (see Johnson 1999 for a similar discussion). For example, archaeologists have developed sophisticated theories for understanding the ways material culture—both textual and artifactual—participated in past societies, but have yet to fully turn to linguistic analysis as a means of interpreting documents (Cipolla 2012a, 2012d). By incorporating such an approach, I gained new insights into the cultural negotiations associated with colonial interaction and ethnogenesis, along with new understandings of the importance of Brothertown writing in these processes. More specifically, this portion of the study demonstrated the significance of ethnonyms and other modes of reference in processes of ethnogenesis and colonial negotiation, in some instances literally creating new cultural monikers and challenging established modes of social classification. Although ethnonyms represent only one part of social identities, this portion of my analysis demonstrates that it is an important one, particularly within the contexts of colonialism. In the chapters that follow I investigate the material and spatial discourses that complemented the linguistic patterns revealed here.

5

Commemoration in the Northeast

HARDSHIP AND CHANGE WERE ALL too familiar for Aaron Poquiantup. He was born a Niantic Indian among the tumult of postrevolutionary New England and spent his childhood and much of his teenage life as part of the Christian Indian communities of coastal Connecticut and Rhode Island. In his later teenage years he set out with his mother and her family in search of a better life in Brothertown, New York (Love 1899:358). In 1795, he was officially assigned lot number 130 on the western periphery of the first Brothertown settlement, the place where he spent most of his remaining days. At some point he married. A miniature headstone in Brothertown, New York, marked with the initials DP and LP also suggests that he and his wife, Lovinia, not only had children but also suffered through the grief of seeing them die young. At age thirty-one Aaron began a two-year term as treasurer for the Brothertown community. Later in life he performed odd jobs, in one instance making a coffin for a fellow community member. During this stage of his life, the Brothertown community began looking westward once again. By the time that he was fifty-four, many of his neighbors and friends had left for Wisconsin, and white farmers took over their former properties. In 1832, Aaron's lot was sold, which hints at the possibility that the Poquiantups aspired to follow their community westward. Unfortunately they never had the opportunity. Lovinia died in the summer of 1835 amid the changing social landscape of Brothertown, New York. Aaron followed several months later. The couple was buried in a small cemetery located in the heart of the first Brothertown settlement. Their surviving loved ones marked the couple's final resting spot with an austere marker of white marble (figure 5.1). It bears the following inscription:

AARON POQUIANTUP
formerly a member of
the Nahantic tribe of
Indians, R.I.
died Dec. 2, 1835
AE 58 y's

Lovinia
his wife died Aug. 14
1835
AE 45 y's.

By the time Aaron died, he was no longer considered Niantic. His physical relocation and the experiences that he shared with his new community had transformed him into a Brothertown Indian.

As with all histories, only a limited data set remains with which to reconstruct past lives, social interactions, and cultural processes at Brothertown. The Poquiantups are no longer here to recount their experiences, nor did they leave behind detailed written or oral narratives. Their historical legacy exists primarily in the archival and archaeological records. The scant archival sources, consisting of several lines in a town ledger book and a stray coffin receipt, offer information on only a few economic transactions. The archaeological record has the potential to offer a broader perspective on their lives, but it remains largely unidentified and unexplored up to this point except for the stones that mark their graves. Such markers are typically among the most easily identified archaeological traces left behind by past peoples. Although sometimes considered less than archaeological in the traditional sense of the discipline, gravestone studies have grown immensely over the past four decades (Bell 1994).

This and the next chapter focus primarily on the interpretation of such traces, contextualizing them in terms of broader patterns of commemoration and social change. This chapter concentrates on the grave markers of Brothertown, New York. The analyzed mounds, stones, and cemeteries span the late eighteenth, nineteenth, and early twentieth centuries. As detailed in chapter 3, the Brothertown Indians established their New York settlement in the 1780s, but began moving west again after five decades. The Brothertown Indians altered their commemoration practices dramatically during this short period, the most obvious change being the replacement of handmade grave markers and burial mounds with purchased stones, such as that

FIGURE 5.1. Aaron and Lovinia Poquiantup's fallen headstone, Brothertown, New York. (Photograph by author)

of the Poquiantups. The differences between these forms of commemoration speak directly to the complexities of colonial endurance in the modern world.

Traditions of Death and Commemoration

Coastal New England

The commemoration practices of the ancestral Brothertown communities of seventeenth- and eighteenth-century New England are vital for this project because they set the framework for what developed in New York. Nascent members of the Brothertown community brought with them memories and traditions of how to treat, mourn, and remember their deceased loved ones and ancestors. As they moved to Brothertown, however, they modified these practices in relation to their new surroundings. Before turning to these cemeteries, I establish a comparative baseline by exploring burial and commemoration practices among several other Native American communities of the Northeast, some of which tie directly into Brothertown history. I also briefly discuss "sacrifice rocks," another type of monument constructed by Native peoples in the area.

Algonquian peoples of the East Coast traditionally understood the world as rife with spiritual power or *manit* (Crosby 2003 [1988]; Simmons 1986). A variety of deities governed this world, the most powerful of which was the Creator, Cauntantowwit—known by several other names depending on the group (Bragdon 1996; Crosby 2003 [1988]:183–92; DeForest 1964 [1851]:21–23; Simmons 1986; Williams 1973 [1643]). Cauntantowwit lived in the southwest and controlled life cycles. At the time of death, one of the deceased's souls—of which there were several—traveled to Cauntantowitt's house to live with the ancestors. Another important deity, Hobbamock, was deeply involved in daily life and was a source of personal spiritual power and knowledge. Residing in the east or northeast, Hobbamock was the spiritual force behind powwows (i.e., shamans). Unlike Cauntantowwit, who remained distant, Hobbamock often appeared in people's visions and dreams. In certain instances the souls of the wicked ended up with Hobbamock, who condemned them to haunt the living rather than letting them continue to Cauntantowitt's house (Crosby 2003 [1988]). Although English colonists often made sense of these beliefs by layering their own Christian sensibilities over them and framing these two deities as diametrically opposed (i.e., God versus Satan), Native cosmology was far more subtle and complex (Simmons 1986). Furthermore, as discussed later, the introduction of Christianity did not simply overwrite and replace these traditional forms of spirituality.

The Narragansett

Due to land development and other types of unintentional discovery, there exists a fairly large corpus of archaeological data concerning Narragansett burial practices of the seventeenth century. The West Ferry Site (RI-84) was a seventeenth-century Narragansett burial ground located on Conanicut or Jamestown Island in Narragansett Bay, Rhode Island. Archaeologists—both professional and amateur—excavated fifty-nine burials over the course of six decades following Euro-American discovery of the site in the 1930s (Simmons 1970; see also McBride 1989, 1990b). Although the excavated graves were unmarked, they contained a variety of funerary items of both Native and European manufacture meant to provision the soul that resided in the chest of the deceased (Crosby 2003 [1988]). As seen in the plan (figure 5.2), the Narragansett consistently oriented the graves of their loved ones so that the tops of their heads pointed to the southwest. This was necessary so that the deceased's other soul—residing in the head—could travel to Cauntantowwit's house (Simmons 1970; see also Bragdon 1996), where the ancestors lived. Graves at the West Ferry Site sat in loose rows and columns, typically with a meter or less separating neighboring interments. Bodies were placed on their sides in the flexed position (Simmons 1970), a configuration that spoke to the cyclical nature of life stages in the Narragansett world. Of note, this tradition of placing bodies in the flexed position extends deep into human antiquity. In fact, archaeologists observe this pattern all over the world, even at ancient sites dating to the Middle Paleolithic Period (Parker Pearson 1999).

Approximately half a century after the discovery of the West Ferry Site, developers in North Kingstown, Rhode Island, accidentally uncovered another seventeenth-century Narragansett burial ground, now known as the RI-1000 site. Archaeologists subsequently excavated the burial ground to preserve information from the burials and protect them from looters (Rubertone 2001; see also Nassaney 1989). Similar to the West Ferry Site, none of the RI-1000 burials were marked above the ground, but they contained a diverse array of Native and European manufactured material culture hidden below. The layout of the RI-1000 site mirrored that of West Ferry; the deceased were consistently placed in the flexed position and oriented on a southwest–northeast axis. More so than those of West Ferry, graves at RI-1000 were organized in tightly spaced rows and columns. The site sat in

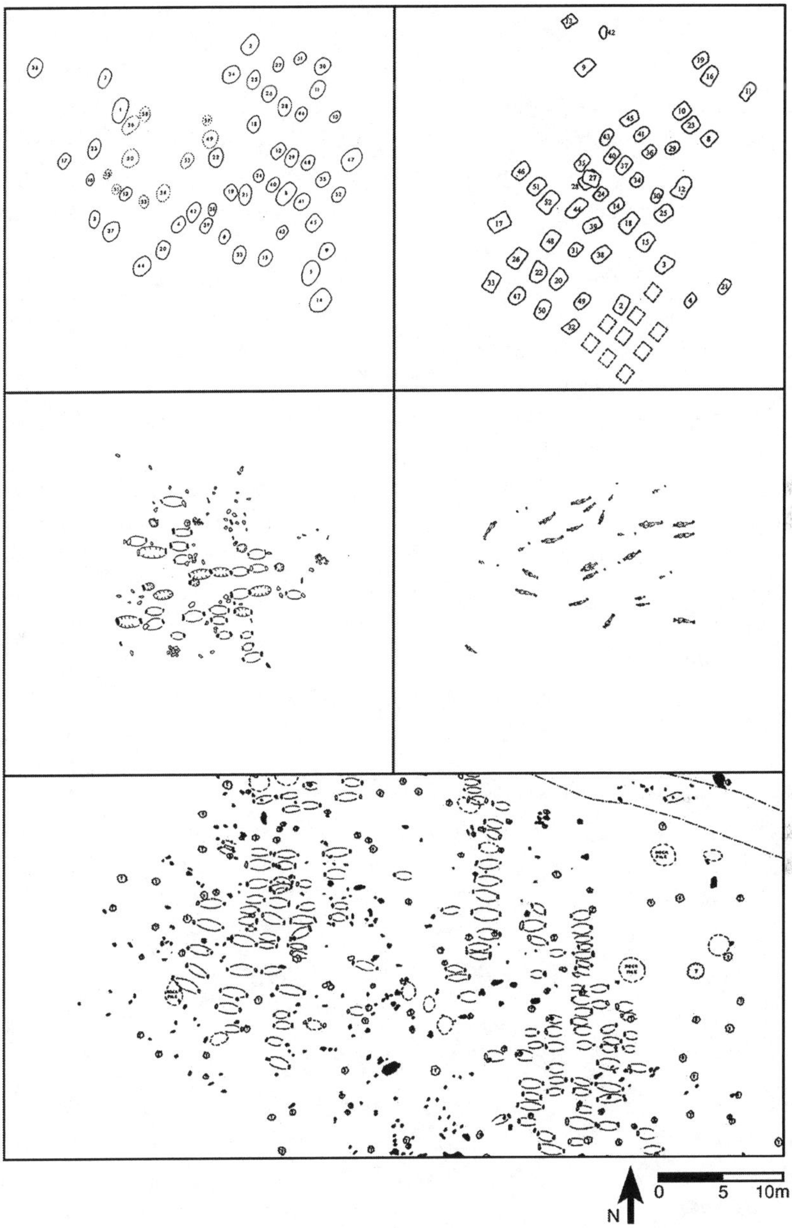

FIGURE 5.2. Plan maps of Native cemeteries of the Northeast, including Narragansett burial grounds RI-84 in the top left (modified from Simmons 1970) and RI-1000 in the top right (from Fitzhugh 1975, courtesy of the Smithsonian Anthropology Department), Mashantucket Pequot burial grounds 72-78 in the middle left (modified from Cipolla 2010) and 72-49 in the bottom (modified from Cipolla 2010), and the Wampanoag burial ground at Waldo Farm in the middle right (modified from Hodge 2005, courtesy of the Society for Historical Archaeology).

close proximity to a Narragansett village, connecting the everyday lives of the site's occupants to their ancestors. As Patricia Rubertone (2001:127) explains, "the dead shared the cultural landscape with the living, for whom this sacred space served as a constant and visible reminder of communal ties that linked generations and connected people to their ancestral homelands." In the case of Brothertown cemeteries discussed shortly, practices of communal remembrance like this were forever transformed with the incorporation of purchased grave markers bearing text inscriptions. Similar to those of Brothertown, later period Narragansett commemoration practices also relied on purchased stones, but the timing and extent of this transition is largely unknown.

The above-the-ground materiality and spatiality of the seventeenth-century Narragansett cemeteries differ markedly from the cemeteries created by Brothertown Indians (and perhaps the Narragansett themselves) in the eighteenth, nineteenth, and twentieth centuries. Although I discuss this issue in further detail later, a few points warrant brief mention here. First, many Brothertown Indians marked the graves of their loved ones above the ground with monuments that still exist today, including small mounds, locally made stone markers, and purchased gravestones. Of course this does not rule out the possibility that some or all of the Narragansett burials of RI-84 and RI-1000 were once marked with more ephemeral monuments that left no physical trace in the present. For instance, Roger Williams (1973 [1643]; see also DeForest 1964 [1851]) mentioned that one of the deceased's garments was often placed on the ground surface above the grave or hung from a nearby tree; once in place, it was taboo to touch such items as they decayed in the open. In this volume, shifts in above-the-ground materiality are considered in terms of their pragmatic effects on memory practices and colonial politics at Brothertown.

Second, the spatial distribution of graves in the Narragansett cemeteries contrasts with those of the Brothertown cemeteries, particularly in Wisconsin (chapter 6). Along with the clear shift in grave orientation—discussed in detail shortly—there is also a subtle difference in how the living placed the dead in relation to one another. The distribution of age groups in the Narragansett burial grounds shows no clear evidence of members of nuclear families being placed together. For example, most of the child burials (individuals up to nine years old) at RI-1000 sit in the center of the burial ground with adolescents or adults situated around them. The few child burials that sit on the periphery of the burial ground tend to have significantly less material culture associated with their graves. This pattern suggests that at the time of their deaths, the children buried on the periphery were perhaps less a part of the community than those situated at the center. If they had buried mothers/

wives, fathers/husbands, and their children (the nuclear unit) together, one would expect to find child burials distributed evenly across the burial ground, rather than concentrated in the center. One would also expect to find small clusters of burials as opposed to evenly spaced rows and columns. As will be demonstrated, Brothertown cemeteries increasingly emphasized nuclear family units and individuals within the community as Brothertown Indians incorporated purchased grave markers and continued to interact with outsiders. These transformations resulted in markedly different forms of social remembrance (and social relation) compared to the seventeenth-century contexts discussed here.

The Mashantucket Pequot

There are several historic cemeteries located on the Mashantucket Pequot Reservation (Kevin McBride, personal communication). Compared to the Narragansett burial grounds already discussed, fewer of these cemeteries have been disturbed by development or looting. All of the data discussed here are thus from noninvasive (above-the-ground) surveys. Because many of these sacred sites have been preserved and protected, they provide a valuable timeline for changes in commemoration among the Pequot before, during, and after the Brothertown movement.

The Mashantucket Pequot have used Cemetery Site 72-49 from the mid-seventeenth century onward. The pre-twentieth-century portion of the cemetery covers an area of approximately forty square meters and contains only one purchased stone bearing a text inscription. All other burials are marked with unmodified fieldstones or handmade gravestones (figure 5.3). Cemetery Site 72-78 is slightly newer, dating to the mid-eighteenth and early nineteenth centuries, and smaller, covering an area of approximately twenty-five square meters. Like the Narragansett, the Mashantucket Pequot organized these cemeteries in tightly spaced rows and columns, with approximately a meter or less separating neighboring interments. Unlike the Narragansett, however, they oriented the stones (and presumably the burials that they mark) in a strictly east–west pattern (figure 5.2).

When considered in relation to the commemoration practices already discussed, the materiality and spatiality of Pequot cemeteries stand out in several regards. The tightly spaced rows and columns found in these cemeteries resemble the spatial distribution of graves in seventeenth-century Narragansett burial grounds, which suggests the possibility of a non-nuclear burial pattern. The names, ages, and familial relations of nearly all of the individuals commemorated in the Pequot cemeteries remain unknown at

FIGURE 5.3. Mashantucket Pequot cemeteries 72-78 (top left) and 72-49 (bottom left), which include handmade gravestones (top right), purchased stones (middle right), and stone piles (bottom right).

this time, so this is only a working hypothesis. In a much more concrete manner, however, the cemeteries speak to several important changes in Pequot commemoration practices through time, some of which may also apply to other contemporaneous Native communities in the area.

With the proliferation of stone monuments in the mid-seventeenth century, these cemeteries demonstrate a clear shift toward more enduring forms of above-the-ground commemoration. The consistent east–west orientation of the markers also hints at the possibility of new forms of spirituality on the Mashantucket Pequot Reservation at this time. Often typified as the classic Christian grave orientation, the east–west pattern of burial is observable all across the globe, even at sites that predate Christian proselytization by centuries (Williams 2006). The pattern is said to tie directly to beliefs in the second coming of Christ from the East. In these instances, the grave markers face west, with the bodies of the deceased buried in front in the supine rather than flexed position, the tops of their heads also pointing westward. On the second coming, the deceased can sit up from this position and face Christ (Cunningham 1989). Moreover, the supine position could relate to specific understandings of the life course; whereas flexed burials referenced the cyclical nature of life, supine burials may have symbolized beliefs in a linear (nonrepeating) pattern. Instead of placing the dead back into the womb of Mother Earth to await rebirth in some new form, the bereaved set the dead to wait for the next stage in the linear progression of Christian ontology (i.e., Judgment Day).

Although the contrast between this pattern and that of the southwest–northeast burial tradition of the seventeenth-century Narragansett should not be understated, it remains unclear whether these burials were oriented differently solely because of Christianity. Despite neat and tidy explanations of grave orientations, many Christian burials do not actually conform to this pattern, and many non-Christian graves do exhibit east–west orientations. Interestingly, Mohegan historian, author, and medicine woman Melissa Tantaquidgeon (Fawcett 2000:41) notes that Mohegan spirits pass from east to west, following the sun's daily path across the sky. The east–west orientations could also result from a number of nonspiritual factors, such as crowding in cemeteries, which may prevent ideal placement of monuments and graves (Parker Pearson 1982) or landmarks such as lakes, mountains, or even roadways in the vicinity of cemeteries that may influence burial patterns. Regardless of the precise reason, the mid-seventeenth century was a time of new materials and spatial patterns in Pequot cemeteries.

In contrast to certain aspects of the layouts of these cemeteries, the dearth of text-bearing markers therein complied with traditional modes of commemoration in the Native Northeast. In many local Native communities, it was prohibited to speak individuals' names after their deaths (Morgan 1962 [1851]; Simmons 1970; Williams 1973 [1643]). For example, Roger Williams (1973 [1643]:248) made note of this practice among seventeenth-century Narragansetts: "They abhorre to mention the dead by name, and therefore, if any man beare the name of the dead he changeth his name; and if any stranger accidentally name him, he is checkt, and if any wilfully name him he is fined; and amongst States, the naming of their dead Sachims, is one ground of their warres; so terrible is the King of Terrors, Death, to all natural men." Just over 200 years later, famed anthropologist Lewis Henry Morgan (1962 [1851]:175) observed parallel practices among the Iroquois, writing, "After the mourning period had expired, the name of the deceased was never mentioned, from a sense of delicacy to the tender feelings of his friends." In other words, the blank grave markers prevalent in eighteenth- and nineteenth-century Native cemeteries of the Northeast may be blank for reasons other than financial hardship. The materiality of these markers supports a specific type of social memory, which may predate European colonialism.

The Wampanoag

Though the Wampanoag of Massachusetts and Rhode Island were not officially involved in the Brothertown movement, the archaeology of their cemeteries is relevant to this study for several reasons. To begin, they spoke a similar language within the Algonquian family, shared similar cultural milieus, and lived in close proximity to several groups that did participate in the movement. Furthermore, like many northeastern Native communities in the eighteenth century, the Wampanoag felt the effects of the Great Awakening, with group members converting to various sects of Christianity at the time.

The Burr's Hill site of Warren, Rhode Island, was a sizable seventeenth-century Wampanoag burial ground (Gibson 1980). Although amateur archaeologists began excavating the site in the late nineteenth century, a professional analysis of the recovered materials did not appear in print for another century. At the time of their discovery, none of the burials were marked. Also—like the other seventeenth-century burials discussed here—most of the individuals interred at this site were placed in the flexed position with the tops of their heads generally oriented to the southwest. The bodies were typically wrapped in mats or blankets or placed with bark boards.

In contrast, the Waldo Farm site—located in Dartmouth, Massachusetts—was an early eighteenth-century Christian Wampanoag burial ground (Hodge 2005). Like many of the eighteenth- and nineteenth-century Pequot burials already discussed, the users of the site marked the graves of their loved ones with both head- and footstones, described by the original excavators of the site as "fieldstones." Most of the individuals buried at Waldo Farm were placed in their respective graves in a nontraditional supine position oriented on a traditional southwest–northeast axis. Also of note, no funerary objects or furnishings were recovered from the Waldo Farm burials. Unlike seventeenth-century Wampanoag burials that were typically furnished with mats, blankets, or bark boards, or the many contemporaneous

Euro-American burials furnished with coffins, individuals buried at Waldo Farm were laid to rest unclothed save for shrouds.

Given these patterns along with the site's proximity to a sizable Quaker population, Christina Hodge (2005) interprets the burials from Waldo Farm as representing a blend of Wampanoag and Quaker burial traditions. The blank gravestones are consistent with both cultural traditions to some extent. As seen in the Pequot cemeteries, it was common practice for Native peoples to mark the graves of their ancestors with blank stones. Quakers traditionally forbade the use of grave markers as well, but some communities accepted the use of blank stones or stones with minimal decoration and inscription information beginning in the early eighteenth century (Bromberg and Shepard 2006). The use of shrouds instead of coffins or clothing also complied with Wampanoag and Quaker traditions; the former commonly buried the dead wrapped in mats or other textiles, and the latter buried their dead in shrouds or minimally decorated coffins. On one hand, the lack of funerary items placed in the graves at the site is unusual for historic Native burial grounds in the Northeast, but common among Quakers. On the other hand, the orientation of the graves (southwest–northeast) is consistent with traditional Native practices but unique among Quaker burial customs.

Sacrifice Rocks

Grave markers were not the only forms of commemoration used by Native groups of the Northeast; they also constructed piles of stone and brush to memorialize important events or individuals and to mark territorial boundaries (Butler 1946; Jett 1994; Rubertone 2001; Simmons 1986). Ethnohistoric sources state that Native Americans added to these heaps—which often sat on the sides or in the forks of paths—on each encounter with them. These monuments, or "sacrifice rocks," as white observers referred to them, thus grew gradually with the passage of time (an indexical sign). Although the precise symbolic meanings of these heaps were unknown to them, colonists moving through the landscapes of New England often made note of such sites, some even observing Native people adding to the piles. One such pile sat near Stockbridge, Massachusetts, the former home of the Stockbridge Indians. Eva Butler (1946) analyzed a rich record of eighteenth- and nineteenth-century commentary on this particular heap and several other notable heaps throughout New England. As evinced from the ethnohistorical literature, such monuments were used throughout the nineteenth century. There is, however, some confusion in distinguishing between these ceremonial stone features and field clearing piles left over from farming the rocky soils of New England. Although such a discussion is beyond the scope of this volume, it is altogether possible that at least some of these features may be both field clearing piles and monuments simultaneously. Ceremonial piles represent a distinct tradition of communal memory making in Native New England. The materiality of memory in this case is similar to that of contemporaneous Native cemeteries and notably distinct from that of neighboring Euro-Americans, who relied largely on texts to mark (and make) memories.

New York

The Brothertown Indians had both Native and Euro-American neighbors in New York, each with their own distinct practices of burial and commemoration. The first Brothertown settlement sat in Oneida Country, part of the larger territory of the "League of the Iroquois," or the "Five Nations" (Morgan 1962 [1851]). Since Christianity spread at a much slower pace in Iroquoian country than it did on the East Coast, it is possible that some of the practices described next were those of non-Christian Native groups.

Europeans and Euro-Americans observed the Oneida and other Iroquoian groups using several styles of burial mound in the eighteenth and nineteenth centuries. For example, in regard to the funerary practices of the League of the Iroquois, an early eighteenth-century observer wrote,

> Their funeral Rites seem to be formed upon a Notion of some Kind of Existence after Death. They make a large round Hole, in which the Body can be placed upright, or upon its Haunches, which after the Body is placed in it, is covered with Timber, to support the Earth which they lay over, and thereby keep the Body free from being pressed; they then raise the Earth in a round Hill over it. They always dress the Corps in all its Finery, and put Wampum and other Things into the Grave with it; and the Relations suffer not Grass or any Weed to grow on the Grave, and frequently visit it with Lamentations. (Colden 1904 [1750], quoted in Bushnell 1920:70–71)

Lewis Henry Morgan (1962 [1851]:172) also observed various Iroquoian groups burying their dead in the sitting position, facing east. In other instances, outside observers described Iroquoian communities surrounding burial mounds with wooden palisades. The number of people buried in each mound varied considerably; some mounds contained large numbers of burials, and others only included the graves of important political and spiritual leaders (Bushnell 1920).

Excavations at the Kleis site, an early historic Iroquois burial ground located in the northwest corner of New York State, offer further clues into Iroquoian burial practices (White 1967). Like many of the seventeenth-century burials of New England, individuals at the Kleis site were placed in their graves in the flexed position, but with the tops of their heads generally oriented to the west instead of the southwest, as was common on the East Coast. The burials also contained a mixture of Native and European-manufactured items similar to many of the East Coast contexts previously discussed.

In contrast to Iroquoian methods of commemoration, the Brothertowns' Euro-American neighbors primarily used purchased stone monuments to mark the graves of their loved ones. For example, Deansboro Cemetery, located in the former Brothertown, New York, contains mainly Euro-American graves. Most of the markers are marble headstones, although the cemetery also houses a fair number of obelisks, ledgers, and other monuments of various shapes and sizes, some made from granite. Stones in the cemetery are generally oriented to the west—perhaps in accordance with Christian traditions—and organized sporadically with some markers grouped in tightly spaced rows and columns and others sitting in smaller clusters or in relative isolation.

Brothertown Cemeteries of New York, 1780–1907

In the late nineteenth century, William DeLoss Love became the first historian to write of Brothertown cemeteries. He focused most of his attention on the large communal burial ground that he believed was the final resting place of Samson Occom, referred to hereafter as Fowler Cemetery. However, he also noted four additional cemeteries in passing: "One was at the foot of the hill where the present cemetery is; another was near the center of Deansville, north of the highway and between the railroad and the river, called the 'Dugaway' burial-place; the third was near John Tuhie's place and the fourth on the farm of Asa Dick. There may have been others" (Love 1899:294–95). In the fall of 2007 my team and I mapped and cataloged two of the cemeteries mentioned by Love. Unfortunately, Dugaway and Tuhie cemeteries remain lost at this time, and the current owner of Fowler Cemetery denied us access, citing issues of liability. Although we were not permitted to formally map and record data from Fowler Cemetery, the owner did take me to the site for a brief visit the previous year, thus enabling a limited discussion of the markers, size, and layout of this important Brothertown burial ground.

In addition to the cemeteries mentioned by Love, our team also located, mapped, and cataloged three other Brothertown burial grounds with the help of the Brothertown Indians and local residents of Deansboro and Waterville, New York (formerly Brothertown, New York, see chapter 3). Although there is a dearth of archival records associated with these cemeteries, the 1795 plot map of Brothertown helped identify the Brothertown Indians who lived on the lots on which the cemeteries sit. For the purposes of the preceding analysis and discussion, I standardize the cemetery names based on the surnames of these eighteenth- and nineteenth-century residents.

Niles Occom Cemetery

Also known locally as the Brothertown Burial Ground, Niles Occom Cemetery sits on a hilltop in the southern half of the historic settlement. Although nestled among a grove of trees situated between two agricultural fields and largely unobtrusive, a road sign prominently marks this cemetery's location. After a quick but steep ascent, visitors to the site find forty-four handmade limestone grave markers hidden among the trees. (I use the term *handmade* henceforth to refer to stones that appear to have been manufactured by the loved ones of the deceased or by specialists within the Brothertown community, as opposed to purchased stones that were manufactured by professional or semi-professional stonemasons.) None of the handmade markers at Brothertown bear inscriptions of any kind.

Although not mentioned in Love's work, this cemetery is the largest Brothertown burial ground of New York cataloged for this book. It sat on the historic boundary between lots 40 and 41. The Brothertown superintendents' book lists widow Patience Occom as living on lot 40 and James Niles II as living on lot 41 (Brothertown Indians n.d.; Cipolla 2010:133–35). Patience, of Mohegan descent, was likely married to Samson Occom's son Andrew Gifford Occom, who died before 1796, and James, a Narragansett Indian from Charlestown, Rhode Island, was a former soldier in the American Revolution (Love 1899:353). The cemetery's location between two lots and the relatively large number of burials within it suggest that the Brothertown Indians used this spot as a communal burial ground between the late eighteenth and early nineteenth centuries.

Skeesuck Cemetery

Commonly referred to as the Dick Family Cemetery, this burial ground sits in the backyard of a residence located in the eastern central portion of the historic settlement. A marker situated in back of the house and only visible from the road by the attentive observer contains several historical inaccuracies: "Historical Marker, Burial Ground of Brothertown Indians. In 1783 Indians from Seven New England Towns Settled This Area. Emigrated to Green Bay, Wisconsin 1850." Here visitors can observe a very different type of commemoration than what was practiced at Niles Occom Cemetery. This burial ground contains fragments of at least fifteen purchased marble headstones, many of which bear text inscriptions. Included among these are the Poquiantup stones discussed in the introduction of this chapter. Unfortunately none of the stones are in situ. All the gravestones currently lie face up, aligned in a loose row between two mulberry bushes. Marker inscriptions firmly date this cemetery to the second quarter of the nineteenth century. The broader historical context of the area and the relatively small number of stones contained within this cemetery indicate that it was a private family burial plot. The names inscribed on the headstones and the genealogical relationships they share with one another add further support for this hypothesis.

Historically, Skeesuck Cemetery was located on the edge of lot 26. Although Love referred to it as part of "Asa Dick's farm," Asa Dick never actually owned the property. Beginning in 1795, the forty-hectare lot was assigned to John Skeesuck, a Narragansett Indian born in Charlestown, Rhode Island (Brothertown Indians n.d.). He was one of the earliest settlers in Brothertown, receiving the lot after serving in the American Revolution. He likely died around 1807, after which time his wife, Anne, took possession of the lot. John Skeesuck II, born in 1782, later inherited this lot from his mother. His cousin married Asa Dick during the second quarter of the nineteenth century, explaining the presence of Asa's gravestone (dating to 1843) in the cemetery. Asa's nineteenth-century popularity remains prominent in local folk memory. For instance, residents still refer to the part of town containing Skeesuck Cemetery as "Dicksville."

Dick Cemetery

Today this cemetery sits in a grove of trees situated between several large agricultural fields, far removed from any roadways. No commemorative sign marks its location, and very few residents even remember that it exists.

Those who do remember refer to it as Kindness Cemetery after Tom Kindness, the last Brothertown Indian who lived in the cemetery's vicinity during the late nineteenth and early twentieth centuries. To reach this cemetery, one must hike through fields and woodlands for about twenty minutes. Only an astute observer notes this collection of ten handmade limestone markers, several of which are broken or toppled and none of which bear text inscriptions. This cemetery sat in the center of lot 37, which was officially assigned to Isaac Dick in 1804 (Brothertown Indians n.d.). The Dick family was Narragansett in ancestry, and came from Charlestown, Rhode Island. Isaac Dick moved to Brothertown in 1799, settling on the lot in question. He died around 1812; in 1835, the lot was sold for his children, Asa, Martha, Isaac, Hannah, and Betsey. The sale reserved "three rods square for the burial plot" (Love 1899:377). The listed size (approximately fifteen meters square) correlates with the current size of this cemetery (approximately twelve by eight meters). The types of grave markers present in this cemetery also resemble other Brothertown markers of the late eighteenth and early nineteenth centuries, thus potentially correlating with Isaac Dick's recorded death date. Like Skeesuck Cemetery, this space functioned as a private family burial ground. In fact, it is highly likely that Dick Cemetery was the predecessor of Skeesuck Cemetery, with different generations of the same family group using these two cemeteries.

Deansboro Cemetery

This is a large public cemetery located on Route 12B in Deansboro, New York. It houses three known Brothertown graves, respectively dating to 1822, 1864, and 1907, all of which are marked by purchased marble gravestones. It is also the only known New York cemetery containing both Euro-American and Brothertown Indian graves.

Shelley Cemetery

This small burial ground sits behind what is now a residence in the southern central portion of the historic settlement. It contains only two grave markers: one handmade limestone marker and one purchased gravestone bearing a date of 1835. Historically, it was located on the eastern edge of lot 68, a twenty-hectare piece of land assigned to Simeon Shelley in 1820 (Brothertown Indians n.d.).

The Shelley surname originated among the Eastern Pequot community in North Stonington, Connecticut (Love 1899:394). As indicated by the date of this lot assignment, Simeon arrived relatively late in Brothertown. Only fourteen years later, he sold the lot to move to Brothertown, Wisconsin, where he died in 1860. His wife was Sabrina Welch, a Stockbridge Indian. Like Skeesuck and Dick cemeteries, this cemetery also functioned as a private family burial ground. The only inscribed stone on the premises marks the grave of Nancy Welch, who was probably Simeon's mother-in-law. The other stone, a miniature handmade headstone, potentially marks the grave of one of the Shelley children.

Fowler Cemetery

Fowler Cemetery sits in a forest near the top of Bogusville Hill in Deansboro. A commemorative roadside sign marks its location, reading, "Historical Marker, Samson Occom, Indian Preacher of the Brothertown Indians, believed to be buried in cemetery 1/4 mile south of here." After a fifteen- to twenty-minute hike through a series of privately owned fields and forests, one finds a large cemetery containing anywhere from 60 to 100 burials dating from the late eighteenth to the early nineteenth centuries. Yet this cemetery's size is not the only dimension that sets it apart from other Brothertown burial grounds of New York. In addition to the typical handmade limestone grave markers of this period and one purchased marble gravestone, this cemetery also contains miniature burial mounds, approximately fifty centimeters in height, fifty or so centimeters wide, and less than two meters in length. It is possible, given the similarities they share with local burial practices, that these miniature mounds represent a fusion of Iroquoian, Algonquian, and Euro-American burial customs of the time. After visiting this cemetery in the late nineteenth century, William DeLoss Love remarked, "There are at least sixty indian graves in this ground, many marked by stones, but more by mounds" (Love 1894). Brothertown Indians interviewed in the late nineteenth century by Love (1899:294) described this cemetery as an early communal burial ground.

Historically, the cemetery sat on lot 105. David Fowler (Montaukett) lived on this lot of just over sixty-one hectares. The lot was conferred to him in 1775 (Brothertown Indians n.d.). Fowler died in 1807, followed by his wife, Hannah, in 1811. As recorded by several historical observers (e.g., Love 1899:298), the inscription on their shared headstone in Fowler Cemetery once read:

DAVID FOWLER
Died March 31, 1807. Aet.
72 years
HANNAH wife of
DAVID FOWLER died
Aug. 1811. Aet. 64 years.

Fowler's lot was also the earliest communal center for the Brothertown Indians. In addition to the cemetery, it contained a barn where meetings and religious services were held. Occom delivered sermons to Brothertown and Stockbridge Indians alike in the Fowler barn and led funeral services in Fowler Cemetery. As indicated on the roadside sign, some believe this cemetery to be the final resting spot of Samson Occom despite a clear lack of supporting evidence.

Dugaway and Tuhie Cemeteries

Love (1899:334) mentioned these cemeteries in passing and depicted their approximate locations on a map. To date each remains unidentified; thus, it is possible that their markers have fallen or otherwise disappeared. Dugaway Cemetery sat on lot 20, which was assigned in 1795 to Benjamin Touee, a Farmington Indian (Brothertown Indians n.d.). In regard to Tuhie Cemetery, Love described its location as "near John Tuhie's place." Tuhie was a Narragansett Indian from Charlestown, Rhode Island. He owned lots 11 and 18, which were assigned to him in 1795. According to Love (1899:364), Tuhie's gravestone inscription read, "John Tuhie Esq. Died December 14, 1811."

Markers

In total, the New York assemblage includes data collected directly from seventy-four Brothertown grave markers dating between the late eighteenth and early twentieth centuries. Most markers date to the period between the founding of Brothertown in the 1780s and the next emigration to Wisconsin in the 1830s and 1840s. The team cataloged stones in Niles Occom, Skeesuck, Deansboro, and Shelley cemeteries, recording raw material, stone type and shape, height, width, thickness, orientation, mason's mark, condition, text inscription, and decorative motif whenever possible. Each stone was also photographed and mapped using a total station.

Raw Materials

A majority of the stones cataloged in New York are handmade grave markers (fifty-five markers, 74 percent) (figure 5.4). The Brothertown Indians probably quarried the limestone used to make these markers from local outcrops, which are abundant in and around the settlement. Although the manufacturing techniques vary between markers, most appear to have been either cut directly from outcrops or knapped from medium-sized limestone fieldstones. Their colors typically vary between different shades of gray, but a few are nearly as white as the purchased marble headstones found in many contemporaneous cemeteries. The remaining nineteen markers in the New York assemblage are white marble headstones shaped and sometimes inscribed by professional or semi-professional stonemasons. The predominance of marble among the purchased stones of Brothertown, New York, is unsurprising because it was the most popular raw material used to make gravestones beginning in the late eighteenth century (Forbes 1927).

FIGURE 5.4. Grave markers in Brothertown, New York. Handmade markers (top and bottom left) and Nancy Welch's purchased stone (right) with inscription, "In Memory of NANCY WELCH, wife of william welch, died may 18 1835, AE 56 Y 7 MO & _ D, depart my friends and dry up you tears I must ly here Till Crist appears."

Types, Shapes, and Sizes

Based on their forms, it seems that all of the handmade markers functioned as headstones (figure 5.5). These monuments are flat stone slabs originally planted vertically in the ground to mark the location of graves. A quarter of the stones (fourteen) bear cortex, indicating that they were shaped from field-stones. I use two criteria for classifying the various types of handmade markers: side angle and top edge. Although just over half of the handmade Brothertown markers were severely weathered or broken, preventing classification,

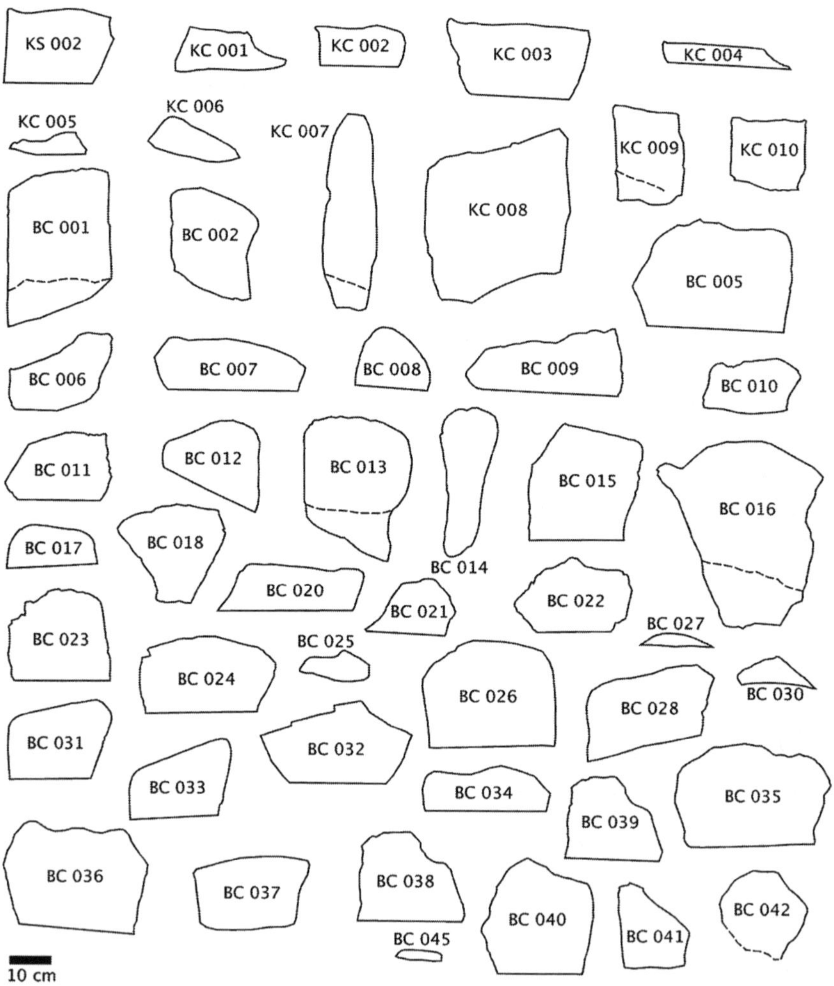

FIGURE 5.5. Shapes of handmade grave markers in Brothertown, New York.

Table 5.1. Handmade Marker Types in Brothertown, New York

	Side angle	Top edge	Occurrence in handmade assemblage
Type A	Parallel	Flat or concave	6 (11%)
Type B	Parallel	Convex	7 (13%)
Type C	Splayed	Convex	9 (16%)
Type D	Splayed	Flat or concave	2 (4%)
Unidentified	—	—	31 (56%)
Total			55 (100%)

four main maker types were defined (table 5.1). Type A stones have parallel sides with flat or concave top edges; type B stones have parallel sides with convex top edges; type C stones have splayed sides with convex top edges; and type D stones have splayed sides with flat or convex top edges. The most prevalent shape (C) is also found in other parts of New York. For instance, a majority of handmade stones erected on Long Island between the late seventeenth and early nineteenth centuries resemble truncated diamonds with their bottom points buried in the earth (Stone 1987:146). Also of note, types A, B, and C resemble purchased stone shapes popular in the eighteenth century, suggesting that their makers may have intended to replicate such shapes.

Only twenty-one purchased stones are known to mark (or have marked) the graves of Brothertown Indians in the New York settlement. The team collected information from seventeen of these. Evidence of the remaining four stones consists of two vacant marble bases meant for headstones and two historically documented headstones. Figure 5.6 depicts purchased headstone shapes found in Brothertown cemeteries in New York and Wisconsin. The cemeteries of Brothertown, New York, include types 1 through 5. The majority of the stones (thirteen, or 76 percent) are type 1, a basic rectangular shape similar to handmade type A. Only one example of each of the other shapes is represented in the collection. They include type 2, with a convex top edge similar to type B; type 3, a more complex shape with a point in the center of the top edge and two smaller points on the tops of each shoulder; type 4, another complex shape with a rounded central point and two embellished shoulders; and type 5, a stone resembling the shape of a Gothic arch, with a rounded cone-like center point and two rounded shoulders.

Types 3 and 4 mimic the shapes of headboards on beds (McGuire 2003 [1988]; Tarlow 1999). Archaeologist Sarah Tarlow sees material metaphors such as these as key components in processes of bereavement and commemoration. In her study of Orkney Island graveyards and cemeteries in the

FIGURE 5.6. Purchased marker shapes from both Brothertown settlements (modified from Mytum 2002 [2001]). (Reproduced by permission of Harold Mytum and the Council for British Archaeology)

United Kingdom, she found that the bereaved used a series of material and textual metaphors to liken death—the great unknown—to more comfortable realms of human experience. The most popular metaphor for death in nineteenth-century Orkney cemeteries was that of sleep. The bereaved likened death to sleep with inscriptions, which often literally spoke of death as a long sleep, and stone forms, which often replicated the shapes of bed headboards or cribs, depending on the age of the deceased. The fact that such metaphors were used thousands of kilometers away in Brothertown cemeteries only adds support to Tarlow's argument, further demonstrating the importance of metaphor in human experience. This pattern may also relate to the interconnectedness of the modern world. The nineteenth-century stonemasons who made these markers likely took influence from broader (global) stylistic trends in the material culture of death and commemoration. As the Brothertown Indians entered this consumer market, they became entangled in global economies and systems of influence. Interestingly, the stones in Brothertown, New York, that mimic the shapes of bed headboards lack any textual references to sleep. This pattern is perhaps a function of the limits of consumer choice. As described shortly, stonemasons often kept blank, preshaped stones on hand. In this instance, those Brothertown Indians who purchased headboard-shaped markers may have only done so because of a lack of alternative shapes in their time of need. It may also be that they could only afford to mark their loved ones' graves with the bare minimum of information and thus opted to leave out textual sleep metaphors, which were sometimes used to complement the shapes of such stones.

From Handmade to Purchased

A major period of change in Brothertown commemoration practices occurred between the 1830s and 1840s. During this time, the Brothertown Indians switched from making their own grave markers out of local limestone to purchasing marble gravestones from professional stone carvers. This switch was not a complete replacement, however. Many of the early handmade stones resemble the shapes of purchased stones used later. There were also continuities in practice. For example, all Brothertown Indians oriented their stones in the same way regardless of marker types.

This material transition began in Brothertown, New York, and the cemeteries of Brothertown, Wisconsin, only contain a few handmade stones. By shifting from manufacturers to consumers of gravestones, the Brothertown

Indians gained access to novel types of grave markers previously unseen in their cemeteries. Not only were purchased stones available in new materials, shapes, and sizes, they also came with inscriptions—both textual and decorative. These novel features certainly offered new means of marking memories of the deceased, yet they also came with limitations. In addition to Brothertown preferences, variables such as the stonemasons' individual styles and larger trends in gravestone consumption patterns played roles in the final forms that purchased stones took. For instance, in her classic study of the stonemasons and gravestones of New England between 1653 and 1800, Harriette Forbes (1927) explained that carvers usually kept a number of blank stones bearing only decorative motifs on hand. Customers chose from the limited array of designs that happened to be available. The carver then customized the stone with an inscription of the customer's choosing. It was also common during this time for carvers to provide a book of suggested inscription formats.

Despite the wide variety of purchased stones available to consumers in Brothertown, New York, most Brothertown Indians chose—or were otherwise limited to—stones of similar shapes. For example, 76 percent (thirteen) of the purchased stones in New York are rectangular (type 1), whereas the most popular handmade shape represents only 16 percent (nine) of the handmade assemblage. Because purchased stones typically bear text inscriptions, it is thus possible that the inclusion of text reduced the need to mark distinctions between stones via other dimensions of materiality, such as shape. However, this reduction in variability is also partially a function of buying stones from a limited number of professional carvers who could reproduce the same shapes time and time again. Also, intentionally or otherwise, the Brothertown Indians communicated information about the deceased via the sizes of their purchased stones, discussed further later.

When the Brothertown Indians began consuming stones with inscriptions, thereby infusing their commemoration practices with enduring semantic meanings, the significance of stone shapes diminished in importance. In other words, marker shapes were homogenized as Brothertown Indians began using text inscriptions to mark memories. Words and phrases began to speak louder than other material properties of the stones on which they were inscribed. As discussed in the conclusion of this chapter and in subsequent ones, this shift represents a fundamental reordering of memory practices at Brothertown, transforming cemeteries from spaces of communal remembrance into spaces of individual remembrance.

Inscriptions

Purchased markers are the only stones in the assemblage with inscriptions of any kind. Out of the twelve inscribed stones, eight are strictly textual and four bear both text and decorative motifs. The twelve stones commemorate a total of fifteen individuals, including eight adults and seven children. These numbers only reflect cataloged stones, excluding the historically documented inscriptions of David and Hannah Fowler and John Tuhie, discussed earlier. When included in the final tally, these stones bring the total number of inscribed stones up to fourteen and increase the number of commemorated individuals to eighteen. The marked ages of the deceased range from two months old to ninety-six years old with an average age at death of forty years. In terms of gender, seven stones commemorate females, six commemorate males, and two commemorate children of unknown sex.

The oldest known inscriptions date to the early nineteenth century and include the stones of David and Hannah Fowler (1807 and 1811), John Tuhie (1811), and Esther Poquenup (1822). However, most inscribed stones date to the time of the Brothertown Indians' second emigration during the 1830s and 1840s. In addition to these, two stones dating to the late nineteenth and early twentieth centuries mark the graves of Brothertown Indians who clearly chose to stay behind in New York after most of their fellow community members had departed for Wisconsin.

Considered as a whole, the inscriptions contain a limited array of biographical information. The range of information displayed includes the deceased's name, the deceased's parents' names, familial relations (e.g., the daughter of . . .), death dates, and ages at death. A few stones also contain information on tribal affiliations, religious identity, and military service. Of note, the full name of the deceased is only included on the stones of adults. In the case of children, the first name and middle initial are explicitly stated, but the reader has to infer the deceased's surname from the name of the parents. Similarly, parents' names only appear on the stones of children, and familial relations (e.g., the wife of, the son of . . .) are only mentioned on stones of children or adult females. Nearly all of the inscriptions (thirteen) include death dates. The only exception to this trend is a stone that presumably commemorates the Poquiantup children, bearing only two sets of initials. Similar to death dates, the age at death usually appears in the inscriptions (ten markers), four of which list the precise age of the deceased to the year, month, and day.

Beyond the information they contain, there are also several patterns in the phrasing of inscriptions that warrant further discussion. For example, four inscriptions begin with the clause, "In memory of"; six begin with the first name, full name, or initials of the deceased; and two begin simply with the verb "died," followed by the deceased's name and death date. The phrasing of the latter group of inscriptions emphasizes the actual event of death, whereas the former two primarily emphasize the memory of the deceased, a pattern discussed further in the next chapter.

The inscriptions typically stress only one characteristic of the deceased's life. For instance, eight discuss familial relations; the relationship listed is presumably that shared between the deceased and the commemorator(s). These include three instances of "the daughter of," two instances of "the son of," and three instances of "the wife of." None of the inscriptions typify the deceased as "the husband of," "the father of," or "the mother of." Women's identities were thus represented as largely contingent on their male relatives (i.e., from males' perspectives) (see also Rainville 1999). Additionally, one inscription emphasizes the military career of the deceased and another emphasizes the deceased's devotion to Christianity. Finally, two inscriptions define the deceased as *former* members of Native groups. These two inscriptions—including the stone of Aaron and Lovinia Poquiantup discussed in the introduction—are the only examples of stones explicitly referencing the Native ancestry of Brothertown individuals in both the New York and Wisconsin assemblages. Similarly, none of the inscriptions contain the ethnonym *Brothertown* (see chapter 4).

Esther Poquenup's inscription presents an interesting, albeit subtle juxtaposition between the two clauses inscribed on the stone. It reads (emphasis added):

In
Memory of
ESTHER POQUENUP,
who *was a member of the Mohegan*
Tribe of Indians
Died Jan 22 1822,
a practiced and exemplary Christian,
Aged 96 years and 3 months.

The first clause, written in the past tense, signifies a former state (i.e., membership in the Mohegan tribe), and the second clause emphasizes the state in which the deceased died (i.e., as a practiced and exemplary Christian). By including the past tense "was" in the first clause and omitting it from the second, intentionally or otherwise, the "author" portrayed Mohegan and Christian identities in opposition to one another.

The inscription on Aaron and Lovinia Poquiantup's stone presents a similar case. It defines Aaron as "formerly a member of the Nahantic tribe of Indians, R.I." The precise meaning of the word *formerly* is unclear in this context. On one hand, it might refer to the state of the deceased (i.e., formerly living, and thus formerly a member of the Niantic). On the other hand, it may refer to his leaving his home settlement in Rhode Island to join the Brothertown community. Because it also equates a location (Rhode Island) with the tribal identity Niantic, the latter is more likely. The location of Aaron Poquiantup's grave in Brothertown, New York (i.e., not in Rhode Island) indexically reinforces the message sent by the tense of the inscription, further emphasizing that the deceased died as something other than a Niantic Indian. The reader is left to contemplate how views of Aaron Poquiantup (including his own) changed after he left his home community of Charlestown for Brothertown.

In addition to text inscriptions, four stones bear inscribed decorative motifs. Romance Wyatt's stone bears an image of a waving flag, which signifies his professional identity as a soldier, and John Skeesuck's stone is decorated with a floral and geometric border design. The stones of Prude Harry and John Dick—both dating to the second half of the nineteenth century—bear the urn and willow motif. In Euro-American cemeteries of the East Coast, carvers introduced the willow motif in the late eighteenth century, and it remained popular throughout the first three decades of the nineteenth century (Linden 1980).

This motif represents the last stage in a sequence of stylistic transformations in colonial gravestones studied by archaeologists James Deetz and Edwin Dethlefsen (Deetz 1989, 1996 [1977]; Deetz and Dethlefsen 1967, 1971; Dethlefsen and Deetz 1966). They were the first archaeologists to systematically record and study this highly predictable sequence of change in gravestone imagery and text in the colonial cemeteries of coastal Massachusetts. The sequence they observed began with the death's head motif, followed by the cherub and urn and willow motifs, respectively. Deetz and Dethlefsen noted that these shifts in imagery also correlated with textual changes in gravestone inscriptions. For example, text inscriptions of stones bearing the death's head motif often begin with the clause "here lies buried"; stones bearing the cherub motif often begin with the clause "here lies the body of"; and stones bearing the urn and willow motif often begin with the clause "in memory of" (see also Fitts 1990). Prude Harry's inscription, which begins with, "In memory of Prude Harry," supports this general pattern of text and imagery.

According to Deetz and Dethlefsen, the earliest gravestones in the sequence reflect Puritanical beliefs emphasizing mortality (see also Ludwig 1966). The death's head motif began as an icon of a human skull meant to signify the ephemeral nature of life. Text inscriptions on these stones augmented the "messages" sent by the motif by stressing the mortality of the deceased. For instance, "Here lies buried . . ." conveys a tone of finality absent in later stages of the sequence. As Puritanical worldviews gave way to beliefs in the immortality of the soul, people began marking the graves of their family members and friends with stones bearing the cherub motif, which represented the enduring soul of the deceased. The text inscriptions of such stones discuss the body and soul as separate entities (e.g., "here lies the body," with no explicit mention of the soul). Finally, as Unitarianism and Methodism became popular in the nineteenth century, New Englanders began using stones bearing the urn and willow motif with inscriptions that spoke only of memories of the deceased. Deetz and Dethlefsen also noted that some markers from this stage in the sequence are cenotaphs, or monuments erected to commemorate those buried elsewhere. For instance, they found one stone that commemorated a sailor who drowned at sea in a shipwreck. Since the Brothertown stones that bear the willow tree conform to this general pattern, like the headboard-shaped stones already discussed, they demonstrate the influences that broader stylistic change in material culture has in local contexts. Although Deetz and Dethlefsen took a structural approach, treating these material patterns as passive reflections of changing mindsets, this volume treats material culture as active, asking how Brothertown grave markers shaped social relations and cultural traditions.

Representing Personhood and Identity

Due to their unique status as text-bearing artifacts, many gravestones break the dichotomy between artifact and text. Beginning with the work of Deetz and Dethlefsen, archaeologists became fascinated with the co-present linguistic and material discourses of gravestones. Deetz and Dethlefsen began by juxtaposing inscribed dates with gravestone imagery in order to gain better understandings of stylistic change (see also Cannon 1989). The myriad gravestone studies preceding Deetz and Dethlefsen demonstrate that they were only scratching the surface of possible comparisons between linguistic and material aspects of gravestones. Here I focus largely on issues of personhood and identity as communicated via a combination of semantic and pragmatic references on the few text-bearing stones present in Brothertown, New York.

In several regards the stone sizes loosely correlate with marked characteristics of the individuals they commemorate. This is most evident in comparisons of adults' stones with those of children. The biggest difference between these dimensions is that of height, with adults' stones standing an average of thirty centimeters taller than children's stones. Randall McGuire (2003 [1988]), James Garman (1994), and Lynn Rainville (1999) found similar results in their cemetery analyses in Broome County, New York; Newport, Rhode Island; and Hanover, New Hampshire, respectively. In terms of inscriptions, children are most often commemorated in terms of their relationship to their parents, as either "daughter of" or "son of." In contrast, adults' stones mark them in terms of other characteristics, such as their relationship to their spouse (only on women's stones), their military service, or as members of certain ethnic or religious groups.

Some correlations also exist between the gender of the deceased and the qualities of the stones that mark their graves. When comparing the stones of those marked as female with those marked as male, the females' stones are generally larger. The biggest difference between the two groups is in stone height, with the stones of females standing an average of forty-two centimeters taller than the stones of males. Interestingly, this difference is larger than the average height differences between the stones of adults and children. It is also more common for inscriptions marking males to begin simply with their full name. This occurs on five males' stones compared to only one female's stone (i.e., a female child sharing a stone with her father).

Spaces

Alongside the artifactual and textual components of cemeteries are the more subtle spatial dimensions. These range in scale from the ways bodies, grave goods, and stones sit in relation to one another to the ways spaces of the dead relate to broader landscape features (Parker Pearson 1999). Archaeologists often correlate particular spatial patterns observed in cemeteries with a variety of different cultural and social phenomena, including but not limited to issues of social organization (Goldstein 1981), identity, and spirituality. Here I consider stone orientations and cemetery locations to gain new insights into spirituality, social relations, and Brothertown history in general.

Stone Orientations

The orientation of nearly all of the in situ stones in Brothertown, New York, was perplexing at first (figure 5.7). Based on the trends discussed in the beginning of this chapter, I anticipated finding one of two possible patterns; either east–west- or southwest–northeast-oriented stones. Instead, stones in Brothertown face approximately southeast–northwest. More precisely the stones face an azimuth of 110/290 degrees rather than the expected 90/270 degrees (east–west) or 225/45 degrees (southwest–northeast).

I first looked for an explanation of this pattern in the immediate landscape features surrounding the cemeteries. The topography in Niles Occom Cemetery offered a possible solution. The ground surface in the cemetery slopes downward on an azimuth of 290 degrees, so it is feasible that its users simply oriented the stones of their loved ones to the natural slope of the land. Unfortunately none of the other cemeteries mirrored this precise topography. Some sit on flat ground, and others sit on slopes angled in varying directions. Moreover, as I began to visit more cemeteries in the area—used by a number of different groups in a variety of time periods—I found that most of the stones faced the same azimuth as the Brothertown markers.

I resolved this issue when I began to consider broader landscape patterns in the area in and around Brothertown. The historic settlement sits in the Oriskany Valley, a sizable northeast–southwest-running valley that cuts across central New York State. The Oriskany Creek and Route 12B run along the valley floor. In the portion of the valley where historic Brothertown sits, the valley floor runs on an azimuth between 20/200 and 30/210 degrees. The orientations of gravestones in nearly all cemeteries in and around Brothertown, New York, are thus perpendicular to the orientation of the valley.

This pattern demonstrates two key points. First, the Brothertown Indians and other communities in the Oriskany Valley may have intended to orient their burials on an east–west axis, but their attempts to do so were obscured by the topography of the landscape. As the sun rose in the east and set in the west, the angle of the Oriskany Valley made it appear to rise slightly south of east and set slightly north of west. Second, these data also serve as proof of the Brothertown Indians' methodology for orienting gravesites. At the very least, the first graves were oriented to points on the horizon where the sun rose and set or toward the valley walls. After the first few interments in each cemetery, those marking subsequent graves may have simply replicated the observed orientation of the standing stones. The only exceptions to this general pattern are the two stones in Shelley Cemetery. Both face precisely west (90/270). Although it is difficult to know exactly why the

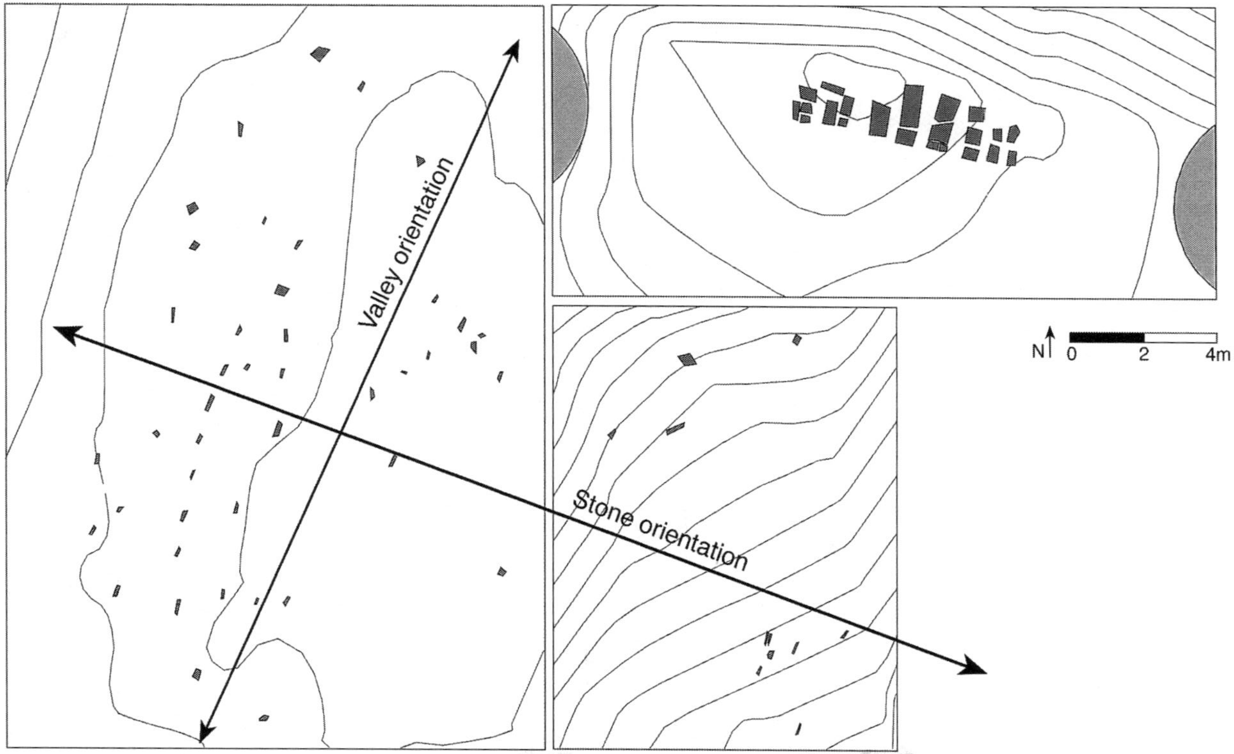

FIGURE 5.7. Plan maps of Niles Occom (left), Skeesuck (top right), and Dick (bottom right) Cemeteries, Brothertown, New York. Of note, stones in Skeesuck Cemetery are not in situ. The orientations of most grave markers in Brothertown, New York, are generally perpendicular to the Oriskany Valley.

orientations of these two stones differ from the rest, the crucial point is that all of the analyzed Brothertown stones of New York—handmade or purchased—were placed in the ground with the same immediate intentions. As with many historical questions, we will never know the precise meanings attached to these intentions. It most likely varied among individuals. Whether members of the eighteenth- and nineteenth-century Brothertown community oriented their stones on an imperfect east–west axis because of its Christian meaning, its relation to the sun's path, or its relation to the valley walls remains unclear.

Cemetery Layouts and Locations

The Brothertown Indians laid out nearly all of their New York cemetery spaces in rough rows with approximately a meter or less separating neighboring stones. This pattern is most evident in Fowler and Niles Occom cemeteries, which have the largest sample sizes, but it is also visible in the plan map of Dick Cemetery (figure 5.7). These spatial patterns are similar to those of the ancestral cemeteries on the East Coast. In this sense, the two most "traditional" Brothertown burial grounds are Niles Occom and Fowler cemeteries in that they contain relatively large numbers of burials sitting in close proximity to one another. Out of all the markers in these cemeteries, the only example of a text-bearing stone marks the graves of David and Hannah Fowler together.

Private and interethnic burial spaces such as Dick, Skeesuck, Shelley, and Deansboro cemeteries strayed further from the ancestral burial traditions of the East Coast. Although the users of Dick, Shelley, and presumably Skeesuck cemeteries continued to place burials in close proximity to one another, they chose to do so in separate cemeteries, each containing between two and fifteen markers, rather than bury their loved ones in communal burial grounds such as Fowler and Niles Occom cemeteries (each containing between 44 and 100 markers). Each of the three Brothertown burials in Deansboro Cemetery sits in its own space with no nearby burials (Brothertown or otherwise). Out of these four burial grounds, Dick Cemetery is the only example that contains only blank handmade markers. All stones in Skeesuck and Deansboro cemeteries were purchased from professional carvers, and many (eight of fifteen) bear text. Shelley Cemetery has one text-bearing stone and one miniature handmade marker, likely marking the grave of a child. As discussed shortly, separate (individualized) cemetery spaces and text-bearing stones fostered new forms of remembrance and inspired new understandings of personhood within the community. In this regard, Skeesuck, Deansboro, and Shelley cemeteries were harbingers of what came later in Brothertown, Wisconsin, cemeteries.

When considering space in Brothertown, New York, more generally, an important distinction between the northern and southern halves of the settlement becomes apparent. I base this interpretation on the relative locations of known communal spaces in the settlement, like the meeting house. This distinction sheds light on the significance of the various cemeteries and their uses within the community.

In his journal entry for November 7, 1785, Samson Occom (2006j [1785]) described the town center, located in the northern half of Brothertown: "Concluded to have a Centre near David Fowlers House the main Street is to run North and South and East and West, to Cross at the Centre." Figure 5.8

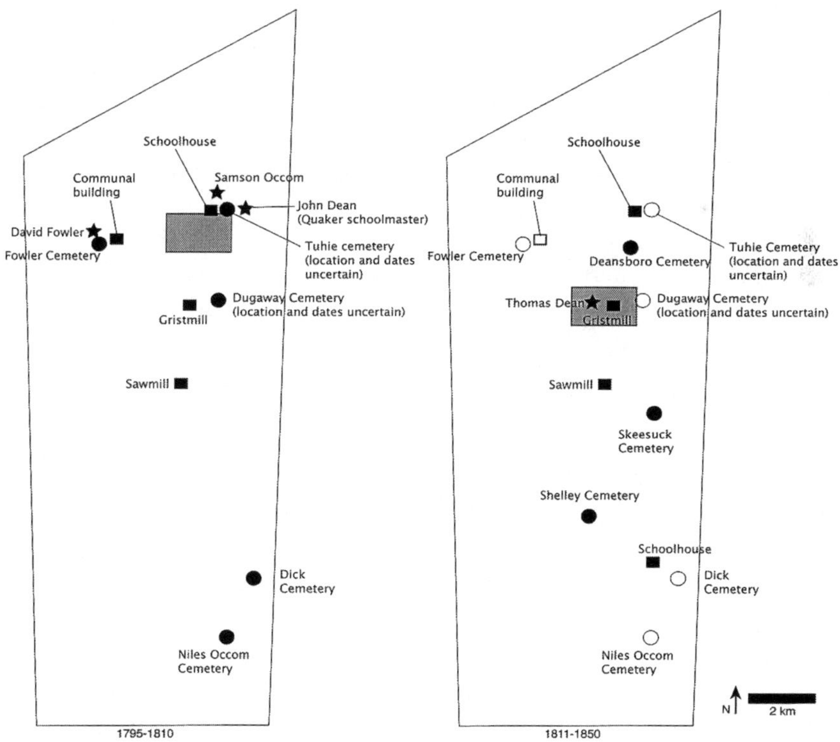

FIGURE 5.8. Maps of Brothertown, New York, showing the locations of cemeteries (circles; black indicates active, white indicates inactive), public buildings (squares), and important Brothertown leaders' homes (stars); the gray areas mark the town center.

highlights the center to which he referred, along with other relevant landmarks in existence up to the first decade of the nineteenth century. As previously noted, the Fowler property was an important communal space: it contained a barn used as a place of worship and a meetinghouse. The northern half of Brothertown also contained Occom's house (until 1791), located on the western half of lot 10 (Love 1899:308); the first schoolhouse, built in 1788 on lot 11; a sawmill built in 1798 on the western part of lot 24; and a gristmill built in 1801 on a creek between lots 16 and 20. There were also four burial grounds located in northern Brothertown: Fowler, Dugaway, Tuhie, and Deansboro cemeteries. Fowler Cemetery was likely the earliest communal burial ground in the settlement. The only other large burial ground in northern Brothertown is Deansboro Cemetery, an interethnic burial ground established in the second quarter of the nineteenth century after Fowler Cemetery had fallen out of use. The dates of Dugaway and Tuhie cemeteries might overlap with those of Fowler Cemetery, but it is unclear when or in what capacity they were used.

In comparison to the northern part of the settlement, the southern half contained fewer communal spaces. A second Brothertown schoolhouse (location unknown) was established there in 1809 (Love 1899:309), and a third was established on Asa Dick's property (lot 36) sometime in the mid-nineteenth century. In contrast to its apparent lack of public buildings and spaces, the southern half of the settlement does contain a number of cemeteries. The Niles Occom burial ground is the only known communal Brothertown cemetery in the area. The other cemeteries in southern Brothertown (Dick, Shelley, and Skeesuck) were private burial plots. Since Shelley and Skeesuck cemeteries were not established until the second quarter of the nineteenth century, Dick Cemetery was probably the only burial ground in southern Brothertown that overlapped temporally with Niles Occom Cemetery.

These patterns show an important distinction between lived spaces and cemetery spaces in Brothertown. The heart of the community was clearly located in the northern part of the settlement and was composed of the only school (until 1809), meetinghouse, and mills, along with the homes of important figures in Brothertown (e.g., the minister, the schoolmaster, many of the political officials). Brothertown Indians living in the southern part of the settlement—including many of the Mohegan-descended Brothertown families discussed in chapter 7—had to travel to engage in certain communal activities. They would have had to walk or ride north to attend school, town meetings, and religious services; to work; and to conduct business at the mills or with the Brothertown Peacemakers (the elected group of Brothertown leaders who dealt with intracommunal disputes and communicated with the superintendents). Although all Brothertown Indians probably shared these important communal spaces in northern Brothertown, the existence of two large contemporaneous communal cemeteries located in opposite sides of the settlement suggests that residents of northern and southern Brothertown used separate cemetery spaces. Based on their respective locations and sizes, it is possible that Fowler and Niles Occom cemeteries served their respective halves of the community.

The 1795–1810 map in figure 5.8 shows no clear relationship between the locations of cemeteries and other communal spaces. Three Brothertown cemeteries (Fowler, Tuhie, Dugaway) sat in close proximity to communal spaces, and two (Niles Occom and Dick) were far removed. A more uniform pattern began to emerge during the second quarter of the nineteenth century; following larger trends in nineteenth-century mortuary practices (see Parker Pearson 1982), Brothertown cemeteries dating to this period were placed relatively farther away from other communal spaces. This trend could be due to several factors. It is possible that with the increase in Euro-Americans living in Brothertown at the time, there was simply no room for new cemeteries in and around the town's communal spaces. It is equally plausible that these patterns relate to emergent social and/or spiritual beliefs that sought increased distance between spaces of the living and the dead. For instance, the increased distance between later-period Brothertown cemeteries and communal spaces stands in stark contrast to the proximity of spaces of the living and the dead around RI-1000 (see previous discussion). All of the active Brothertown cemeteries in New York during the second quarter of the nineteenth century also contained text-bearing stones. As the Brothertown Indians began placing the ancestors farther away from communal spaces, they increasingly used inscriptions to commemorate the dead as unique individuals rather than as unspecified members of the community of ancestors.

Ancestry and Commemoration

The Narragansett and Eastern Niantic

The Narragansett and Eastern Niantic, originally from Charlestown, Rhode Island, are the most widely represented ancestral group within the cemeteries of Brothertown, New York. For instance, it is highly likely that all of the stones in Dick and Skeesuck cemeteries mark graves of Charlestown Indians or their descendants. Both cemeteries are small family plots—the former dating from 1800 to 1830, and the latter dating from 1830 to 1848. Although there are no names inscribed on any of the stones in Dick Cemetery, Isaac Dick, a Narragansett Indian from Charlestown, lived on this lot. Historical documents suggest that he had a family burial plot on his land, adding further support for this hypothesis. The resident of the lot on which Skeesuck Cemetery sits was also a Charlestown Indian, and the inscriptions contained within exclusively list the names of former Charlestown residents. Of note, one inscription bears the name Harriet Fowler—a Montaukett surname—but marks the grave of the daughter of Asa Dick, a descendant of the Charlestown Narragansett. I return to this stone later because it speaks to the roles of consanguineal and affinal kinship ties in shaping the memories of women. In addition to the gravestones in private Charlestown plots, Prude Harry's stone (Deansboro Cemetery) marks the grave of a descendant of the Charlestown Indians; the stone dates to the late nineteenth century. Finally, Tuhie Cemetery, which remains lost at this time, was possibly a Charlestown cemetery since the resident of the lot in which it sat (John Tuhie) was a Narragansett Indian from Charlestown. In total, there are potentially twenty-six stones commemorating Charlestown Indians or their descendants in the cemeteries of Brothertown, New York.

The Mohegan

Esther Poquenup's stone (Deansboro Cemetery) is the only clear example marking the grave of a Mohegan-descended individual in Brothertown, New York. Although the surname Poquenup is either Pequot or Niantic in origin, the inscription on the stone describes Esther as descended from the Mohegan. This is because she had Mohegan parents, but she married Samson Poquenup, a member of the Mashantucket Pequot. Like Harriet Fowler's stone, this stone speaks to the influence of consanguineal kinship ties in shaping memories of women. Although the laws of Brothertown mimicked the androcentric dimensions of white Christian society of the time, reducing Native women's political authority (Jarvis 2010; Murray 1998a), certain Brothertown women were remembered primarily in terms of their direct kin rather than their husbands' bloodlines.

In addition to Esther Poquenup's stone, there are other possible Mohegan gravestones in Niles Occom and Fowler cemeteries. Patience Occom—a Mohegan-descended Brothertown Indian—owned part of the land on which Niles Occom Cemetery sits, but since all of the stones are handmade, it is impossible to determine the identities of those whom they commemorate.

Of note, the settlement patterns analyzed in chapter 7 show a significant number of Mohegan-descended Brothertown Indians living in this corner of the settlement. Additionally, Fowler Cemetery is said to contain the grave of the most famous Brothertown Indian, Samson Occom, who was also Mohegan in descent.

The Eastern Pequot

The most likely Eastern Pequot marker in New York is the handmade stone in Shelley Cemetery. Simeon Shelley, an Eastern Pequot, owned the land on which this cemetery sits. The only other stone in the cemetery is that of Nancy Welch, Simeon's mother-in-law. Because this small cemetery was a family plot, it is very possible that the handmade stone marks the grave of one of Simeon's children.

The Montaukett

The only known Montaukett stones in Brothertown, New York, are those in Fowler Cemetery, which remain uncataloged at this time. The cemetery contains the graves of several Montaukett Indians, including those of David, Hannah, and Jacob Fowler.

The Stockbridge

In addition to the East Coast ancestries represented in Brothertown, New York, there is also one stone commemorating a Stockbridge Indian named Nancy Welch. It sits in Shelley Cemetery, which was owned by Simeon Shelley. His wife was Sabrina, daughter of Nancy and William Welch. It is the only cemetery in Brothertown, New York, known to contain the grave of a Stockbridge Indian.

The Mashantucket Pequot, Western Niantic, and Tunxis

Although there are no gravestones in the New York assemblage that explicitly represent these groups, it is certainly possible that some of the handmade stones or mounds mark burials of Mashantucket Pequot, Western

Niantic, or Tunxis individuals. For example, the resident of the lot that contained Dugaway Cemetery was a Tunxis Indian from Farmington, so it is possible that it contained at least one Tunxis grave.

Comparing Ancestral Tribal Groups

Among handmade stones marking the graves of individuals from different ancestral groups, there are no significant differences in heights, thicknesses, widths, or volumes. Of note, Niles Occom Cemetery—a communal plot—exhibits the widest variety of stone shapes. For example, it contains two shapes that are absent from any of the other Brothertown cemeteries (types B and D) and a relatively higher percentage of stones bearing cortex. The relatively wide variety of stone shapes found in Niles Occom Cemetery could relate to the fact that multiple ancestral groups used the cemetery, but it is most likely a function of sample size; because more people used this cemetery, it exhibits a greater variety of stone manufacturing techniques.

The most explicit means by which gravestones marked social distinctions is with their text inscriptions. However, ancestral tribal affiliations were rarely mentioned. In the New York assemblage, there are only two examples of this phenomenon (Aaron Poquiantup and Esther Poquenup). Beyond these exceptions, Brothertown gravestones were not used as explicit media for marking tribal ancestries. Similarly, the name "Brothertown" does not appear in any of the stone inscriptions. This contrasts starkly with the patterns found in written discourse (chapter 4), highlighting the distinctions between grave marking and other forms of writing (Cipolla 2012d).

The Brothertown Indians also used space to mark social distinctions. The distribution of gravestones in several distinct cemetery spaces is most telling in this regard. A majority of the early Brothertown cemeteries (i.e., Fowler and Niles Occom cemeteries) were used communally and thus likely multitribal. In contrast, Dick Cemetery, dating to the first quarter of the nineteenth century, seems to contain only the burials of Narragansett Indians and their descendants. The dates of this cemetery overlap with the dates of both Fowler and Niles Occom cemeteries. This is to say that the Dick family chose to bury their relatives in a separate burial plot rather than in one of the communal Brothertown cemeteries. The other known private Brothertown cemeteries are Shelley Cemetery (1820–35), which probably postdated the two communal cemeteries, and Skeesuck Cemetery (1830–48), another plot containing only the graves of Charlestown Indians and their descendants. This pattern suggests that the Charlestown Indians were the only group in Brothertown that consistently maintained separate cemetery spaces. In fact, the only known stone representing a Charlestown descendant that is not surrounded by other Charlestown grave markers is that of Prude Harry, located in Deansboro Cemetery. Given the relatively late date of her death (1880s), it is almost certain that her loved ones had no choice but to bury her in Deansboro Cemetery because all other Brothertown burial grounds in New York had fallen out of use by that time. As discussed in chapter 3, the Charlestown community is the only group represented in Brothertown that had a faction of Baptists when on the East Coast. In this light, it is possible that religious differences (rather than ancestral tribal distinctions) led some Charlestown Indians to use and maintain separate cemetery spaces in Brothertown. As discussed in the next chapter, certain Charlestown descendants replicated this pattern in the cemeteries of Brothertown, Wisconsin.

Based on these observations, cemetery discourses in Brothertown, New York, were somewhat silent in regard to ancestral tribal affiliations. The only detectable means by which these distinctions were communicated in cemeteries was through inscriptions (and only on rare occasions). Space played an important role in marking social distinctions, but it seems to have marked religious rather than ancestral tribal differences. Of course, family identities, which are obviously tied to tribal distinctions, played a role in the spatial groupings of burials. The stones of Shelley Cemetery likely commemorate people from two distinct consanguineal groups (i.e., the Stockbridge and the Eastern Pequot) that were related through marriage (affinal ties). In this case, immediate family relations played a greater role than did tribal ancestry when it came to choosing a final resting place.

Discussion and Conclusion

As Brothertown Indians like the Poquiantups mourned their losses and commemorated their loved ones, they simultaneously remade their collective identity while negotiating the politics of colonialism in the modern world. In small incremental steps experienced and executed during the warp and weft of their lives, members of the community continually altered their connections to one another and to outsiders. The materiality of their New York cemeteries offers invaluable perspectives on these processes.

Intracommunal Relations

First and foremost, the New York cemeteries speak to the Brothertown Indians' changing relationships to one another between the late eighteenth and mid-nineteenth centuries. The most prominent transformation in commemoration practices during this period was the replacement of small burial mounds and handmade markers with purchased stones, typically bearing text inscriptions. As the Brothertown Indians replaced their mute mounds and markers with stones bearing the names and biographical information of the deceased, processes of memory and conceptions of personhood were also reconfigured.

Like the East Coast cemeteries, the earliest Brothertown cemeteries were spaces of communal remembrance that the living visited to mourn and remember their collective ancestry and history. From a pragmatic viewpoint, handmade stones and burial mounds did not preserve the locations of specific individuals' graves. In fact, it is plausible that each stone or mound marks the grave of more than one person. The layouts of these cemeteries also had a communal emphasis. Grave distributions replicate those of ancestral cemeteries on the East Coast; markers (and presumably grave shafts) sit in close proximity to one another, with only a meter or so separating neighboring gravesites. Not altogether different from seventeenth-century beliefs in the community of deceased ancestors living in Cauntantowwit's house, a visit to such a cemetery entails physically interacting with memories of multiple ancestors rather than specific individuals. The nature of this form of remembrance is especially evident in the controversy surrounding the precise location of Samson Occom's grave. By the time that William DeLoss Love (1894, 1899, n.d.) went searching for Occom's grave in the late nineteenth century, its location had been forgotten, even by the Brothertown Indians he interviewed. At the time of Occom's death in the late eighteenth century, the Brothertown Indians commemorated their dead in such a way that they were remembered as a collectivity rather than as unique individuals. The most famous Brothertown Indian of all time was no exception to this trend.

Some may argue that these early forms of commemoration were due largely to economic factors. Perhaps the Brothertown Indians used blank handmade stones and mounds because they simply could not afford professionally made stones with inscriptions. Such constraints were clearly influential in their choice of markers, but were not deterministic. As a whole, the Brothertown community increased its economic self-sufficiency as time passed (Jarvis 2010:156–58). During the early nineteenth century, thousands of hectares of land were made suitable for agricultural production by Brothertown hands. Farms in Brothertown produced tens of thousands of bushels of grain and thousands of bushels of potatoes each year. They kept hundreds of livestock and cut hundreds of thousands of feet of fence to bind and protect their new farmlands. Similarly, Brothertown women produced thousands of yards of cloth each year. These figures demonstrate that the Brothertown Indians were not an altogether impoverished group. Furthermore, professionally made gravestones were not overly expensive. Although prices of professionally made grave markers certainly fluctuated temporally and from region to region, gravestones in early nineteenth-century New Jersey ranged between $4.25 and $14 each (Veit and Nonestied 2008:58). It is safe to say that such costs were akin to those in the area of Brothertown, New York, if not more expensive. Additionally, certain receipts in the Brothertown record book indicate that Brothertown Indians typically paid between $2 and $3 for coffins, presumably not much less than it would cost for a modest, professionally made grave marker. It is thus reasonable to suggest that at least some of the Brothertown Indians who used handmade markers did so for reasons other than economic necessity.

The complete lack of inscriptions among the handmade assemblage further supports this interpretation. Members of the Brothertown community not only possessed the skills to quarry and shape limestone grave markers, they also spoke and wrote in the English language. These two factors attest to the fact that Brothertown Indians had the ability to inscribe their handmade grave markers but chose to refrain from doing so. This pattern contrasts sharply with an assemblage of handmade stones cataloged on Long Island, New York, most of which mark the graves of Europeans and Euro-Americans who died between the late seventeenth and early nineteenth centuries (Stone 1987). From 1780 to 1830, such stones represent between 4 and 10 percent of the cataloged Long Island assemblage by decade (notably, far less that the Brothertown community). Many of these Long Island stones originally bore the initials of the deceased along with death dates. Contrary to popular belief, such stones were not limited to poor individuals or Quakers alone (Stone 1987:146). This comparison suggests that the Brothertown Indians who used handmade stones might have had distinct cultural preferences from Europeans and Euro-Americans who used similar stones on Long Island. The use of intentionally blank handmade stones at Brothertown resembled ancestral memory practices, which placed heavy emphasis on the community of ancestors rather than on individuals.

The Brothertown record book provides further evidence for these communal emphases. For example, it contains coffin receipts that speak to the strength of communal bonds in Brothertown, New York (Brothertown Indians 1827c, 1827d). The most interesting of these reads, "William Floyd Esqu one of the Superintendents of the affairs of the Brothertown Indians Sir pleas to pay Aaron Poquiantup the sum of two Dollars it being for making a Coffin for William Peters Decest Who Was Chargeable to the town and

Charge it to the account of Brothertown and oblige yours—[signed] William Dick, Asa Dick, Eliphalet Marthers, Brothertown, May 17, 1827" (Brothertown Indians 1827c). In certain instances the community thus paid to furnish the burials of its members. William Peters' case is all the more interesting given the fact that the Brothertown community recognized him as black or of mixed ancestry (Silverman 2010:155). As documented in their record book, the Brothertown community took measures to push individuals like Peters out of the community beginning in the late eighteenth century (discussed further in chapter 8). Despite such efforts, Peters remained with the community for several more decades, and the Peacemakers even supplied payment for his coffin out of communal funds, demonstrating that he was in fact part of the community, at least in death. Presumably communal funds were only used for such purposes when a Brothertown family lacked financial means to furnish the burial of their deceased loved one or when an individual died who had no family members. The funds for these coffins were probably taken out of the Brothertown Indians' New York account, which was generated from the sale of half of their original land in 1795 (chapter 3).

These specific examples of commemoration and funerary practices complement other historically documented dimensions of the New York community. Historian Brad Jarvis notes the heavy emphasis on community and family in Brothertown, New York. For example, instead of tending to their agricultural fields as individual and family units, farming was a communal activity in Brothertown, and "Men, women, and children labored together throughout the year, often singing religious songs while they worked" (Jarvis 2010:119).

As the Brothertown community incorporated inscribed stones into their commemoration practices, they began transforming Brothertown cemeteries into spaces of individual remembrance, thus altering memory processes and the relationships between members of the living community and their ancestors. From a pragmatic perspective, inscribed stones enabled the living to visit the precise location of an individual's grave and read their specific biographical information. In the long run, inscriptions thus allowed Brothertown Indians to remember their unique places within the community as part of particular lineages and histories. Although this shift probably related in part to economic changes within the community, it also tied to new conceptions of personhood that emphasized individuality in the (living) present and the (dead) past. Although the New York cemeteries contain a handful of such markers, the Brothertown Indians did not truly embrace these new forms of commemoration until they reached Wisconsin, the subject matter of the next chapter.

In addition to an increased emphasis on individuality in the Brothertown community, the New York cemeteries also speak to the significance of ancestral tribal identities. Similar to the written discourses analyzed in the previous chapter, the cemeteries suggest that members of the Brothertown community saw themselves as part of a single tribe (albeit with a variety of religious outlooks), rather than as part of a conglomerate of several distinct tribal groups. For example, there are only two inscriptions that include ancestral tribal ethnonyms. The fact that this practice was so rare suggests that such distinctions were not necessarily important within the Brothertown community.

Subtleties in the phrasing of these inscriptions also speak to Brothertown perspectives on identity transformation and ethnogenesis. The stones of Esther Poquenup and Aaron and Lovinia Poquiantup frame the ancestral tribal identities of the deceased in the past tense. The wording of the inscriptions shows an interesting perspective of tribal identity and its relation to shared landscapes, implying close connections between tribal membership and shared geographical space (see discussion of brotherhood in chapter 4).

Anne McMullen's interpretation of changes in Mohegan basket decor between the eighteenth and nineteenth centuries (1987:120–23; see also Fawcett 2000:41; Fitzgerald 2008; Tantaquidgeon and Fawcett 1987) provides an intriguing analog. She saw these changes as linked directly to the politics of the Brothertown movement, particularly to the tensions between new members of the Brothertown community and those they left behind on the East Coast. Such baskets often bear medallions—interpreted as representing groups of people, such as the Mohegan—and borders or stockades, interpreted as representing reservation or other land boundaries (figure 5.9). Baskets manufactured at Mohegan prior to the Brothertown movement use the same type of stamps both inside and outside the borders, whereas baskets manufactured during and after the founding of Brothertown, New York, use different medallions outside of the represented land boundaries. Following McMullen's logic, the Mohegan who chose to remain on their reservation in Connecticut during the late eighteenth century intentionally marked distinctions between themselves and their relatives and friends who chose to join the Brothertown movement, portraying tribal and communal identity as fundamentally contingent on a shared landscape. They depicted the individuals and families who left the reservation as something other than Mohegan.

The lack of the ethnonym "Brothertown" in the inscriptions of Brothertown Indians' gravestones is also significant. This pattern juxtaposes those discussed in chapter 4, likely because these two forms of discourse (i.e.,

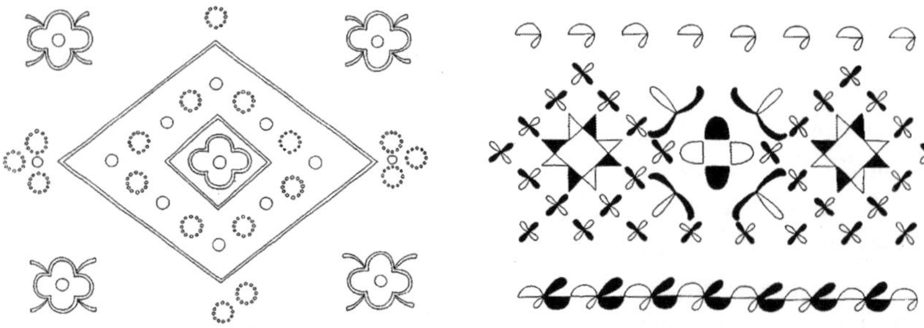

FIGURE 5.9. Mohegan basket designs discussed by McMullen (1987:115). The design on the left predates the Brothertown movement; according to McMullen, the central diamond-shaped border represents the Mohegan land boundaries, and the four-domed medallion within represents the Mohegan people. Those Mohegan peoples represented outside of the boundaries of Mohegan land are similar to those within. The design on the right dates to the early nineteenth century; according to McMullen, the distinction between medallions inside and outside of the Mohegan land boundaries was meant to deny the Mohegan ancestries of those individuals who had joined the Brothertown movement. (Courtesy of the American Indian Archaeological Institute Press)

writing and commemorating) operated on distinct social registers. Since the primary visitors to Brothertown cemeteries in New York were Brothertown Indians, they were also the only intended receivers of gravestone discourses. This pattern suggests that Brothertown community members were comfortable with their own senses of identity and felt no need to explicitly mark their loved ones in terms of tribal or ethnic identities.

Intercommunal Relations

While the transition to purchased stones changed the ways in which Brothertown Indians related to one another and to their respective pasts, it also made Brothertown cemeteries look more like those of Euro-Americans. The Brothertown burial grounds containing only purchased stones were ambivalent spaces (Ashcroft, Griffiths, and Tifflin 1989; Bhabha 1994:145–74; Liebmann 2008b:5–6) in the sense that, if experienced by non-Brothertown individuals, they likely gave no impression of "Indian-ness." These changes indexically marked the Brothertown community as similar to Euro-American communities and distinct from contemporaneous Native communities that used more "traditional" forms of commemoration. As with the ethnonym "Brothertown" discussed in chapter 4, this transformation had the potential to challenge accepted norms of social classification of the time, further blurring the lines between Indian and Euro-American essences.

Because it would have been rare for Euro-Americans to visit the cemeteries of Brothertown, New York, in the nineteenth century, what difference did these changes really make? As discussed in the next chapter, the Brothertown cemeteries of Wisconsin were much more public than those of New York. If these transformations had no pragmatic effect on non–Brothertown Indians in New York, they certainly made differences in Wisconsin Territory, where the Brothertown Indians petitioned for US citizenship by explicitly arguing that they occupied an interstitial position between white and Indian societies (chapter 4). The materiality of their Wisconsin cemeteries, which relates closely to that of their later-period New York cemeteries, supported their written arguments.

Cemetery Discourses

Although their primary purpose was to help the living cope with their losses and mark memories of the dead (see Tarlow 1999), the Brothertown cemeteries of New York also shaped conceptions of personhood and identity, in turn altering intra- and intercommunal relationships. The Brothertown Indians negotiated their identities by entangling spatial, material, and linguistic discourses.

Beginning with spatial discourses, it seems that most Brothertown stones in New York were meant to face west and (potentially) replicate Christian burial patterns, which were distinct from those of many seventeenth-century Algonquian communities. Moreover, some Brothertown Indians used spatial segregation to mark religious distinctions within the community as evinced by separate cemetery spaces kept by Narragansett-descended Baptists from Charlestown. In terms of material discourses, certain handmade Brothertown grave markers mimicked the shapes of popular (Christian) Euro-American gravestones of the time, and purchased stones later transformed Brothertown cemeteries into ambivalent spaces, indistinguishable from Euro-American cemeteries. With these stones came inscribed words and phrases, which diminished the importance of other pragmatic aspects of grave markers in Brothertown, New York. In other words, the messages written on their faces came to speak louder than the markers' other physical attributes. This logocentric shift was just one part of a much larger transformation in the ways the Brothertown Indians imagined their community. In the next chapter, I track these changes across the cemeteries of Brothertown, Wisconsin, and beyond.

6

Commemoration in Wisconsin

HANNAH DICK'S GRAVE SITS IN a small cemetery in the northwest corner of Brothertown, Wisconsin, adjacent to the lot where she spent the last twenty-one years of her life. It is the only Brothertown cemetery bounded by stone walls reminiscent of the vernacular architecture of New England. Such walls cleaved the landscape of Charlestown, Rhode Island, the place that Hannah called home for the first thirty-two years of her life. Her marker, a modest marble gravestone, faces the tranquil waters of Lake Winnebago to the west (figure 6.1). It reads:

HANNAH DICK
DIED
Aug. 6 1855,
Aged 88 y'rs.
& 7 mo's.
Like the corn, fully ripe
To the grave thou hast come
and thy saviour in mercy
Has gathered thee home.

Elegant as it is, this brief inscription omits many of the details and textures of Hannah's remarkable life. Like the few purchased stones of Brothertown, New York, this stone's design and inscription were clearly shaped by the constraints of consumer choice. Despite these limitations, a brief consideration of Hannah's life reveals the cultural nuances of her formulaic gravestone inscription. When contextualized, the seemingly homogenized (i.e., mass-produced and "store bought") message that marks her grave invokes memories of her unique life history and identity as a Brothertown Indian. Read in isolation and ignorance, however, they suggest that she was no different from any other nineteenth-century Wisconsinite.

FIGURE 6.1. Hannah Dick's headstone, Brothertown, Wisconsin.

Hannah was one of the few Brothertown Indians to experience life on the East Coast and in both Brothertown settlements. She was born in 1767 to Daniel and Mary Potter, both Narragansett Indians living in Charlestown (Love 1899). She married William Dick, another Narragansett Indian, and in Rhode Island they had several children together—of which there was eventually a total of eleven. In 1799 the Dick family moved to Brothertown,

New York, where they lived on lot 135. At age forty-seven, Hannah experienced the heartbreak of losing William after nearly thirty years of marriage. She persevered, however, remaining in Brothertown for two more decades before departing for the Wisconsin settlement at age sixty-seven. In 1834 she traveled among one of the earliest groups of settlers. With her daughters Abigail and Thankful and their families, she rode a schooner, *The Navigator*, from Buffalo to Green Bay (Love 1899:325) before making the southward journey to the new Brothertown. There she spent her remaining years living on lot 2. She died at the ripe age of eighty-eight after witnessing the transformation of the new Brothertown from forest to farmland and experiencing the relief of becoming a US citizen with official land rights. When she died, she knew that the Brothertown community was finally safe from the land struggles that had spurred them to their new home.

Hannah may have associated the stone walls that surrounded the small cemetery near the corner of her property with her ancestral homelands on the East Coast. Since it was a family plot, it is possible that she even played a part in its construction. After all, she was known for her adherence to certain traditional practices; for instance, she was one of the last fluent speakers of Algonquian in the entire Brothertown settlement (Heller n.d.). Perhaps it was she who suggested the idea to her family members, likely the people who sought out the fieldstones—much less abundant in this area of Wisconsin compared to reservation lands back east—and constructed the walls. And perhaps it was these memories of Hannah that led her loved ones to choose the epitaph quoted above when marking her grave within those traditional walls. Although metaphors likening death to a homecoming (usually assumed to be in heaven) were common in the late nineteenth century (Tarlow 1999), "home" in this case may have evoked images of the stories that Hannah told of the East Coast. Her stone is the only marker in and around Brothertown to use this metaphor in the 1850s. All other stone inscriptions that liken death to a homebound journey date to the 1860s and later. Half of them mark the graves of Brothertown Indians, the next oldest of which commemorates John Johnson, who died in 1860. Like Hannah, he was born on the East Coast and had the experience of living in each Brothertown settlement. The reference to corn on Hannah's epitaph is also interesting in several regards. It may have held special meaning for her loved ones given the significance of maize in the diets and spiritual beliefs of Native peoples of the Northeast for hundreds of years prior (Chilton 2005, 2008; Ferguson 2010; Hart 2008). Likewise, maize was associated with women given its symbolic designation as one of the "three sisters" and its important place in women's work. Finally, by likening Hannah's life to that of corn, the inscription hints at beliefs in a cyclical nature of life stages as opposed to the linear progression of life iterated in many Christian ontologies (see chapter 5).

This chapter extends the work of chapter 5 to consider the cemeteries and grave markers in and around Brothertown, Wisconsin. As exemplified with Hannah Dick's stone, such markers provide insights into identities, memory processes, and social relations at Brothertown between the 1830s and the early 1900s. When the Brothertown Indians relocated to Wisconsin, they physically distanced themselves from the landscape and associated material legacies of their settlement in New York. In spite of these changes, memories and identities endured, albeit in new configurations. Since the Brothertown stones of Wisconsin closely resemble those of their non-Brothertown neighbors, I also compare them with cemeteries and stones of neighboring groups to identify subtle distinctions in commemoration between insiders and outsiders.

Brothertown Cemeteries of Wisconsin, 1830–1910

A total of 521 grave markers were cataloged in Wisconsin, 270 of which mark the graves of Brothertown Indians. The team collected most of these data (504 markers, 97 percent) from four cemeteries situated in or nearby Brothertown (figure 6.2). The remaining stones were cataloged in four additional cemeteries ranging from 25 to 240 kilometers away from the settlement.

Union Cemetery

About a kilometer and a half northwest of Brothertown's historic (and current) town center sits Union Cemetery, the largest Brothertown burial ground by far. Surrounded by farmland and facing Lake Winnebago to the west, this was the earliest formal burial ground in the new settlement where Brothertown Indians put their loved ones to rest, mourned their losses, and remembered the dead. Informed visitors will note several differences between this cemetery and those of Brothertown, New York. It contains approximately twelve times the stones of the largest New York cemetery, and its markers are nearly all store bought and much more diverse, including ledgers or flat slabs, stone lecterns, and obelisks, along with headstones. With its many markers glimmering in the open air of the comparatively flat Wisconsin landscape, this cemetery is much more prominent to the passerby

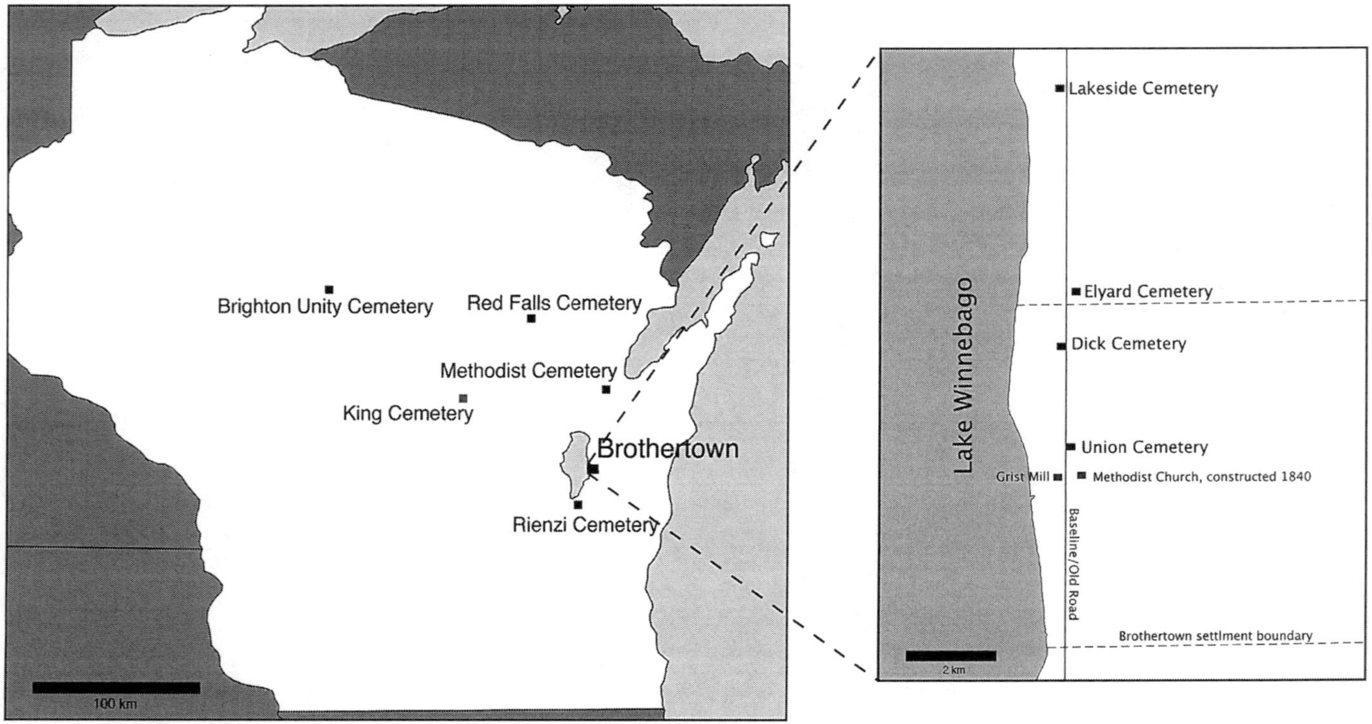

FIGURE 6.2. Map of Wisconsin cemetery locations.

than the hilly, forested, and partially hidden cemeteries of New York. Finally, the nineteenth-century users of this burial ground differed markedly from those of the New York cemeteries. Similar to other burial grounds discussed in this chapter, Union Cemetery contains large numbers of both Native and non-Native graves.

The Brothertown Indians established Union Cemetery in the 1830s, and it remains in use today. With only a few exceptions, Brothertown graves sit in the southern half of the cemetery, separated from the northern half by a rough footpath. As of June 2009, Union Cemetery contained a total of 526 grave markers. Out of these, 306 date between 1830 and 1910, 203 (66 percent) of which mark the graves of Brothertown Indians. For each individual commemorated with an inscribed stone, membership in the Brothertown Indian community was determined using land records in conjunction with the genealogical research of William DeLoss Love (1899) and Rudi Ottery, a Brothertown Indian (Ottery n.d.; see also Ottery and Ottery 1989). Former Brothertown tribal genealogist Caroline Andler also helped with this process. The monuments referred to as Brothertown stones in this volume thus mark the graves of individuals who were (and are) identified as members of the group by other Brothertown Indians both past and present. Brothertown records (Brothertown Indians n.d.) contain invaluable information on lot assignments within the community from the late eighteenth century onward (chapter 7); these records provide useful genealogical information along with rare documentation of land disputes within the community related to interethnic marriages (see discussion of Sarah Pendelton in chapter 8). Combined, these sources help distinguish the grave markers of insiders from those of outsiders—a comparatively complex task when considered in relation to the Brothertown markers and cemeteries of New York, most of which look different (e.g., handmade markers) or sit in separate cemeteries from non-Brothertown stones.

The sign on the cast-iron entrance gate to the cemetery reads, "Union Cemetery, 1911," glossing over the burial ground's deeper Native past. As of 1840, the cemetery sat between the northwest corner of lot 24 (owned by Phebe Fowler) and the southeast corner of lot 25 (owned by Sarah Dick). Phebe's family (surname Kindness) was originally from the Eastern Pequot Reservation. Phebe married David Fowler (II) in Brothertown, New York; he died in 1836 and never made it to Wisconsin. Much less is known of Sarah Dick. Although she was part of one the biggest family lines in the Brothertown community (Narragansett in origin), the finer details of her life are unknown.

Dick Cemetery

This cemetery contains the grave of Hannah Dick. It sits in the northwest corner of the settlement—just over three kilometers north of the town center—and is the only Brothertown burial ground currently bounded by stone walls. The small stone structure of Dick Cemetery is clearly visible from Lakeshore Drive (originally known as Baseline or Old Road), the westernmost of three parallel roadways constructed in the 1830s that still run north to south through the settlement. After entering through its cast-iron gate, visitors observe the smallest Brothertown Indian cemetery in Wisconsin: a collection of nineteen gravestones. All seemingly mark the graves of Brothertown Indians.

Dick Cemetery dates to the mid- to late nineteenth century (1840–70). Like Dick and Skeesuck cemeteries of New York, it functioned as a private burial plot used almost exclusively by Baptist descendants of Charlestown Indians. It sat on the northeast corner of lot 3, just next to Hannah Dick's property. As of 1840, Cynthia Dick owned the land on which it currently sits. Her family (surname Wauby) was either Narragansett or Pequot. She married Thomas Dick (II) in Brothertown, New York, but suffered a tragedy in 1832 after arriving in the new settlement: a group of Menominee Indians reportedly murdered her husband (Love 1899). Thomas' father, Thomas Dick (I), had been a leader of the Baptist community in Brothertown, New York. Despite her ties to her husband's family and the proximity of their cemetery to her property in Wisconsin, after her death in 1871, Cynthia's loved ones chose to bury her in Union Cemetery. Like the stones of Harriet Fowler and Esther Poquenup discussed in chapter 5, this choice demonstrates the endurance of women's consanguineal identities even after they had acquired new surnames, affinal kinship ties, and religions affiliations.

Elyard Cemetery

Nearly five kilometers north of the town center and just outside of the Brothertown boundary line lies Elyard Cemetery. Part of the current-day town of Quinney, Elyard Cemetery literally sits in the middle of a modern planting field. Like Dick Cemetery, it is small in size, containing only twenty-two grave markers. Older residents of the area informed me that Elyard Cemetery once contained many more markers than it does currently. They also recalled that the cemetery once had stone walls surrounding it much like those that still bound Dick Cemetery. Given its current location, it is likely that farming practices have affected this cemetery, reducing the number of visible markers. Elyard Cemetery's small size and comparatively remote location make it difficult to spot from the roadway, but it is still visible to the keen observer. During the warmer months, miniature American flags placed near the graves of veterans help this cemetery stand out on the landscape. Within, visitors will find markers akin to those of both Union and Dick cemeteries.

Taking its name from its late nineteenth-century non-Native landowner, Elyard Cemetery was in use between the mid-1850s and the early twentieth century. Of the twenty-two markers that it currently contains, twenty predate 1910. Like Dick Cemetery, this burial ground also appears to have been used as a semi-private burial plot. Caroline Andler informed me that a number of the individuals buried in this cemetery were of mixed Native, European, and African ancestry. The surnames of those buried in the cemetery support this interpretation. Approximately half of the inscribed names are those of documented Brothertown families, and a quarter are both Brothertown and Stockbridge in origin (i.e., surnames that were present in both communities in the eighteenth and nineteenth centuries). The remaining names are non-Indian surnames known to have married in to either of the communities during the nineteenth century. The location of this burial ground just outside of Brothertown boundaries may correlate with the interstitial position of its users—between Native American, African American, and Euro-American.

Lakeside Cemetery

Almost ten kilometers north of Brothertown center sits Lakeside Cemetery, a large communal burial ground located in current-day Stockbridge, Wisconsin. An enormous, gnarled cottonwood tree marks the entrance to this cemetery and likely dates to the nineteenth century or earlier. The tree dominates the skyline—rivaled only by an occasional grain storage silo—and therefore serves as an excellent landmark for the cemetery. Visitors to this public burial ground will find a variety of markers akin to those in the other Wisconsin cemeteries. The oldest stones in Lakeside Cemetery date to the mid-nineteenth century, and the burial ground is still used today. As of 2009, it contained 211 grave markers, 157 of which predate 1910. Of these, only eleven (7 percent) are known to mark graves of Brothertown Indians. In addition, Stockbridge Indians, Euro-Americans, and African Americans are interred in this cemetery.

Distant Wisconsin Cemeteries

As mentioned previously, Brothertown stones were also cataloged in cemeteries located between 25 and 240 kilometers away from Brothertown. These stones represent only 6 percent of the Brothertown grave markers cataloged in Wisconsin. In total there are seventeen stones in four cemeteries.

The closest of these burial grounds is Rienzi Cemetery, located in Fond du Lac, just twenty-five kilometers south of Brothertown. It was founded in the mid-nineteenth century and contains forty hectares of land. Although Rienzi Cemetery is known to contain several Brothertown gravestones, only one was located and cataloged for this volume (date of death not specified). The next burial ground is a Methodist cemetery located in Oneida, Wisconsin, just over seventy kilometers north of Brothertown. This cemetery contains a number of Euro-American and Native gravestones, including Oneida and Brothertown markers. Of note, there appears to be an "Indian" section of burials in the rear of the cemetery, some marked with handmade stones. Although this cemetery is known to contain at least two Brothertown stones, only one was located (date of death unspecified). The third burial ground is Red Falls Cemetery, located in Gresham, Wisconsin, approximately 145 kilometers north of Brothertown. This is another large cemetery containing both Euro-American and Native gravestones, including Stockbridge, Munsee, and Brothertown markers. A total of ten Brothertown stones were located and cataloged there, ranging in dates between 1860 and 1907. The fourth burial ground is Brighton Cemetery, located in Unity, Wisconsin, 240 kilometers northwest of Brothertown. Five Brothertown stones were cataloged in this cemetery, ranging in dates from 1882 to 1903.

In addition to these cataloged cemeteries, there are other Brothertown gravestones located across the Midwest. For example, King Cemetery (see figure 6.2) is known to contain several Brothertown stones, and there are fairly significant numbers of Brothertown stones reported in Long Prairie and Little Falls, Minnesota (Caroline Andler, personal communication).

Markers

In total, the Wisconsin assemblage includes data collected from 270 Brothertown grave markers dating between the second quarter of the nineteenth century and the first decade of the twentieth century. These stones mark the graves of at least 317 individuals. For comparative purposes, data were also collected from 251 non–Brothertown Indian monuments in Union and

Lakeside cemeteries, marking the graves of at least 303 individuals. The oldest of these stones date to the mid-nineteenth century.

Raw Materials

In contrast to the New York assemblage, nearly all (98.5 percent) of the Wisconsin markers were purchased from professional stone carvers. During the nineteenth century several carvers operated out of nearby Fond du Lac (figure 6.3). To purchase a marker for a loved one, it would have taken Brothertown Indians many hours to make the journey during the warmer months. The frigid Wisconsin winters offered a more efficient pathway, however, freezing the waters of Lake Winnebago and thereby opening up a direct route across the lake. A majority of these purchased stones are made from marble, but small quantities of granite and concrete markers are also present in the assemblage (table 6.1). In regard to the few handmade stones in the Wisconsin cemeteries, all are made from limestone, which is abundant in and around Brothertown. Comparatively, the non-Brothertown assemblage contains relatively more markers made from granite and fewer made from marble, along with several metal markers.

Types, Shapes, and Sizes

The Wisconsin assemblage is considerably more diverse (figure 6.4) than the New York assemblage. Although they contain no mounds, the Wisconsin cemeteries include headstones, obelisks, ledgers or flat slabs, and several other types of grave marker (see table 6.1). Part of the Egyptian revival in American cemeteries, obelisks are four-sided stone pillars with pyramidal tips (Mytum 2002 [2001]). Their presence in Brothertown cemeteries of Wisconsin speaks not only to new forms of commemoration within the community but also to the local effects of consumerism in the modern, globally connected world. For another example of these global influences, note the background of the stone carver advertised in figure 6.3; he was born in Germany, gained work experience in New York City, and subsequently started his business in Fond du Lac.

Compared to the other markers, ledgers have a much lower profile. They face upward with their inscribed faces nearly flush with the ground surface. In addition to these forms, there are also several stone lecterns and one stone urn marking Brothertown graves in Wisconsin—each life-sized.

S. EUDEMILLER, Marble and Granite Works, Established 1862.

As "in the midst of life we are in death" is being constantly verified, it should cause everybody to prepare for that inevitable event, and especially induce those of us who survive our relatives and friends to do all we can to keep in affectionate remembrance the memory of the deceased. One of the most enduring outward signs of this is to mark their last earthly resting place by some monument which shall be an ever present reminder of their worth and affection. This is usually done by selecting some substantial, ornate and lasting material such as marble or granite. This system has been in vogue for centuries, and has become very common of late among all classes. While this is right and proper, yet, in adopting this course, we ought to go to the dealer who is practical and honorable and who possesses valuable facilities for satisfying our various wants, and who, in the matter of designs and facilities, may be able to gratify our varied tastes and financial circumstances. In doing this we know of no better place to go to for anything in this line, under any condition of circumstances, than Sebastian Eudemiller's, located at 409 Main street. He is a practical man of many years' experience and one of the most conscientious gentlemen following this business with whom we are acquainted. He is a native of Hesse-Darmstadt, Germany, and came to this country in 1846 a practical stonecutter, finding employment with Fisher & Bird, the great marble dealers of 464 Houston street, New York city, with whom he remained until 1861. Here he had a very varied and long experience, and on locating in Fond du Lac in the last named year was well prepared for business on his own account, and which he established in 1862, 1887 therefore, records the twenty-fifth year of his business career here, which makes him the oldest continuous practical marble and granite worker in the city. During this time he has been one of the most laborious and vigilant business men in this vicinity, and produced designs requiring the peculiar skill he is known to possess. These monuments may be found in every cemetery in this vicinage, an inspection of which will demonstrate his superior ability, while the prices of the same have been regarded very reasonable. He makes a point of securing his material from first hands, and there is nothing in the marble or granite line but what he can produce and at the most moderate figures. During his career in this city he has maintained a valuable business name, contributed liberally to the city's advancement and served a number of years with much credit in the city council.

FIGURE 6.3. Advertisement for Sebastian Eudemiller's Marble and Granite Works in Fond du Lac, Wisconsin, City Directory, 1887–1891.

Table 6.1. Raw Materials and Marker Types in the Wisconsin Assemblage

Raw Material	Brothertown	Non-Brothertown	Marker Type	Brothertown	Non-Brothertown
Marble	259 (93%)	158 (63%)	Headstones	219 (81%)	113 (45%)
Granite	15 (5%)	88 (35%)	Ledgers	10 (4%)	62 (25%)
Concrete	1 (<1%)	0 (0%)	Obelisks	28 (10%)	41 (16%)
Limestone	4 (1%)	0 (0%)	Other	13 (5%)	35 (14%)
Metal	0 (0%)	5 (2%)			
Total	270 (100%)	251 (100%)	Total	270 (100%)	251 (100%)

Comparatively, the non-Brothertown assemblage of Wisconsin consists of similar types of marker albeit in slightly different proportions, with far fewer headstones and many more ledgers and obelisks.

Each of these marker types came in a variety of shapes and sizes. Headstones, representing 81 percent of the Brothertown Indian assemblage, exhibit the greatest diversity. While rectangular (type 1, $N = 96$) or semi-rectangular (type 2, $N = 61$) headstones were the most popular, Brothertown Indians also marked the graves of loved ones with thirteen additional headstone types, several of which are shaped like headboards (chapter 5). A few uniquely shaped markers also take the form of three-dimensional hearts, buildings, leaves, or cylinders. In addition, there are two handmade shapes (types A and B) present in the assemblage along with the obelisks, lecterns, and single urn-shaped marker already mentioned.

Table 6.2 compares the mean size of grave markers for Brothertown Indians and non–Brothertown Indians in Wisconsin. Neighboring non-Brothertown markers of marble are considerably larger, with an average estimated volume greater than twice the size of Brothertown markers of the same material. This pattern ties directly to the higher proportion of large marker types (e.g., obelisks marking two of more individuals) found in the non-Brothertown assemblage. Although the Brothertown markers of granite appear much larger than do non-Brothertown markers of the same material, this pattern may be skewed due to the small sample size of granite markers in the Brothertown Indian assemblage (see table 6.1). Overall, these disparities may be the result of cultural preferences, economic differences, or perhaps time scale. Since the Brothertown Indians began purchasing grave markers in Wisconsin well before other non-Native populations moved to the area (approximately two decades), it is possible that the differences in frequency of raw material, marker types, and sizes between the two assemblages are the result of regional

FIGURE 6.4. New types of grave marker used in Brothertown, Wisconsin, included lecterns (top left), obelisks (top right), and ledgers or flat slabs (bottom). (Photographs by author)

Table 6.2. Mean Marker Size (cm) in the Wisconsin Assemblage

	Brothertown	Non-Brothertown
Marble		
Height	71	87
Width	37	42
Thickness	12	22
Granite		
Height	77*	55
Width	67*	62
Thickness	39*	31

*Denotes small sample size

stylistic trends in grave marker consumption. As explored shortly, however, a close comparison of the two groups also speaks to distinct understandings of personhood, commemoration, and community.

Inscriptions

In stark contrast to the New York assemblage, nearly all Brothertown stones in Wisconsin bear text. Out of the 270 cataloged stones, 251 (93 percent) have legible text inscriptions. Of the remaining stones, 3 percent once bore text but are now illegible from weathering and 4 percent are blank handmade markers like the majority of stones in the New York assemblage. The oldest inscribed stone in Brothertown, Wisconsin, marks the grave of Joseph Palmer, a Brothertown Indian who was murdered in 1836 (see later discussion). Most of the Brothertown stones date to the mid-nineteenth century, although all decades between 1830 and 1910 are represented. Of the inscribed markers, 158 (58 percent) also bear some sort of decorative motif ranging in extravagance from simple border designs to popular nineteenth-century gravestone iconography like the urn and willow.

The earliest non–Brothertown Indian stones in Union and Lakeside cemeteries date to the 1850s, approximately two decades after the Brothertown Indians settled in the area. Beginning in the 1880s, the number of non-Brothertown stones in these cemeteries surpassed the number of Brothertown Indian stones. This was the period when Brothertown Indians began moving away from Brothertown (chapter 3). Of note, the largest portion of the non-Brothertown sample dates to the 1890s and 1900s, and the largest portion of the Brothertown Indian sample dates to the 1850s and 1860s. Of the 251 non-Brothertown stones, 95 percent bear legible text inscriptions and 57 percent have inscribed decor.

Texts

Technically speaking, not all of the gravestone texts in the Wisconsin assemblage are actual inscriptions. In fact, inscription was only one of three methods used to mark texts or decor on gravestones; relief and inlaid markings are also present in the assemblage. Inscription consists of removing stone so that the missing raw material forms the characters of texts and the remaining raw material forms the negative shapes of the characters. Relief is just the opposite: stone is removed so that the remaining stone forms the characters of texts and the absent stone forms the negative space. Finally, with inlaid texts, the carver inscribes characters on the stone face and subsequently fills in the inscriptions with a different type of raw material—usually another color of stone.

The most readily used method for marking texts in the Wisconsin assemblage was through a combination of inscription and relief. This combination accounts for the majority (65 percent, N = 165) of text-bearing stones in the assemblage. Typically, relief lettering was used to emphasize certain portions of the text—most often the first name of the deceased—and inscribed lettering was used for all other parts of the text. The next most common methods of marking text on the Wisconsin stones were inscription only, relief only, or a combination of inscribed and inlaid lettering.

The 270 stones commemorate a total of at least 317 individuals (table 6.3). Of note, two stones are family plot markers and thus do not commemorate specific individuals. Although the majority of the stones commemorate single individuals, just under 15 percent (thirty-nine) of the stones in the Brothertown Indian assemblage are known to commemorate between two to five individuals each. Certain people also have more than one marker. This usually occurs only with married couples or pairs of parents and children. In such cases, two individuals are marked with three stones: one commemorating the two people together, with separate stones marking the specific interment locations of each individual. Comparatively, the number of individuals commemorated per stone in the non-Brothertown assemblage range from one to eight, with a majority of the stones commemorating single individuals. Although the non-Brothertown assemblage contains fewer individually

Table 6.3. Number of Persons Commemorated per Grave Marker in the Wisconsin Assemblage

	Brothertown		Non-Brothertown	
Persons per marker	Number of markers	Number of persons	Number of markers	Number of persons
1	199 (74%)	199 (63%)	163 (65%)	163 (54%)
2	30 (11%)	60 (19%)	27 (11%)	54 (18%)
3	6 (2%)	18 (6%)	3 (1%)	9 (3%)
4	2 (<1%)	8 (2%)	3 (1%)	12 (4%)
5	1 (<1%)	5 (1%)	3 (1%)	15 (5%)
6	0 (0%)	0 (0%)	1 (<1%)	6 (2%)
8	0 (0%)	0 (0%)	1 (<1%)	8 (2%)
1 person/2 stones	2 (<1%)	1 (<1%)	6 (2%)	3 (1%)
2 people/2 stones*	0 (0%)	0 (0%)	2 (<1%)	2 (<1%)
2 people/3 stones	6 (2%)	4 (1%)	27 (11%)	18 (6%)
3 people/3 stones*	3 (1%)	3 (1%)	3 (1%)	3 (1%)
Family plot makers	2 (<1%)	0 (0%)	1 (<1%)	0 (0%)
Undetermined	19 (7%)	19 (6%)*	11 (4%)	11 (4%)*
Total	270 (100%)	317 (100%)	251 (100%)	303 (100%)

*Denote estimated numbers for blank or illegible markers.

marked graves than the Brothertown Indian assemblage (i.e., one stone per person), it exhibits many more examples of graves of single individuals or couples marked with several monuments each.

Most inscriptions on Brothertown stones begin with the name or initials of the deceased. A majority of these lead off only with the first name. Inscriptions beginning with full names or initials follow in proportion, and a few texts start simply with the surname or surname initial of the deceased. Another group of inscriptions begin with the familial relations or roles that the deceased held in life for the bereaved. Examples of this type include "Brother," "Children of . . . ," and "Our Mother." Other inscriptions begin with metaphors likening death to more comfortable realms of human experience. These include inscriptions that frame death as a journey (e.g., "Gone Home" or "Farewell") or as sleep (e.g., "At rest"). The non-Brothertown assemblage mirrors these basic patterns.

None of the Brothertown stones in Wisconsin make explicit mention of tribal or religious identities. The inscriptions on most of the markers typify the deceased in terms of their part in the nuclear family. The most popular of these represent the deceased as "Wife of . . . ," "Daughter of . . . ," or "Son of . . ." In most cases inscriptions emphasize a single familial role, however, there are a few exceptions in which two roles are mentioned. Examples of these typify the deceased as "Daughter and Wife," or "Mother and Wife." The only other dimension of identity explicitly mentioned in the Wisconsin inscriptions are those relating to military service. In two cases, both military service and familial relations are mentioned together. Since the US government commissioned the military stones, it comes as no surprise that they frame the deceased's life almost solely in terms of their former military service. In most cases these stones exclude basic biographical information such as dates of birth and death. Only military ranks and company numbers are included in such inscriptions.

Patterns in the text inscriptions speak to the roles that family, gender, and age played in the Brothertown community. Within the Brothertown Indian assemblage, only 32 percent of the text inscriptions include the full name of the deceased (table 6.4). The remaining inscriptions offer only the first name. As discussed in chapter 5, the reader must infer the full name by other co-textual clues in the inscription. For example, Phebe Fowler's stone typifies her as "Phebe, wife of David Fowler," despite the fact that she was a widow long before her own death and that she lived in Wisconsin on her own for nearly three decades. Like her stone, many inscriptions in Brothertown cemeteries define the deceased in relation to other persons. The deceased is most often defined by his or her relationship to parents or a husband. I return to these patterns when I compare stone forms with the marked biographical qualities of those they commemorate. The non-Brothertown assemblage exhibits comparatively high frequencies of full names, demonstrating that non-Brothertown residents emphasized the individuality of the deceased more than their Brothertown Indian neighbors did. The comparatively high number of individuals commemorated as "children of" on Brothertown Indian markers supports this interpretation. Instead of commemorating their children as unique individuals, Brothertown Indians of Wisconsin often defined their deceased children primarily in terms of the relationships they had

Table 6.4. Represented Personhood on Grave Markers in the Wisconsin Assemblage

	Brothertown	Non-Brothertown
Full name	101 (32%)	149 (49%)
Wife of . . .	48 (15%)	34 (11%)
Children of . . .	91 (29%)	47 (16%)
Other	77 (24%)	73 (24%)
Total	317 (100%)	303 (100%)

with their parents, at least in much higher frequencies than did their non-Native neighbors.

Other inscription patterns demonstrate shifting forms of commemoration within the Brothertown community. As discussed in chapter 5, some stones emphasize memories of the event of death and loss experienced by the living community, whereas others emphasize memories of the deceased's life and biography. In the Wisconsin assemblage, nearly half of the text inscriptions include just the death date, and less than a quarter include both birth and death dates. The lack of birth dates may relate directly to record keeping (or lack thereof). It is altogether possible that precise dates of birth were unknown in many instances, particularly for tribal elders. The community's relatively early embrace of the English language and colonial forms of record keeping combated these processes of forgetting to a certain degree. Regardless of the precise cause of these patterns of remembrance, they still had pragmatic effects, shaping the ways in which community members conceived of their ancestors over the long term. Other co-textual clues demonstrate these differences. For instance, the verb *died* appears in just over half of the text inscriptions. For example, James Niles' inscription reads, "JAMES NILES DIED SEP. 7. 1863 AGED 82 Y's," and Francis Dick's stone simply lists his full name, birth date, and death date: "FRANCIS F DICK, OCT. 7, 1864, JULY 11, 1890." The former emphasizes the end of a life, and the latter emphasizes the duration of a life. In these two cases, the gravestones mediate slightly different social processes, one emphasizing bereavement and loss, the other emphasizing the biography of the deceased. Inscription data on the age of the deceased also tie to these themes; some text inscriptions include the precise age of the deceased at time of death in terms of years, months, and days.

Epitaphs like the one found on Hannah Dick's stone are a frequent occurrence in the Brothertown Indian assemblage. Typically found at the bottom of text inscriptions, epitaphs often appear in the form of a brief poem or verse concerning loss, death, or the afterlife. Like Hannah Dick's epitaph, most focus on the current status of the deceased. They typically imply or state directly that the deceased is in heaven, resting, immortal, or simply elsewhere. For example, Harriet Dick's (she was the daughter of Hannah Dick's husband's brother's son) epitaph reads,

Ere sin Could blight or sprit fade,
Death came with fondly care,
The opening bud to Heaven conveyed,
And bade it blossom there.

Inscriptions like this portray the deceased as capable of enduring death in some fashion—spiritually or otherwise—making it possible for a future reunion between the deceased and their surviving loved ones. Also within this group are epitaphs that speak of the dead as living on in the memories of their loved ones. For example, William Coyhis' epitaph reads, "Gone but not forgotten." Of course, perspectives such as this do not operate on beliefs in the afterlife or heaven specifically. Other epitaphs in the assemblage focus on the deceased's life, the event of death, and spiritual understandings of death, whereas still others present moralistic messages for the living, describe the process of bereavement, and discuss the possibility of a future reunion between the (then) living and the deceased. Finally, one group presents instructions for the bereaved or the deceased, urging the former not to grieve and the latter to rest in peace.

Overall, text inscriptions of the Wisconsin stones speak—directly or indirectly—to a number of issues, including familial relations, gender, age, professional identities, perspectives on death, and processes of bereavement. Issues of racial and ethnic identity and/or colonial and community politics are almost completely absent from the inscriptions of Brothertown Indians. The only exception is found on Joseph Palmer's marker, the oldest inscribed stone in the assemblage. It reads,

JOSEPH PALMER
DIED
July 3, 1836
AE 42 yrs.
He was murdered by the Stockbridge Indians in Stockbridge.

This is the only inscription in the Wisconsin assemblage in which the word *Indian* appears. This pattern remained even after the Brothertown Indians came to share cemetery space with individuals who were clearly not Brothertown, nor Indian. The wording on Palmer's stone hints at some animosity between the Brothertown and Stockbridge communities at the time of the monument's erection. Although two specific Stockbridge Indians, the Konkapot brothers, were known to have murdered Palmer, the inscription on his stone frames the event as if the entire Stockbridge community were at fault. In this instance, the inscription represents the offending Konkapot brothers' membership in the Stockbridge Indian community as the most important aspect of difference between them and the deceased. The stone implicitly marks a difference between the Stockbridge and Brothertown communities. The fact that both groups were Christian Indian communities who shared neighboring settlements in New York and Wisconsin and intermarried frequently did *not* erase distinctions between the two groups, the most prominent of which was their origins. In opposition to the Brothertown, the Stockbridge—also known as "the Mohican" (not to be confused with Mohegan)—trace their ancestry to the Hudson River Valley of New York and western Massachusetts (Frazier 1992; Silverman 2010).

Imagery

In total, 158 stones in the Brothertown Indian assemblage bear some sort of nonlinguistic decorative motif. Of these, 130 have imagery that occupies a central position in the stone design, and 28 have only border decorations typically consisting of simple geometric or floral designs. The number of stones bearing central imagery is one of the most prominent differences between the Brothertown and non-Brothertown assemblages. Nearly half of the stones marking Brothertown graves bear central imagery, compared to just under a quarter of the cataloged non-Brothertown stones (table 6.5). This pattern likely stems from economic differences between the two groups in the mid-nineteenth century. It is altogether possible that Brothertown Indians had more money to spend on grave markers than their non-Native neighbors did during this time. However, different cultural preferences might have contributed to this pattern. Perhaps Brothertown Indians preferred to mark memories of their loved ones using a combination of words and images rather than just words alone.

Common themes represented in the decorative motifs are Christianity, military service, companionship, love, and nature. The most prevalent motifs are the military shield and the willow tree. Other popular designs include lambs (for children), various floral designs, the Bible (or unspecified book), clasped hands, and hands pointing upward. I categorize these motifs in regard to six general themes: (1) personal accomplishments or character of the deceased, (2) current status of the deceased/spiritual understandings of death, (3) mortality, (4) social relations, (5) Christianity, and (6) bereavement. What follows is a loose interpretation of the potential meanings of these types of imagery. It is highly likely that the imagery discussed here held other contextual and personal meanings for the Brothertown Indians who purchased and viewed the stones in the nineteenth century.

The most common motifs are those that emphasize the personal accomplishments or character of the deceased. The only accomplishments explicitly highlighted are those relating to military service, represented by the

Table 6.5. General Image Themes Organized in Order of Popularity among the Brothertown Indians of Wisconsin

Type	Brothertown Frequency	Non-Brothertown Frequency
Personal accomplishments or character of the deceased		
Military shield	31 (11%)	11 (4%)
Lamb (1 depicting a lamb underneath a willow tree)	9 (3%)	9 (3%)
Dove	4 (1%)	4 (1%)
Sword with curtain/veil	1 (<1%)	0 (0%)
Sword with rifle	1 (<1%)	0 (0%)
Anchor	0 (0%)	2 (<1%)
Cannons	0 (0%)	1 (<1%)
Status of the deceased or spiritual interpretations of death		
Willow	22 (8%)	6 (2%)
Hand pointing up	9 (3%)	3 (1%)
Laurel wreath	9 (3%)	3 (1%)
Book/Bible	7 (2%)	3 (1%)
Hand reaching down	2 (<1%)	0 (0%)
Lamb	See above	See above
Dove	See above	See above
Angel	1 (<1%)	0 (0%)
Birds	1 (<1%)	0 (0%)
Hand holding book open	1 (<1%)	0 (0%)
Mortality		
Flower (unidentified)	8 (3%)	11 (4%)
Rose	8 (3%)	0 (0%)
Book/Bible	See above	See above
Urn	5 (2%)	1 (<1%)
Branch with fruit	2 (<1%)	0 (0%)
Leaf	1 (<1%)	0 (0%)
Relationships		
Clasped hands	5 (2%)	3 (1%)
Heart	1 (<1%)	1 (<1%)
Christianity		
Book/Bible	See above	See above
Church bells	1 (<1%)	0 (0%)
Cross	1 (<1%)	1 (<1%)
Bereavement		
Willow	See above	See above
Subtotal	130 (48%)	59 (24%)
Border designs only	28 (10%)	83 (33%)
No imagery	97 (36%)	96 (38%)
Unknown	15 (6%)	13 (5%)
Grand Total	270 (100%)	251 (100%)

high frequencies of military shield designs and other military-related motifs. The dove and lamb motifs each symbolize the character of the deceased. The dove, which conventionally denotes purity and peace, and the lamb, which denotes innocence (Keister 2004:74–80) were both popular choices when marking the graves of Brothertown children. I also include the dove and lamb in the next category because it is possible that these images refer to the current peaceful state of the deceased.

Motifs that speak to the current status of the deceased or spiritual understandings of death are also standard occurrences in the Brothertown assemblage. Although I include the willow design in this category because it may stand for the peaceful state of the deceased for some, I also include it under the category of bereavement, discussed shortly. Because laurel leaves do not wilt easily, some interpret images of the laurel wreath on grave markers as denoting eternity and immortality (Keister 2004:48). The book likely represents the Bible, but also may have denoted the completion of a life when depicted as closed, or openness to God when depicted as open (Keister 2004: 112–13). The hand pointing upward suggests that the deceased has gone to heaven. Similarly, images of birds likely symbolize the spirit of the deceased. Also included in this general category are images of the lamb and the hand reaching down—representing the hand of God.

Third are motifs that represent mortality in various forms; these include mostly plants and flowers, which denote the cyclical and fleeting nature of life (Keister 2004:41). Also included in this category are images of the urn and the book. Fourth are motifs that symbolize personal relationships (likely between the bereaved and the deceased); included in this category are the clasped hands of friendship or marriage and the heart. Fifth are motifs that depict Christian symbols such as the Bible, cross, and church bells; and sixth are motifs that relate to the process of bereavement. The only image included in this category is the willow or weeping willow motif, which denotes grief and sorrow in certain contexts (see also chapter 5).

Personhood and Identity

Similar to the New York assemblage, correlations exist between the materiality of the Wisconsin stones and the qualities of the person or people whose grave(s) they mark. In particular, the number of persons commemorated per marker and the deceased's age and gender each influenced their commemorators to purchase certain types of monument and include or omit certain types of information in the inscriptions. In other words, these qualities of personhood were communicated via the pragmatic dimensions of the analyzed markers. To be sure, this is not to say that Brothertown Indians or others carefully calculated the ways in which relative stone height, for example, spoke of the deceased, although this possibility cannot be fully ruled out. Despite the lack of clear evidence for intentionality, trends in Brothertown gravestone consumption made differences in the ways the dead were remembered, and they offer insights into intracommunal social relations.

The Brothertown Indian stones of Wisconsin mark the graves of individuals ranging in age from a few days to ninety-three years old. I divide the stones into the following four groups depending on the age of the deceased at time of death: (1) newborn to two years old; (2) three to nineteen years old, (3) twenty to fifty-nine years old, and (4) sixty years and older. These groupings facilitate a comparison of stones memorializing infants, children/adolescents, younger adults, and older adults. I also compare stones marking the graves of females versus those marking the graves of males.

Marker Forms

Brothertown Indians used a variety of memorial types to mark the graves of single individuals, the most popular of which was the headstone. The majority of double graves are also marked with headstones. When it came to marking the graves of three or more individuals, however, Brothertown Indians typically used obelisks. The average size of markers thus correlates with the number of persons commemorated per marker. This pattern is only partially attributable to the use of different marker types for different numbers of people. For instance, a comparison of headstones that mark the graves of single individuals versus those marking the graves of two people shows an average height increase of thirteen centimeters for double graves (table 6.6). In other words, larger stones tend to mark more burials than smaller stones, or relative gravestone sizes iconically represent the relative number of people commemorated.

There is also a strong correlation between the age of the deceased and the variety of monument types and shapes used to mark their graves (table 6.7). The Brothertown Indians used a wider variety of stone types and shapes to commemorate older individuals. Each of the first two age groups contains three memorial types, and the last two groups contain four memorial types each. Although headstones are the most common monument type found across all age groups, the two adult groups are also slightly more varied in

Table 6.6. Comparing Headstone Size versus Number of Persons Commemorated

	Sample	Height (cm)	Width (cm)	Thickness (cm)
Brothertown				
Headstones marking single individuals	180	63	35	7
Headstones marking two or more individuals	21*	76	48	8
Undetermined	18			
Total	219			
Non-Brothertown				
Headstones marking single individuals	100	64	36	9
Headstones marking two or more individuals	4*	113	69	23
Undetermined	9			
Total	113			

*Denote small sample sizes. Of note, larger monuments such as obelisks were typically used to mark graves of two or more individuals.

their distributions of memorial types compared to the stones of infants and children/adolescents. This pattern also holds for the variety of headstone shapes marking all age groups. More variation exists within the older age groups. For example, the most popular headstone shape—rectangular (type 1)—represents 90 percent (nineteen of twenty-one) of the youngest age group in the Brothertown Indian assemblage and just under 40 percent of the oldest (nine of twenty-three). Furthermore, there are only three different shapes among the headstones of infants compared to seven shapes present in the oldest adult age group. Stones marking the graves of older individuals are generally larger than stones marking the graves of younger ones. For instance, average headstone sizes increase consistently between the four arbitrary age groups with an average difference in height of more than thirty centimeters between stones marking infants' graves and stones marking members of the oldest group. These general patterns are magnified in the non-Brothertown assemblage with even greater increases in marker diversity from youngest to oldest.

In terms of relative distributions of memorial types, women and men were commemorated in similar fashions, with slightly more obelisks marking the graves of women. The same holds true with a comparison of headstones shapes between the two groups. The female group exhibits seven different headstone shapes and the male group exhibits eight. The most distinct difference is that between relative proportions of the two most popular headstones shapes (types 1 and 2). The ratio of type 1 to type 2 stones in the female group

Table 6.7. Comparing Grave Marker Type by Age and Gender of the Deceased.

	Headstones	Ledgers	Obelisks	Other	Total
Brothertown					
Age 0–2	21 (88%)	2 (8%)	1 (4%)	0 (0%)	24 (100%)
Age 3–19	24 (89%)	2 (7%)	0 (0%)	1 (4%)	27 (100%)
Age 20–59	38 (74%)	3 (6%)	5 (10%)	5 (10%)	51 (100%)
Age 60+	23 (77%)	2 (7%)	4 (13%)	1 (3%)	30 (100%)
Monuments marking more than one individual					44
Undetermined					94
Total					270
Female	82 (83%)	5 (5%)	8 (8%)	4 (4%)	99 (100%)
Male	79 (88%)	4 (5%)	3 (3%)	4 (4%)	90 (100%)
Monuments marking more than one individual					44
Undetermined					37
Total					270
Non-Brothertown					
Age 0–2	11 (65%)	5 (29%)	1 (6%)	0 (0%)	17 (100%)
Age 3–19	15 (60%)	7 (28%)	2 (8%)	1 (4%)	25 (100%)
Age 20–59	22 (43%)	16 (31%)	6 (12%)	7 (14%)	51 (100%)
Age 60+	18 (36%)	22 (44%)	5 (10%)	5 (10%)	50 (100%)
Monuments marking more than one individual					51
Undetermined					57
Total					251
Female	36 (44%)	30 (37%)	8 (10%)	7 (9%)	81 (100%)
Male	55 (58%)	25 (26%)	9 (10%)	6 (6%)	95 (100%)
Monuments marking more than one individual					51
Undetermined					24
Total					251

mirrors that of the entire assemblage, whereas the male group contains an unexpectedly high number of type 2 stones along with a relatively low number of type 1 stones. This pattern relates directly to the shapes of military stones (almost always type 2). Similar to the New York assemblage, the stones of women are generally larger in size than the stones of men, but the difference is virtually imperceptible (i.e., on average two centimeters taller and one centimeter wider). Comparatively, the non-Brothertown assemblage contains slightly more headstones marking the graves of males and a considerably larger difference between headstone sizes of males and females. On average, headstones marking the graves of women stand ten centimeters taller than those marking the graves of men.

Inscription Content

For both Brothertown and non-Brothertown assemblages, inscriptions associated with older individuals tend to include a wider variety of information compared to those of younger individuals. For example, in the Brothertown Indian assemblage, the stones of infants typify those whom they commemorate as either daughters or sons, whereas the children/adolescent stones typify the deceased as daughters, sons, or wives. The younger adults' stones typify those they commemorate as wives, daughters, sons, daughters *and* wives, mothers, and soldiers. Finally, the older adults' stones typify the deceased as wives, mothers *and* daughters, mothers *and* wives, and sons.

Full names are most numerous on the stones of older individuals, and the frequencies increase from the youngest to the oldest age group (table 6.8). Conversely, familial roles and the names of parents steadily decrease in frequency from the youngest to the oldest age group. Although wives' names

Table 6.8. Comparing Inscription Content by Age and Gender of the Deceased

	Full Name	Birthdate	Precise Age	Imagery	Family Role	Military	Sample Size
Brothertown							
Age 0–2	3 (12.5%)	5 (21%)	18 (75%)	8 (33%)	21 (87.5%)	0 (0%)	24
Age 3–19	7 (26%)	7 (26%)	16 (59%)	14 (52%)	20 (74%)	0 (0%)	27
Age 20–59	16 (32%)	13 (26%)	19 (38%)	18 (36%)	31 (61%)	1 (2%)	51
Age 60+	22 (73%)	9 (30%)	9 (30%)	14 (47%)	8 (27%)	0 (0%)	30
Female	21 (21%)	23 (23%)	42 (42%)	41 (41%)	80 (81%)	0 (0%)	99
Male	64 (71%)	17 (19%)	22 (24%)	60 (67%)	23 (25.5%)	27 (30%)	90
Non-Brothertown							
Age 0–2	4 (23.5%)	4 (23.5%)	10 (59%)	10 (59%)	11 (65%0	0 (0%)	17
Age 3–19	3 (12%)	8 (32%)	10 (40%)	11 (44%)	17 (68%)	0 (0%)	25
Age 20–59	33 (65%)	31 (61%)	13 (25%)	24 (47%)	25 (49%)	1 (2%)	51
Age 60+	35 (70%)	15 (30%)	9 (18%)	19 (38%)	24 (48%)	3 (6%)	50
Female	34 (42%)	24 (30%)	16 (20%)	29 (36%)	53 (65%)	0 (0%)	81
Male	57 (60%)	28 (29%)	27 (28%)	50 (53%)	35 (37%)	14 (15%)	95

do not appear in any Brothertown Indian inscriptions, husbands' names are fairly common on the stones of adults, particularly within the younger adult group. Birth dates, which are somewhat rare in the Brothertown Indian assemblage, occur most frequently in the inscriptions of adults, both young and old, and children/adolescents. Precise ages at death, including years, months, and days old, are more frequent on the stones of infants and children/adolescents.

Imagery was used most frequently to adorn the markers of children/adolescents and older adults; in these groups, approximately half of the stones bear imagery compared to only 36 percent of the younger adults' stones and 33 percent of the infants' stones. With ten distinct types, the child/adolescent group also displays the widest array of imagery. The stones of adults, both young and old, follow with eight and nine types each. Comparatively, the stones of infants bear only five image types. Each of the age groups has at least two unique image types not found in the other groups. With five unique image types, the older adult group is most diverse. Types of imagery found only on stones of older adults are the Bible/book, hand reaching down, shield, sword with rifle, and sword with curtain/veil. The child/adolescent stones follow with three unique image types: church bells, doves, and the lamb under a willow tree. The infant and younger adult stones follow with two unique images each: angels and crosses for infants, and the hand holding a book open and hearts for younger adults. Of note, the willow motif occurs much more frequently on adults' stones.

Gender differences are also evident in inscription content. Beyond the basic biographical information that they contain, stone inscriptions often emphasize certain vectors of the deceased's social identity. In the Brothertown Indian assemblage, this is considerably more common in the inscriptions of women (81 percent) than in those of men (59 percent). The inscriptions in the assemblage typify women only in terms of the familial roles they occupied in life, whereas they typify men in terms of familial roles or military service. Most of the inscriptions on women's stones typify them as daughters, wives, or mothers, and some inscriptions typify the deceased in terms of multiple familial roles, such as daughter and wife, mother and daughter, or mother and wife. The inscriptions on men's stones typify them as soldiers, sons, fathers, brothers, or as fathers and soldiers. The full name of the deceased is also more prevalent on the stones of men, a pattern directly related to the practice of defining the deceased in terms of their relationship to husbands or parents. For example, Oscar and Ellen Johnson's stone reads,

OSCAR JOHNSON
MAR. 28. 1842.
AUG. 26. 1907.
ELLEN J.
HIS WIFE
APR. 16. 1844.
NOV. 21. 1901.

This practice also links directly to the relatively high proportion of familial roles and husbands' names listed in women's inscriptions.

The relatively higher frequencies of death dates, ages of the deceased, the word *died*, and epitaphs found on women's stones relate to the formula of military stones, all of which mark the graves of men. Military stones omit such information, which explains the elevated proportions of these categories on women's stones. For example, M. V. Charles' stone simply reads,

M.V. CHARLES
CO. A.
21 WIS. INF.

Compared to the stones of Brothertown men, 67 percent of which bear imagery, women's stones are more modest, with only 41 percent bearing decor. Again, the prevalence of military-related imagery on the stones of men explains the comparatively high frequencies of imagery found there. The military motifs account for nearly half of the gravestone imagery on men's stones. The stones of women bear fifteen types of imagery, and the stones of men bear fourteen. The two groups overlap on only seven imagery types. The remaining types are unique to their respective groups. Images of the angel, bells, book, branch with fruit, cross, and dove are restricted to the stones of women, and images of the heart, shield, sword/rifle, and urn are restricted to the stones of men.

These analyses suggest that, even more so than their neighbors, Brothertown Indians placed great emphasis on age. With old age came increased status; becoming a tribal elder meant special treatment, at least in death. For Brothertown women, age was particularly important because it might have been one of the few identity vectors with which women could achieve special status in their community. As opposed to Brothertown men, who could perhaps enhance their status through economic prosperity, political success, or military bravery, women had far fewer avenues open to them that led up the social hierarchy at Brothertown. In their ancestral settlements on the East

Coast, this was not the case because women could take on and inherit roles as political leaders (Rubertone 2012). Traditional gender relations were challenged by the Brothertown system of politics, modeled after white (androcentric) Christian society. Precise ages were thus carefully remembered and recorded in the inscriptions of Brothertown women, at least more so than they were for Brothertown males or white neighbors, both male and female (see table 6.8).

Spaces

The spatial dimensions of mortuary practices include orientations of markers and burials, layouts of cemeteries, and distributions of formal cemetery spaces across landscapes (chapter 5). Each of these dimensions was subject to change as the Brothertown movement took shape and new generations of Brothertown Indians reproduced funerary traditions. The first generations to relocate to Wisconsin did so free of the direct material and spatial constraints of their ancestral East Coast and New York burial grounds. As they started anew in this foreign landscape, spatial patterns shifted to fit emergent understandings of self and community in ways that matched the material and textual patterns already discussed.

Stone Orientations

To reiterate, Native American burial orientations on the East Coast generally shifted from southwest to west during the eighteenth century. A majority of the grave markers in Brothertown, New York, face an azimuth of 110/290 degrees (see figure 5.7). Based on the topography in the area, particularly its location in the southwest-running Oriskany Valley, I interpret the orientations of the New York stones as the result of several factors. The Brothertown Indians likely intended to orient their loved ones' burials to the east, but shifted the orientation slightly in relation to the walls of the valley, or to the sun's setting and rising points as modified by the valley. Since the landscape of Brothertown, Wisconsin, is comparatively level, the chances are significantly less that topography influenced gravestone orientations there as it did in New York.

An initial look at any of the Wisconsin cemeteries supports this interpretation (figures 6.5 and 6.6). Most of the Brothertown stones therein face precisely west. Unlike the orientations of stones in New York, the westward-

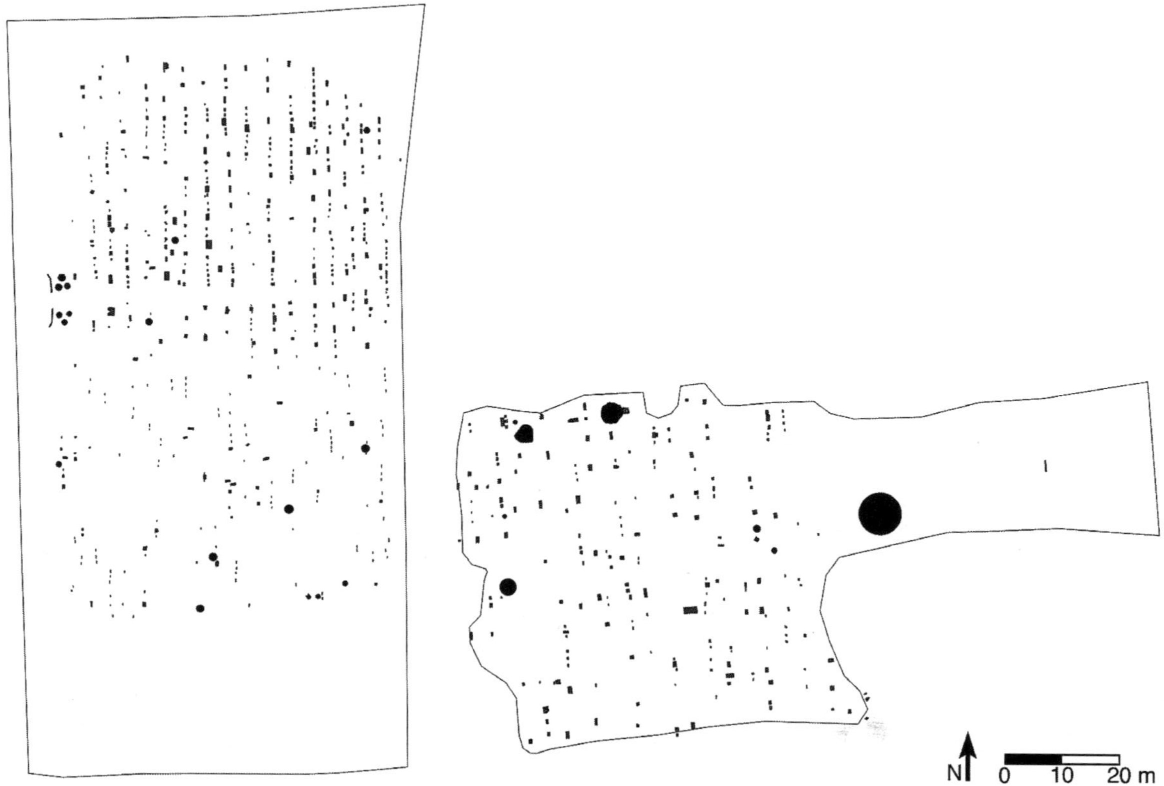

FIGURE 6.5. Plan view maps of Union (left) and Lakeside (right) Cemeteries; gray shapes represent markers, black circles represent trees.

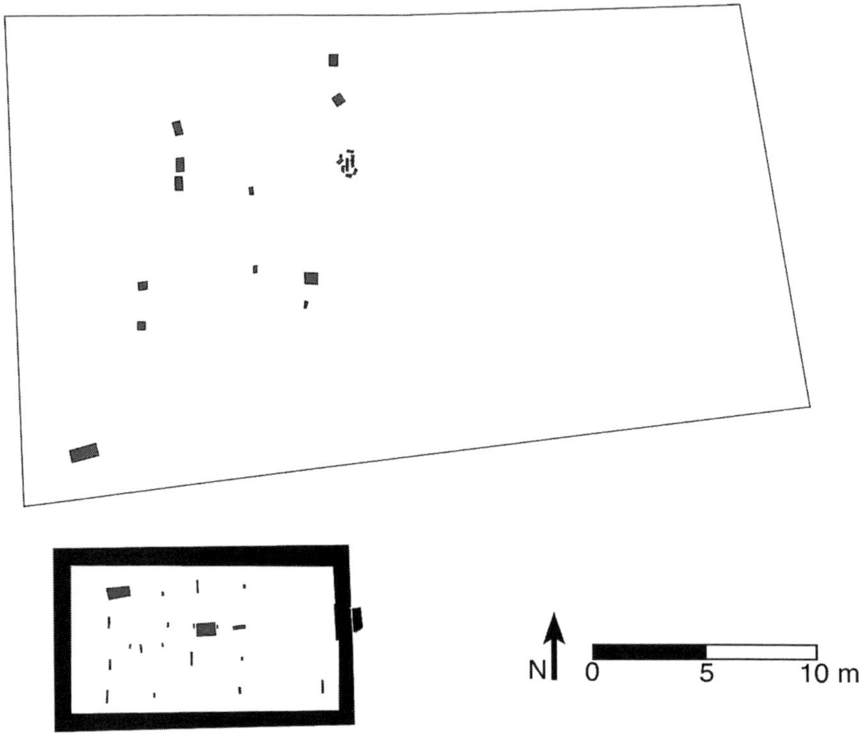

FIGURE 6.6. Plan view maps of Elyard (top) and Dick (bottom) cemeteries; gray shapes represent markers, black outline represents stone wall.

facing stones of Wisconsin face an azimuth of 270 degrees. These include 202 (88 percent) of the in situ stones. Other stones face east (just over 11 percent) or south (less than 1 percent). Comparatively, stone orientations of the non-Brothertown assemblage of Wisconsin are more variable. Just over half of the non-Brothertown markers face west (54 percent), 26 percent face east, and the remaining 20 percent face a variety of directions (i.e., north, northwest, south, southeast). These disparities between Brothertown and non-Brothertown stone orientations may relate to the diversity of the non-Brothertown Indian population living in and around Brothertown during the second half of the nineteenth century.

Cemetery Layouts

The two largest interethnic burial grounds in the area—Union and Lakeside cemeteries—each exhibit distinct distribution patterns of Brothertown and non-Brothertown burials. Most Brothertown stones sit in the southern half of Union Cemetery, and most non-Brothertown stones sit in the northern half. This spatial pattern makes sense because the Brothertown Indians founded Union Cemetery and used it exclusively for two decades prior to Euro-American settlement in the area. As new people moved into the region, they chose to bury their dead just to the north of the Brothertown burials, creating the segregated pattern seen today. This pattern attests to the social and cultural distinctions at play in the heart of mid-nineteenth-century Brothertown, Wisconsin. In contrast, the Brothertown stones of Lakeside Cemetery are evenly dispersed among the non-Brothertown stones. As people began interring their loved ones there, ethnicity was not a major factor influencing burial locations. This pattern may be due to the fact that Lakeside Cemetery served a more ethnically diverse community than did Union (see foregoing discussion).

The Brothertown Indians organized most of their Wisconsin burials in loose rows running north to south. In contrast to their New York cemeteries, however, they used a much less uniform pattern of distribution. Most Wisconsin markers sit in isolation or in small clusters of two to six stones. The only exception to this pattern is the northern part of Union Cemetery, which contains most of the recent (post-1910) non-Native burials in the cemetery. This section is more crowded than the Indian half. A ground-penetrating radar survey of the southern half of Union Cemetery demonstrated that the clustered pattern on the Indian half accurately represents the nineteenth-century layout of graves (Cipolla 2010:528). Although the geophysical survey identified several unmarked burials in the cemetery, their presence does not change our understandings of the original cemetery layout. The sparse distribution of stones and groups of stones in the Brothertown Indian half of the cemetery (southern half) is *not* the product of bad preservation or lost stones but the result of intentional clustering of stones marking the graves of immediate family members. This pattern matches up closely with those of the later-period cemeteries of Brothertown, New York.

Cemetery Locations

All of the known cemeteries of Brothertown, Wisconsin, sit on the western edge of the settlement near the shore of Lake Winnebago. The Brothertown Indians constructed a communal building that served as a church, meetinghouse, and school near Union Cemetery in the early 1830s. In 1842 a Methodist church was built on the corner of Thomas Commuck's land, lot 23. A town center subsequently emerged just south of the church along Military

Road, now Highway 151. Thus at first, Union Cemetery sat in the center of the community. By the 1840s, however, the communal center had shifted slightly to the southeast, only about a kilometer and a half away from the burial ground. All other Brothertown cemeteries in Wisconsin were far removed from this communal center, some separated by many kilometers.

In addition to the obvious distinctions in location, the cemeteries also differ in terms of the physical aspects of their stones, inscription forms, demographics, and family names. In spite of these disparities, the cemeteries share similar stone orientations (i.e., most monuments face west) and organizational schemes (loose rows of monuments running north to south).

Union Cemetery is the largest Brothertown burial ground in Wisconsin with the greatest temporal span of use, beginning in the 1830s and extending to the present. The cemetery is diverse in terms of memorial types, shapes, sizes, imagery, text inscriptions, and the number of individuals commemorated by single markers. The stones in Union Cemetery are also generally larger than the stones of other cemeteries in the collection. The monuments within commemorate individuals from forty-nine different Brothertown families, the most numerous of which are the Fowlers (originally from Montauk), the Johnsons (originally from Mohegan), and the Dicks (a Narragansett family line originally from Charlestown, Rhode Island).

Dick Cemetery is the smallest burial ground of Brothertown, Wisconsin; it came into use approximately a decade after Union Cemetery and fell out of use about forty years later. The stones of Dick Cemetery are less elaborate than the stones of the other cemeteries. It contains the highest frequency of blank stones and one of the lowest frequencies of stones bearing imagery. Furthermore, its stones are relatively smaller than those of the other cemeteries. The inscriptions found in Dick Cemetery generally contain only the most basic information concerning the deceased. Although stones in other cemeteries often reference the deceased's family or professional identity, stones in Dick Cemetery mainly emphasize names, death dates, and age of the deceased. In terms of demographics, the cemetery houses only two known men's graves. It is also unique in that its markers commemorate single individuals only.

Located just north of Brothertown, Elyard and Lakeside cemeteries contain comparatively small numbers of Brothertown gravestones. The Brothertown Indians began using Elyard Cemetery approximately two decades after Union Cemetery came into use and stopped after 1910. They began using Lakeside Cemetery three decades after they founded Union and continued into the twentieth century. Compared to the other cemeteries, the markers in Elyard Cemetery are diverse in size and imagery, whereas those of Lakeside Cemetery are generally larger than the markers found in the other cemeteries.

Ancestry and Commemoration

The inscribed grave markers of Wisconsin only represent five of the seven ancestral tribes documented as contributing to the Brothertown movement. These include stones marking the graves of Narragansett, Eastern and Mashantucket Pequot, Mohegan, and Montaukett descendants. Surnames known to have originated in the Niantic and Tunxis communities are completely absent. Given this dearth along with the small number of plots claimed by individuals of Niantic and Tunxis ancestry in Brothertown, Wisconsin (chapter 7), it seems that these two ancestral groups played a comparatively lesser role in the Brothertown community than the other tribal groups did. In addition to the represented East Coast surnames, there are also several names of unknown tribal ancestry among the Brothertown stones along with Stockbridge, Oneida, and Euro-American surnames, some of which are known to have married in to various Brothertown family lines during the nineteenth century.

Of all the represented groups, stones marking the graves of Narragansett descendants are most numerous, with forty-nine known examples representing nine surnames. Stones marking the graves of Montaukett descendants are the next largest group, with thirty-one stones representing only one surname (Fowler). Mohegan stones follow in frequency with twenty-seven stones representing two surnames. Respectively, sixteen stones represent four surnames of Eastern Pequot origin, and four stones represent two surnames of Mashantucket Pequot origin. The oldest stones in most of the ancestral tribal assemblages date to the 1840s and the most recent stones date to the first decades of the twentieth century.

For the most part, grave markers and cemeteries of Brothertown, Wisconsin, show little evidence for ancestral tribal distinctions within the Brothertown community. There are no notable distinctions in stone forms. In terms of spatial distributions, Montaukett and Mashantucket Pequot markers only appear in a single cemetery (Union), whereas stones marking the remaining groups are dispersed across two or more cemeteries each. The reason for the division of Narragansett stones between Union and Dick cemeteries relates to differences in religious outlook (chapter 5). Those buried in Dick Cemetery were Baptists, and those buried in Union Cemetery practiced other forms of spirituality, most likely Methodism. The spatial distributions of the stones also show that there were no tribal neighborhoods among the multitribal cemeteries of Brothertown, Wisconsin. Instead, immediate familial relations governed decisions on where to bury loved ones as seen in the spotty distribution of various tribal groups across Union Cemetery (figure 6.7).

Differences between the texts of grave markers shed light on subtle distinctions in the ways that various ancestral groups commemorated the individuality of their deceased. On one hand, the Mashantucket Pequot, Narragansett, and Eastern Pequot assemblages contain the highest frequencies of stones marking single graves. The inscriptions in these assemblages also exhibit the highest frequencies of full names and the lowest frequencies of references to familial roles and names of others, such as the deceased's parents or husband. On the other hand, the Montaukett and Mohegan assemblages contained the lowest relative frequencies of stones marking the graves of single individuals; the inscriptions in these assemblages exhibit the lowest relative frequencies of full names of the deceased and the highest frequencies of others' names. The former groups thus defined their deceased loved ones as individuals more so than the latter groups, who often defined their deceased loved ones in terms of the relationships they had with others (i.e., a communal form of remembrance). Of note, military stones are distributed fairly evenly throughout the five represented ancestral groups, ranging from 6 to 25 percent of each ancestral tribal marker assemblage; the patterns just described are thus unrelated to the limitated information contained in military stone inscriptions.

Stockbridge Commemoration

The town of Stockbridge sits just north of Brothertown, Wisconsin; it was the nineteenth-century home and reservation of the Stockbridge Indians, established contemporaneously with Brothertown. Although a few Stockbridge Indians chose to bury their loved ones in Lakeside Cemetery during the third quarter of the nineteenth century, most used a separate cemetery located just a few kilometers to the north of the current town center. This cemetery contains stones dating to the latter three-quarters of the nineteenth century. It currently houses approximately seventy gravestones and many unmarked graves according to the memorial plaque situated at the entrance to the cemetery.

With the exception of overall size, Stockbridge Cemetery closely resembles Union Cemetery. It contains mainly marble headstones along with

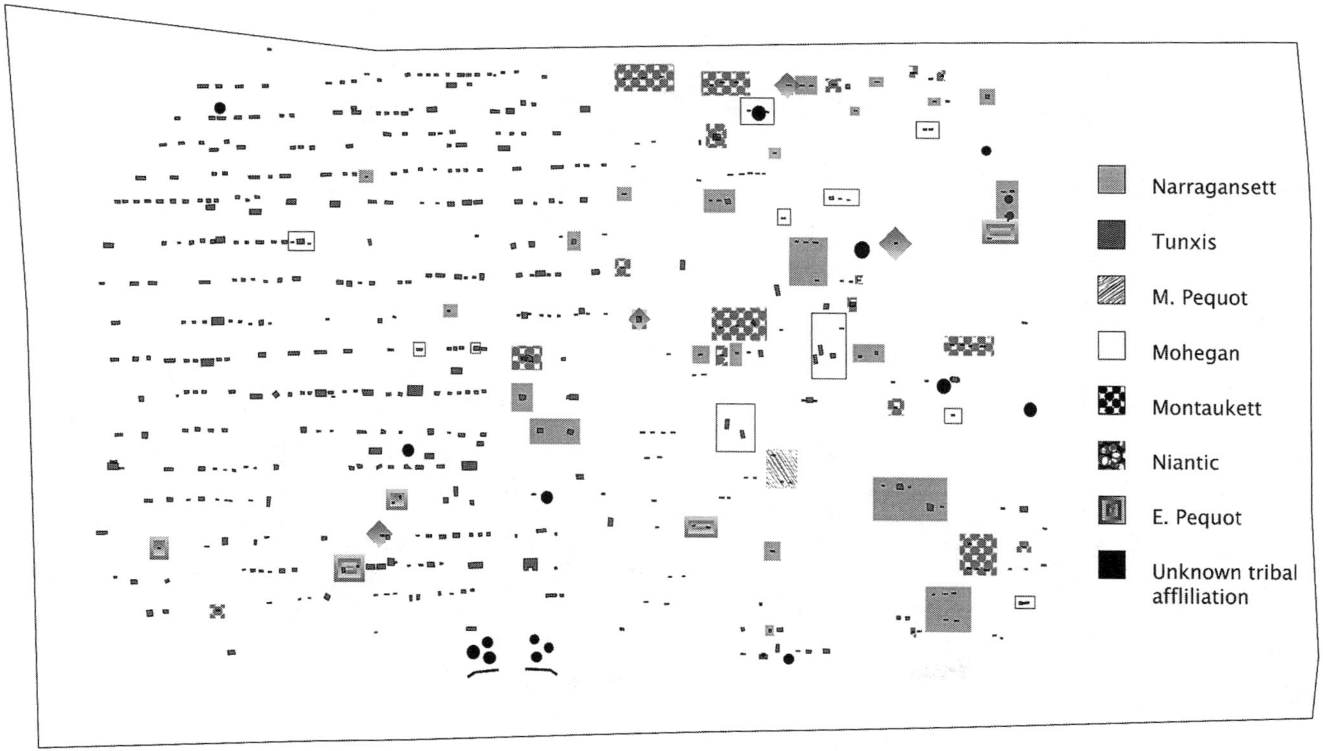

FIGURE 6.7. Distribution of graves by tribal ancestry in Union Cemetery, Brothertown, Wisconsin.

several marble obelisks and a few granite monuments of various shapes and sizes. The most popular headstone shapes are the same as in Brothertown cemeteries, though this cemetery also contains several purchased shapes not present in Union, along with a greater number of handmade stones. The Stockbridge likely fashioned the latter from local limestone; the markers closely resemble Brothertown handmade stones (chapter 5). Decorative motifs on the stones include the open book, military shield, willow tree, clasped hands, hand pointing upward, and lamb. Inscriptions often define the deceased in terms of their relationships to other individuals and tend to emphasize the event of death over the deceased's accomplishments in life. The stones are also arranged on an east–west axis with most of their inscriptions facing west. Similar to those of Union Cemetery, the stones in Stockbridge Cemetery sit in small clusters representing groups of immediate family members.

Oneida Commemoration

Approximately seventy kilometers north of Brothertown, just outside of the Oneida Reservation sits a Methodist cemetery that houses a number of Native graves. The cemetery's proximity to the Oneida Reservation suggests that most blank handmade stones therein might mark the graves of Oneida Indians. Since the Oneida arrived in current-day Wisconsin at the same time as the Brothertown and the Stockbridge, these stones might represent burials dating to the 1830s and 1840s. A majority of the handmade stones sit on a small crest in the rear central portion of the cemetery. Unlike Brothertown and Stockbridge handmade stones, these markers are occasionally inscribed with dates. The stones are tightly aligned in rows and columns, similar to the cemeteries of Brothertown, New York, and the East Coast. Based on the positioning of the few texts in this "Indian" section, most burials face west. In contrast, most non-Native gravestones in this cemetery face east, toward the roadway.

Discussion and Conclusion

When the Brothertown Indians relocated to Wisconsin they adopted new forms of commemoration. This is most evident in their rather abrupt and nearly complete switch to purchased stones during the 1830s and 1840s. Compared to the markers of New York, the Wisconsin stones are generally more diverse in terms of memorial types and shapes, inscription techniques, and imagery. They are also substantially larger and distributed in distinct spatial configurations. These cemetery transformations articulated with evolving social relations, both within the community and between community members and outsiders.

Intracommunal Dynamics

In the previous chapter I argued that new commemorative practices and materials of Brothertown, New York, began a reconfiguration process, transforming Brothertown cemeteries into spaces of individual remembrance. The cemeteries of Wisconsin continued in a similar direction, increasingly emphasizing individuality and immediate family relations over other communal ties. These changes are partially crystallized in the stone forms, inscriptions, and spatial distributions of the new Wisconsin cemeteries. Shifting memory practices also tied to other communal changes. As Brothertown Indians came to define the present community in terms of a past divided into specific genealogies and family histories, individuals and family groups simultaneously made choices to sell their land and move away from the community they and their ancestors had lived with for as long as eight decades in some cases.

This pattern shows through in the locations and dates of Brothertown cemeteries in Wisconsin. With the passage of time, community members chose to bury their loved ones in cemeteries located farther and farther away from their new home and center. The community primarily used Union Cemetery in the 1830s, located in the heart of Brothertown. The 1840s saw some Brothertown Indians create a private cemetery space, specifically, Hannah Dick's family, who founded Dick Cemetery, located near the northern boundary of the settlement. A decade later, certain community members began using Elyard Cemetery, located just outside of the settlement, and the 1860s saw Brothertown Indians begin interring their loved ones in Lakeside Cemetery, located in the town of Stockbridge, several kilometers north of Brothertown. The Brothertown stones of Rienzi, Methodist, Red Falls, and Brighton cemeteries—each located between 25 and 240 kilometers away from Brothertown, Wisconsin—also speak to the nature and timing of these departures.

During this period, the materiality and spatiality within Brothertown cemeteries also shifted. Between the 1830s and early 1900s, there were roughly three periods of change. In the earliest period, Brothertown Indians only used headstones to mark the graves of their loved ones. The inscriptions they chose often explicitly defined the deceased in terms of their relationships to other people. They also tended to emphasize the event of death and loss as experienced by the community of mourners, rather than memorializing the life and personal accomplishments of the deceased.

Between 1850 and 1880, Brothertown Indians diversified their cemetery material culture. For instance, markers dating to this time period display the widest array of stone shapes and imagery. Also, while most community members continued to use headstones during the period, a few Brothertown Indians chose to mark the graves of their loved ones with obelisks, whose markedly increased heights continue to stand out among Brothertown cemetery landscapes.

During the late nineteenth and early twentieth centuries, Brothertown grave markers diversified even more. Headstones diminished in popularity compared to earlier periods as Brothertown Indians increased their use of obelisks, ledgers, and other specially-shaped markers. The inscriptions they chose during this period also represent a shift. In contrast to earlier inscription patterns, the texts came to emphasize the individuality of the deceased and to memorialize their lives rather than their deaths.

With time came a shift in the represented personhood of the deceased. The average number of individuals commemorated per stone decreased through time as the number of stones commemorating single individuals generally increased. Stone inscriptions came to emphasize this individuality rather than defining the deceased in relation to other persons (e.g., as "the daughter of . . ."). In a similar fashion, inscriptions shifted from primarily emphasizing the events of death and loss, as experienced by the deceased's surviving loved ones, to commemorating the deceased's life and accomplishments as unique individuals. Last, the spatial distribution of gravestones in small clusters of immediate family members also attests to this shift in represented personhood. These changes informed and took shape from new conceptions of individuality and memory processes among the Brothertown community.

The Wisconsin cemeteries also speak to the existence of a breadth of religious and spiritual outlooks within the community in the nineteenth and early twentieth centuries. Although early community leaders such as Samson Occom and Joseph Johnson undoubtedly saw Christianity as a central unifying tenet of the Brothertown community, religiosity clearly differentiated factions within the community as time passed. Some Brothertown Indians expressed religious differences by using distinct cemetery spaces. As they had in New York, the Dick family and other Brothertown Baptists maintained a separate cemetery space in Wisconsin. Compared to other Brothertown markers of the time, the gravestones of Dick Cemetery are less elaborate. It is possible that the Brothertown Baptists were of comparatively limited economic means or simply believed in modest forms of commemoration, perhaps out of fear of idolatry. The wide varieties of inscription in the Wisconsin assemblage, only some of which discuss beliefs in an afterlife, also speak to the breadth of spirituality among the nineteenth-century Brothertown community. Brothertown individuals and families living in Wisconsin thus practiced at least a few different types of spirituality, each with slightly different understandings of death and the afterlife or lack thereof.

Intercommunal Dynamics

More so than those of New York, the Brothertown cemeteries of Wisconsin appear almost identical to contemporaneous Euro-American cemeteries. Although these transformations in cemetery material culture and space clearly shaped the ways in which the Brothertown Indians remembered their pasts and related to one another, they also allowed the community to reclassify itself to a degree and to achieve certain goals. Although the New York cemeteries were indexically marked as non-Euro-American by the presence of "Indian" stones and a few inscriptions discussing the tribal identities of the deceased, the Wisconsin cemeteries contain only a few handmade stones and no inscriptions discussing tribal or Indian identities of Brothertown individuals. The ambivalent nature of the Brothertown grave markers of Wisconsin certainly shaped Euro-American perspectives on the community, especially those Euro-Americans who shared cemetery spaces with Brothertown Indians. Such changes blurred the lines between Indian and Euro-American, thus challenging dominant modes of social classification. As discussed in chapters 3 and 4, during this time period the Brothertown Indians also explicitly argued their case for US citizenship and associated land rights by virtue of their unique position between white and Indian worlds. Their cemeteries quietly reinforced such arguments.

In general there are no major distinctions between the gravestones of Brothertown Indians and those sharing cemetery spaces with them in Brothertown, Wisconsin. Since all residents of Brothertown—Indian or white—probably purchased their loved ones' stones from local carvers, this comes as no surprise. The comparisons made here thus demonstrate the homogenizing nature of consumption and its tendencies to blur cultural and social distinctions in certain ways.

Several minor disparities between the two assemblages do, however, hint at subtle differences between the Brothertown Indians and their non-Indian neighbors of Wisconsin. Some differences may be economic in nature. For example, at first, Brothertown Indians purchased markers that were slightly more expensive than the stones used by their white neighbors. As summarized in table 6.5, Brothertown Indians purchased relatively more stones bearing imagery that occupied a central position in the stone design, whereas outsiders purchased many more stones with only border designs. This pattern might also relate to different cultural preferences for marking memories; it could be that Brothertown Indians preferred to use a combination of words and images to mark their loved ones' graves. As time passed, some of these patterns shifted. Economic hardship partially influenced Brothertown Indians to begin leaving Brothertown in the second half of the nineteenth century. Those individuals and families who remained in Brothertown during and after this time marked the graves of their loved ones with monuments of the same or similar cost as those used by their white contemporaries.

Other differences point to slight distinctions in personhood, bereavement, and commemoration between the Brothertown Indians and their Euro-American neighbors. Overall, inscriptions in the Brothertown assemblage define the deceased in terms of their former relationships with other persons and focus on the event of death and loss as experienced by the surviving community, while inscriptions in the non-Brothertown assemblage tend to highlight the deceased as "atomic" individuals, emphasizing their accomplishments in life. As time passed, however, the text inscriptions on Brothertown stones came to mirror those of their non-Brothertown neighbors. While the texts inscriptions of the oldest Brothertown stones of Wisconsin suggest a more "corporate" conception of personhood (following Strathern 1988, as *dividuals* rather than *individuals*) among the community, actual burial practices offer a contrasting pattern. As discussed previously, I attribute these distinctions to a combination of economic factors and different conceptions of personhood between Brothertown Indians and their neighbors.

Cemetery Discourse

The Brothertown cemeteries of Wisconsin "speak" both of the deceased and the living via combinations of linguistic, material, and spatial discourses operating on various planes of consciousness and intentionality. This analysis demonstrates the ways in which texts, images, spatial arrangements, and forms of grave markers complement one another. Though none of the inscriptions discuss Christianity explicitly, the images on the stones and their spatial orientations often mark them (pragmatically) as Christian burials. Similarly, the forms and sizes of grave markers in Wisconsin convey the relative number of persons commemorated and the age and gender of the deceased; these qualities reinforce the direct semantic messages inscribed on the markers' faces.

Considering the entire sequence of Brothertown grave markers and cemeteries between 1780 and 1910, words, things, and spaces each fluctuated in their respective discursive importance through time. At first, the actual forms of grave markers were the primary means of signifying social distinctions in Brothertown cemeteries. It is thus possible that community members intentionally marked social distinctions between the dead via physical differences between grave markers. During this time, certain community members also began marking social relations with space, particularly by creating and using separate burial grounds, such as Dick and Skeesuck cemeteries of New York.

With the increase of purchased stones bearing inscriptions during the 1830s and 1840s, texts became the primary means of marking the unique qualities of the deceased. In other words, inscriptions became the central means of distinguishing between graves because most markers from this period were of similar shape, size, and color. The Brothertown Indians also continued to use space as an important social diacritic. In fact, when creating new cemetery spaces in Wisconsin, they organized their cemeteries in small clusters of immediate family groups; in these new configurations, space between stones represented the nature of genealogical ties between the dead (or lack thereof). Finally, stone forms became important for marking social distinctions once again beginning in the 1850s, as certain Brothertown individuals and families came to afford more extravagant styles of cemetery material culture, such as granite markers.

7

Spatial Practices at Brothertown

> Brothers, We thank you for the good offers you have been pleased to make us of the privilege of Having Lands in your cuntry for us to live upon and we expect in the course of this fall or in the Spring and with your consent to make choise of a spot to build our fire place.
>
> —Brothertown Peacemakers, 1811

IN AN EFFORT THAT ULTIMATELY led them to current-day Wisconsin, the Brothertown Indians sought out yet another new communal land base in the early nineteenth century. As outlined in chapter 3, they first looked to present-day Indiana, writing the letter quoted above to the leaders of a multitribal community then residing in the area (Jarvis 2010). Although not the intention of early leaders like Samson Occom and Joseph Johnson, *mobility*—the physical act of withdrawal from one spot to another—came to constitute a central theme in Brothertown history (Cipolla 2013a). To persevere in the ever-changing political and social landscape of the United States, the Brothertown Indians made and remade their "fire places" in several "spots" across northeastern North America. As they moved into new landscapes in New York, Wisconsin, and beyond, the Brothertown Indians continually negotiated their identities, their relations to one another, and their places in the modern world.

In the previous chapters I examined the ways writing and commemoration—each tethered to issues of landscape and spatial practices in their own ways—speak to shifts in the intra- and intercommunal dynamics of Brothertown history. The textual, material, and spatial patterns revealed and discussed therein demonstrate the negotiated nature of colonial histories, with both insiders and outsiders playing parts. Here I narrow my focus to examine the intracommunal dynamics further. I consider the differences that mobility and continually starting anew made for the Brothertown community and for the production of their history. As in previous chapters, I argue that with each new spot, with each new communal fire place, came new opportunities that critically shaped the ethnogenesis and endurance of the community. More specifically, I investigate nineteenth-century residential patterns in both Brothertown settlements. Systematic analyses of the detailed plot maps and record books associated with the settlements offer new insights into the emergence and transformation of the community. Not only is such a perspective rare in terms of Native histories of the nineteenth century, it also adds a unique point of comparison for the documents and cemeteries analyzed and discussed previously.

The Place of Space in Brothertown Ethnogenesis

The settlement patterns analyzed in this chapter resulted from practices that likely spanned a range of consciousness. Although they clearly had the potential to do so, I do not argue that spatial configurations of settlements simply resulted from intentionally discursive practices designed to create or bolster social boundaries. Similar to Michel de Certeau's (1984:93) observations on pedestrians moving through the crowded streets of Manhattan, "whose bodies follow the thicks and thins of an urban 'text' they write without being able to read," I see Brothertown settlement patterns as the long-term and aggregated outcomes of fairly short-term decisions on the part of individuals and families. Like the paths described by Certeau, decisions on where to live were influenced by the particular contexts in which they took place, but also reflexively shaped those contexts in ways unbeknownst to their practitioners (see chapter 2). Taking influence from practice theorists like Certeau, I approach Brothertown settlement patterns in terms of their long-term results. Although the individuals and families who created and shaped the patterns discussed in this chapter may have done so unconsciously or on levels of what Anthony Giddens (1984) calls "practical consciousness," the resulting patterns still had pragmatic effects in the world. These patterns were part of the fabric of the everyday lives of Brothertown Indians and therefore informed their identities and their relations to one another.

Analyzing Brothertown Land Records

A rich collection of archival materials speaks directly to the history of land claims and ownership in the Brothertown settlements. Commissioned by

New York State in the late eighteenth century, the first survey of Brothertown, New York, generated the oldest documents concerning lot division and settlement patterns in Brothertown. These are comprised of field notes and a survey map (New York Surveyor General 1795). The map shows the earliest lot divisions, and several record books discuss or at least note the individuals and families who lived on each lot through time (Brothertown Indians n.d.; Curtis 1785; New York State Superintendents 1785).

Following the initial survey, the (non-Native) superintendents of the Brothertown community documented land transactions such as lot assignments, reassignments, and land disputes. A typical entry lists the lot number, lot size, name of the person to whom the lot was assigned, name of the superintendent who assigned the lot, date of assignment, and additional remarks, which occasionally include limited information on why lots were assigned or reassigned. For example, the remarks section for Lot 30—a piece of land originally assigned to David Wauby in July 1797—explains, "Died without Issue and assigned to the widow of David Wauby by the Superintendents 21 April 1817." Of course, the Brothertown Indians also kept records of such transactions since the Peacemakers typically settled internal disputes before reporting their findings to the superintendents. Combined, these two perspectives provide a remarkably complete history of settlement patterns in Brothertown, New York, up through 1830.

Landownership in Wisconsin was also well documented. In 1840, just after the Brothertown Indians gained US citizenship, a Euro-American named George H. Featherstonhaugh (1840) completed the first detailed survey of the new Brothertown. Along with property boundaries, his map lists lot numbers and landowners. In contrast to the New York settlement, where the majority of landowners actually lived on their assigned lots, at least some of the Wisconsin lots in the eastern half of the settlement were never actually occupied by their owners. This is evinced by the presence of the same landowners' names on multiple lots across the settlement. For this reason, the Wisconsin settlement data are not as useful as those of New York in terms of neighborhood analysis. In spite of this caveat, the map offers valuable information on neighborhoods in the western part of the settlement in and around the communal center (see chapter 6). Wisconsin State commissioned two subsequent surveys of Brothertown in 1893 and 1920. The resulting maps show dwindling numbers of Brothertown names marked on land parcels, further illustrating the results of the late-nineteenth-century Brothertown population dispersal introduced in chapter 1 and elaborated on in chapters 3 and 6.

In many cases, Brothertown Indians chose their lots on a first come, first served basis. In the end, however, the superintendents officially approved these choices (see chapter 3). Unfortunately, the specific reasoning behind most lot assignments was never recorded. Community members likely favored certain lots over others based on a variety of factors. A particular lot's estimated potential for agricultural production and proximity to landscape features, communal spaces, and certain neighbors potentially shaped these decisions. In the analysis that follows, I focus primarily on the last factor, assessing the significance that tribal ancestry played in shaping Brothertown Indians' decisions on where to live. Did individuals and families of the seven tribal ancestries at Brothertown maintain separate residential areas or "neighborhoods" (see Giddens' discussion of ethnic segregation, 1984:10)? If so, did these neighborhoods persist through time and space as the Brothertown Indians moved from New York to Wisconsin? For that matter, are there connections between shifts in settlement patterns and other known communal changes? For example, as the name "Brothertown" replaced the ancestral tribal names of its members (e.g., Mohegan, chapter 4) and came to signify a unified tribal entity rather than a settlement, did residential patterns also shift?

Using the data already summarized, settlement maps were made depicting the ancestral tribal affiliations of the individuals and families who lived on each lot in Brothertown by decade. The detailed genealogical histories compiled by William DeLoss Love (1899) and Rudi Ottery (n.d.) provided information on the ancestral tribal affiliation of each family line. Caroline Andler—then tribal genealogist of the Brothertown Indian Nation—also provided valuable information on these affiliations. In total, four maps were made of the New York settlement showing these patterns between 1800 and 1830. Two maps were compiled for the Wisconsin settlement, showing the distribution of landowners by ancestral tribal affiliation in 1840 and 1893.

Considered together, the maps illustrate shifting spatial distributions of the seven ancestral tribal groups at Brothertown during the nineteenth century. For each period represented by a map, the number of lots claimed or owned by individuals or families of each ancestral tribal group were tallied. The frequencies at which all lots of one ancestral tribal group bordered lots claimed by other tribal groups were also determined. To do this, the total number of contiguous lots of one ancestral group was divided by the total number of contiguous lots. For instance, in 1800 there was a total of sixty-five lots abutting Narragansett-claimed lots. Out of these, twenty (31 percent) were claimed by other Narragansett descendants, and thirteen (20 percent) were claimed by Tunxis descendants. The resulting figures roughly gauge the frequency at which lots of one ancestral group shared borders with lots of each other ancestral group. To check the statistical significance of these initial findings, *p*-values were calculated for each of the frequencies. This calculation determines the degree to which the frequencies matched up or contrasted with the expected patterns of a completely random distribution. Those that contrast greatly with the expected patterns are considered nonrandom and therefore highly meaningful for this analysis.

Ancestral Tribal Spaces in Brothertown

Not all ancestral tribes were represented equally in Brothertown's population. Consistently between 1800 and 1840, Brothertown Indians of Narragansett descent outnumbered all other ancestral tribal groups. During the first three decades of this period, Narragansett-descended Brothertown Indians claimed 31–44 percent of all lots in Brothertown, New York (table 7.1). Continuing this pattern, the same group owned 44 percent of the lots in Brothertown, Wisconsin, as of 1840. Also fairly consistent between 1800 and 1830, Montaukett-, Mohegan-, and Tunxis-descended Brothertown Indians claimed 15–25 percent of the lots of Brothertown, New York, each. During the later decades in New York, the numbers of Tunxis properties decreased and by 1840, only 2 percent of the lots in Wisconsin had been claimed by descendants of the group. In Wisconsin, Montaukett- and Mohegan-descended Brothertown Indians continued to claim a relatively large number of lots, and the Pequot presence—both Eastern and Mashantucket—shot up, indicating that many Pequot-descended Brothertown Indians skipped over Brothertown, New York, and moved directly to Brothertown, Wisconsin.

Table 7.1. Number of Lots Owned by Members of Each Ancestral Tribal Group at the Brothertown Settlements between 1800 and 1840

	1800	1810	1820	1830	1840
Narragansett	20 (31%)	41 (40%)	46 (42%)	53 (44%)	172 (44%)
Tunxis	13 (20%)	15 (15%)	13 (12%)	13 (11%)	10 (2%)
M. Pequot	3 (5%)	7 (7%)	7 (6%)	8 (7%)	38 (10%)
Mohegan	10 (15%)	16 (16%)	17 (15%)	20 (16%)	46 (12%)
Montaukett	16 (25%)	17 (16%)	22 (20%)	20 (16%)	65 (17%)
Niantic	1 (1%)	2 (2%)	0 (0%)	0 (0%)	5 (1%)
E. Pequot	2 (3%)	4 (4%)	6 (5%)	7 (6%)	55 (14%)
Total	65 (100%)	102 (100%)	111 (100%)	121 (100%)	391 (100%)

Figures for 1800, 1810, 1820, and 1830 are from Brothertown, New York; figures for 1840 are from Brothertown, Wisconsin.

In 1800 several small residential clusters of ancestral tribal groups existed in Brothertown, New York (figure 7.1). These included small concentrations of Narragansett, Montaukett, and Mohegan descendants. Most Narragansetts and Montauketts lived in and around the communal center (figure 5.8) with Narragansetts in the far northeast corner and Montauketts in the northern central portion of the settlement, most notably represented by David Fowler's farm and Fowler Cemetery. In contrast, Mohegan residences were comparatively far removed from the communal center, with most Mohegan descendants living in the southeast corner of Brothertown near Niles Occom Cemetery. Although Tunxis descendants were more numerous than Mohegans at this time, there was little in the way of Tunxis residential clustering as of 1800. Though most Tunxis descendants lived in the northern part of the settlement—near the communal center, their lots rarely abutted one another. As already indicated, far fewer individuals of Eastern Pequot, Mashantucket Pequot, and Niantic ancestry had claimed lots in Brothertown by this time, precluding tribal clustering for these groups. The southwest corner of the settlement remained largely unassigned by 1800, to be held communally for future generations of Brothertown Indians.

Quantitative analysis supports these interpretations, demonstrating that lots claimed by Narragansett, Mohegan, and Montaukett descendants bordered lots claimed by individuals of the same tribal ancestry more so than lots claimed by individuals of other tribal ancestries (table 7.2). Respectively, 46 and 47 percent of the boundaries of lots claimed by Narragansett and Montaukett descendants abutted lots claimed by individuals or families of the same tribal ancestry. For Mohegan-claimed lots, just over 30 percent of their boundaries abutted other Mohegan properties. Each of these frequencies has a high statistical significance, meaning that members of these ancestral tribal groups lived next to each other in frequencies far greater than one would predict if lots had been distributed randomly.

As of 1810, these patterns still existed. Table 7.3 shows that a majority of Narragansett-, Montaukett-, and Mohegan-claimed lots shared boundaries with lots claimed by individuals of the same tribal ancestry. Again, these are the only groups to cluster together in statistically significant numbers. Although some Narragansett descendants remained concentrated in the northeast corner, new Narragansett clusters also appeared. One developed in the central portion of the settlement in the general area of the two mills (chapter 5). The other appeared to the southeast, in the area of Dick Cemetery. It is possible that these separate Narragansett clusters represent different religious factions within the group, as discussed in chapters 5 and 6. In comparison to the previous decade, the frequency of contiguous

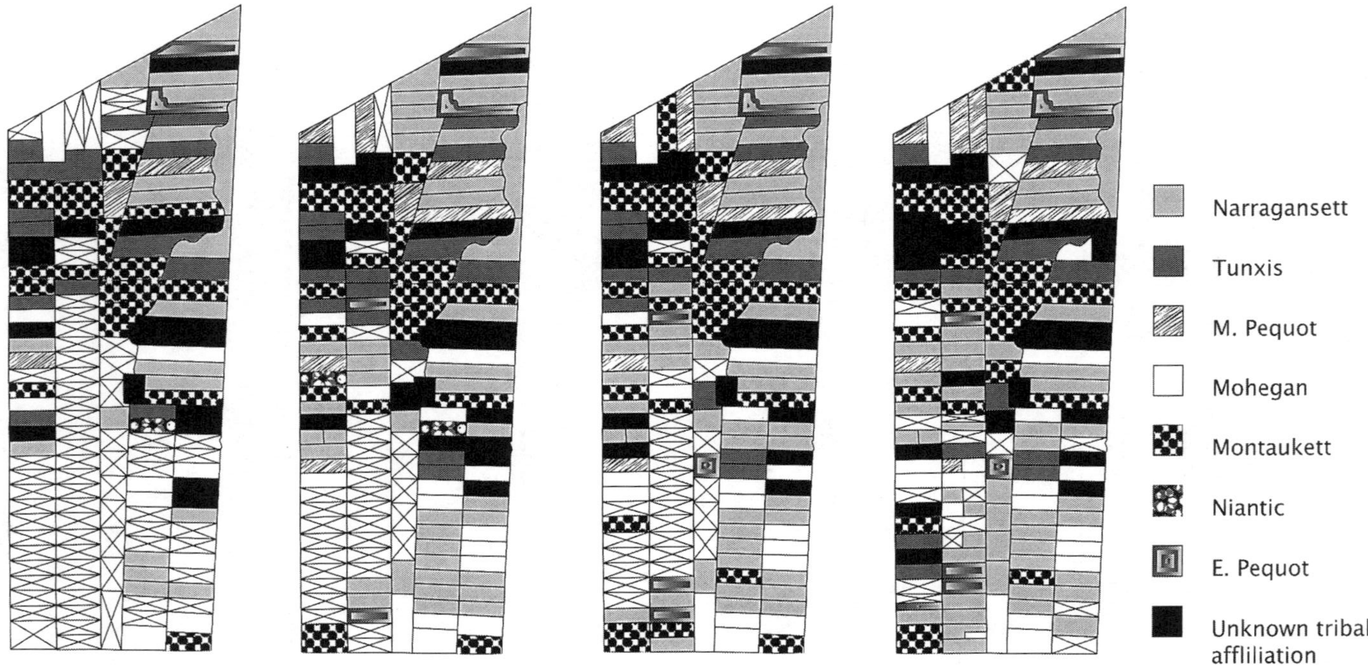

FIGURE 7.1. Distribution of lots occupied by individuals and families of different tribal ancestries in Brothertown, New York, in 1800 (far left), 1810 (center left), 1820 (center right), and 1830 (far right); plots marked with an X were unassigned.

Table 7.2. Quantitative Analysis of 1800 Map Data Displaying the Number and Percentage of Bordering Lots by Tribal Ancestry

	Narragansett	Tunxis	M. Pequot	Mohegan	Montaukett	Niantic	E. Pequot
Narragansett	24 (46%)*	8 (21%)	5 (45.5%)	2 (15%)	7 (12%)	1 (50%)	5 (71%)
Tunxis	8 (15%)	7 (18%)	1 (9%)	4 (31%)	15 (27%)	1 (50%)	2 (29%)
M. Pequot	5 (10%)	1 (3%)	0 (0%)	0 (0%)	5 (9%)	0 (0%)	0 (0%)
Mohegan	2 (4%)	4 (11%)	0 (0%)	4 (31%)*	3 (5%)	0 (0%)	0 (0%)
Montaukett	7 (13%)	15 (39%)	5 (45.5%)	3 (23%)	26 (47%)*	0 (0%)	0 (0%)
Niantic	1 (2%)	1 (3%)	0 (0%)	0 (0%)	0 (0%)	0 (0%)	0 (0%)
E. Pequot	5 (10%)	2 (5%)	0 (0%)	0 (0%)	0 (0%)	0 (0%)	0 (0%)
Total	52 (100%)	38 (100%)	11 (100%)	13 (100%)	56 (100%)	2 (100%)	7 (100%)

Note: Columns represent the total number of lots representing a particular tribal group and rows represent the types and frequencies of neighboring lots. Asterisks mark statistically significant frequencies as determined by p-values. Please note that despite the small Mohegan sample size for this decade, the next four decades analyzed (tables 7.3–7.6) consist of more robust samples and show consistent numbers of abutting Mohegan lots.

Table 7.3. Quantitative Analysis of 1810 Map Data Displaying the Number and Percentage of Bordering Lots by Tribal Ancestry

	Narragansett	Tunxis	M. Pequot	Mohegan	Montaukett	Niantic	E. Pequot
Narragansett	72 (57%)*	10 (22%)	9 (41%)	16 (33%)	8 (14%)	3 (43%)	9 (56.25%)
Tunxis	10 (8%)	8 (18%)	2 (9%)	6 (13%)	15 (26%)	0 (0%)	4 (25.25%)
M. Pequot	9 (7%)	2 (5%)	2 (9%)	3 (6%)	5 (9%)	1 (14.25%)	0 (0%)
Mohegan	16 (12%)	6 (13%)	3 (14%)	15 (31%)*	6 (10.5%)	1 (14.25%)	1 (6%)
Montaukett	8 (6%)	15 (33%)	5 (23%)	6 (13%)	20 (35%)*	1 (14.25%)	2 (12.5%)
Niantic	3 (2%)	0 (0%)	1 (4%)	1 (2%)	1 (2%)	1 (14.25%)	0 (0%)
E. Pequot	9 (8%)	4 (9%)	0 (0%)	1 (2%)	2 (3.5%)	0 (0%)	0 (0%)
Total	127 (100%)	45 (100%)	22 (100%)	48 (100%)	57 (100%)	7 (100%)	16 (100%)

Note: Columns represent the total number of lots representing a particular tribal group and rows represent the types and frequencies of neighboring lots. Asterisks mark statistically significant frequencies as determined by p-values.

Narragansett-claimed lots increased overall by more than 10 percent. This coincided with more than a doubling of Narragansett-claimed lots from the previous decade, suggesting that some Narragansett-descended Brothertown Indians arrived a few decades after the founding of the settlement. Such was certainly the case for Thomas Commuck, who arrived in Brothertown in 1825 (chapter 3). Consistent with the previous decade, Montaukett descendants remained clustered in and around the heart of the settlement, and Mohegan descendants maintained their residential cluster in the southeast corner of Brothertown.

In 1820 some of the tribal clusters remained and others began to dissipate (table 7.4). Montaukett and Mohegan residences remained clustered in

Table 7.4. Quantitative Analysis of 1820 Map Data Displaying the Number and Percentage of Bordering Lots by Tribal Ancestry

	Narragansett	Tunxis	M. Pequot	Mohegan	Montaukett	Niantic	E. Pequot
Narragansett	64 (45%)	11 (27.5%)	14 (56%)	17 (32%)	23 (30%)	0 (0%)	13 (62%)
Tunxis	11 (8%)	5 (12.5%)	2 (8%)	6 (11%)	13 (17%)	0 (0%)	3 (14%)
M. Pequot	14 (10%)	2 (5%)	2 (8%)	2 (4%)	5 (6.5%)	0 (0%)	0 (0%)
Mohegan	17 (12%)	6 (15%)	2 (8%)	18 (34%)*	8 (10%)	0 (0%)	2 (10%)
Montaukett	23 (16%)	13 (32.5%)	5 (20%)	8 (15%)	25 (32.5%)*	0 (0%)	3 (14%)
Niantic	0 (0%)	0 (0%)	0 (0%)	0 (0%)	0 (0%)	0 (0%)	0 (0%)
E. Pequot	13 (9%)	3 (7.5%)	0 (0%)	2 (4%)	3 (4%)	0 (0%)	0 (0%)
Total	142 (100%)	40 (100%)	25 (100%)	53 (100%)	77 (100%)	0 (100%)	21 (100%)

Note: Columns represent the total number of lots representing a particular tribal group and rows represent the types and frequencies of neighboring lots. Asterisks mark statistically significant frequencies as determined by p=values.

statistically significant numbers, and Narragansett descendants spread across Brothertown, interspersing their residences with other ancestral tribal groups. Clusters of Narragansett descendants are visible on the map in the northeast, central, and southeast portions of the settlement, but not in numbers exceeding what would be expected in a random distribution. The Montaukett maintained their residential cluster in the northern central portion of the settlement while expanding southward. Likewise, the Mohegan maintained their residential cluster in the southeastern portion of the settlement while spreading westward. As in previous decades, Tunxis-claimed lots remained dispersed among lots claimed by individuals of other tribal ancestries and Niantic, Mashantucket Pequot, and Eastern Pequot descendants claimed relatively few lots.

By 1830 Narragansett descendants had spread across all of Brothertown, causing the frequency of contiguous Narragansett-claimed lots to spike once again (table 7.5). As in 1800 and 1810, tribal clusters of Montauketts, Mohegans, and Narragansetts existed. Narragansett-descended Brothertown Indians still had a residential cluster in the northeast corner of the settlement, but most Narragansett descendants lived in either the central or southeastern portions of Brothertown by this time. In fact, their numbers had increased so much that most other ancestral tribal groups at Brothertown began sharing lot boundaries with Narragansett descendants more so than with any other group (including their own) at this time. In spite of these changes, Montaukett and Mohegan descendants maintained their respective residential clusters in northern central and southeastern Brothertown. Consistent with the maps from previous decades, the 1830 map demonstrates the relatively

Table 7.5. Quantitative Analysis of 1830 Map Data Displaying the Number and Percentage of Bordering Lots by Tribal Ancestry

	Narragansett	Tunxis	M. Pequot	Mohegan	Montaukett	Niantic	E. Pequot
Narragansett	112 (55%)*	9 (24%)	13 (45%)	29 (46%)	27 (39%)	0 (0%)	15 (53%)
Tunxis	9 (4.5%)	4 (10.5%)	3 (10%)	7 (11%)	10 (14%)	0 (0%)	5 (18%)
M. Pequot	13 (6%)	3 (8%)	4 (14%)	5 (8%)	4 (6%)	0 (0%)	0 (0%)
Mohegan	29 (14%)	7 (18.5%)	5 (17%)	17 (27%)*	2 (3%)	0 (0%)	3 (11%)
Montaukett	27 (13%)	10 (26%)	4 (14%)	2 (3%)	24 (34%)*	0 (0%)	3 (11%)
Niantic	0 (0%)	0 (0%)	0 (0%)	0 (0%)	0 (0%)	0 (0%)	0 (0%)
E. Pequot	15 (7.5%)	5 (13%)	0 (0%)	3 (5%)	3 (4%)	0 (0%)	2 (7%)
Total	205 (100%)	38 (100%)	29 (100%)	63 (100%)	70 (100%)	0 (100%)	28 (100%)

Note: Columns represent the total number of lots representing a particular tribal group and rows represent the types and frequencies of neighboring lots. Asterisks mark statistically significant frequencies as determined by p=values.

low numbers of lots owned by Niantic, Mashantucket Pequot, and Eastern Pequot descendants.

Figure 7.2 depicts settlement patterns of Brothertown, Wisconsin, in 1840 and 1893. Consistent with the patterns discussed thus far, Narragansett-descended Brothertown Indians were ubiquitous in the new settlement, owning a majority of the land as of 1840. However, instead of clustering in the northeast corner of the settlement as they did in New York, Narragansett descendants established a residential concentration in the northwest of Brothertown, Wisconsin, abutting the eastern shore of Lake Winnebago. Similarly, Mohegan descendants lived mainly in the southwest corner of the new settlement, also choosing spots close to Lake Winnebago. Rather than establishing residential clusters like the Narragansett and Mohegan descendants, Brothertown Indians of Montaukett ancestry spread fairly evenly throughout the new settlement. The 1840 data also speak to a sharp increase in the number of lots owned by both Mashantucket Pequot and Eastern Pequot descendants compared to previous decades. Both groups maintained residential clusters in the south-central portion of the new Brothertown.

In the late nineteenth century, William DeLoss Love (1899:328) briefly mentioned a part of Brothertown, Wisconsin, known as "Pequot" in a discussion of Brothertown history: "At first they [the Brothertown Indians] named their town Deansborough, though a certain locality was called Pequot. It was also known as Manchester. The name is now Brothertown, in remembrance of their old home." In a letter sent to Milwaukee, Wisconsin, in the mid-nineteenth century, Commuck (1851) also self-addressed his envelope, "Pequot Wis." Although these sources omit any discussion of Pequot's

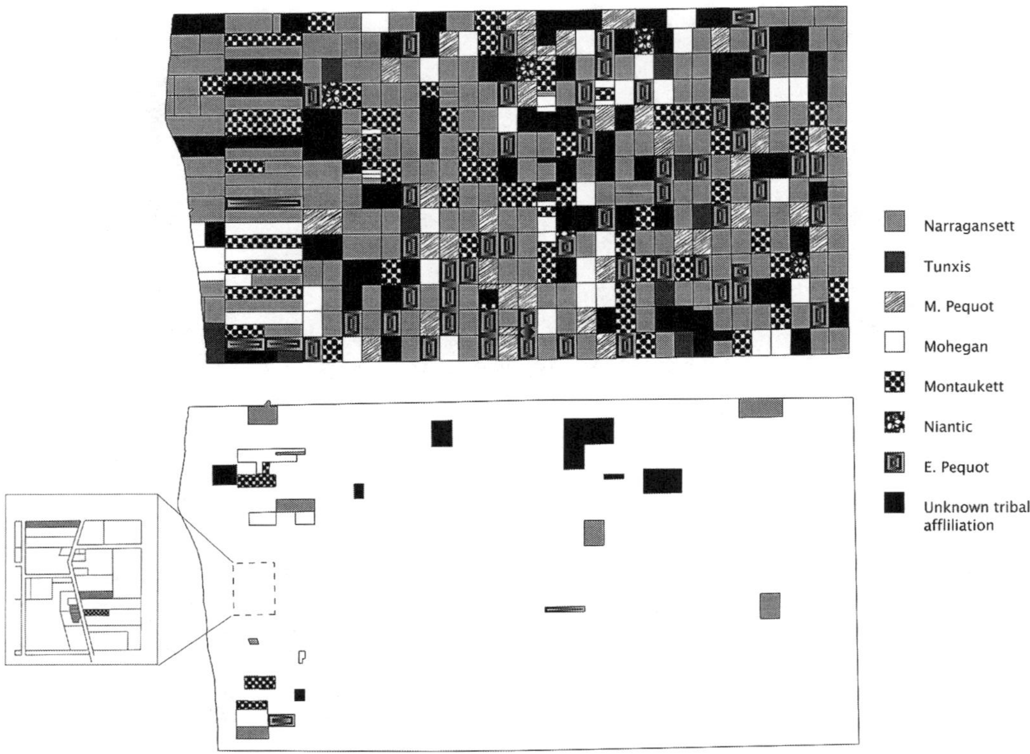

FIGURE 7.2. Distribution of lots occupied by individuals and families of different tribal ancestries in Brothertown, Wisconsin, in 1840 (top) and 1893 (bottom).

location in Brothertown, the concentration of Pequot descendants—both Mashantucket and Eastern—in the south-central part of the settlement provides an invaluable clue to its potential location.

Quantitative analysis of the 1840 data (table 7.6) supports this hypothesis. Excluding Niantic descendants, all other ancestral tribal groups neighbored lots owned by Narragansett descendants more than lots owned by any other group in Brothertown, Wisconsin. Despite the prevalence of Narragansett-owned lots, for the first time in Brothertown history both Eastern Pequot– and Mashantucket Pequot–owned lots abutted lots owned by members of the same ancestral group in statistically significant numbers. When combined, Pequot-owned lots (both Eastern and Mashantucket) abutted other Pequot owned lots 28 percent of the time.

By the late nineteenth century, Euro-Americans owned most of the land in Brothertown, Wisconsin. Although Brothertown Indians owned nearly every lot depicted in the 1840 map, the settlement consisted of only thirty Brothertown-owned lots by 1893 (figure 7.2). Despite these transformations, Narragansett-descended Brothertown Indians still owned more lots than any of the other ancestral tribal groups at the time. By 1920, only a handful of Brothertown Indians owned land in the settlement; it is said that the last Brothertown Indian to actually live in Brothertown, Wisconsin, moved away sometime during the 1970s.

The 1901 tribal roll discussed in chapter 3 offers invaluable clues into the ancestral tribal composition of Brothertown, Wisconsin, and the two largest Brothertown "satellite" communities of Long Prairie, Minnesota, and Fond du Lac, Wisconsin, at the turn of the twentieth century. Brothertown, Wisconsin, remained home to the largest portion of the Brothertown Tribe

Table 7.6. Quantitative Analysis of 1840 Map Data Displaying the Number and Percentage of Bordering Lots by Tribal Ancestry

	Narragansett	Tunxis	M. Pequot	Mohegan	Montaukett	Niantic	E. Pequot
Narragansett	300 (50%)*	13 (41%)	45 (35%)	53 (33%)	109 (49%)	2 (14.25%)	76 (39%)
Tunxis	13 (2%)	0 (0%)	1 (<1%)	5 (3%)	3 (1.5%)	1 (7%)	9 (5%)
M. Pequot	45 (7.5%)	1 (3%)	20 (16%)*	14 (9%)	15 (7%)	3 (21.5%)	30 (16%)
Mohegan	53 (9%)	5 (16%)	14 (11%)	32 (20%)*	32 (14%)	3 (21.5%)	20 (10%)
Montaukett	109 (18%)	3 (9%)	15 (12%)	32 (20%)	38 (17%)	3 (21.5%)	23 (12%)
Niantic	2 (<0.5%)	1 (3%)	3 (2%)	3 (2%)	3 (1.5%)	0 (0%)	2 (1%)
E. Pequot	76 (13%)	9 (28%)	30 (23%)	20 (13%)	23 (10%)	2 (14.25%)	32 (17%)*
Total	598 (100%)	32 (100%)	128 (100%)	159 (100%)	223 (100%)	14 (100%)	192 (100%)

Note: Columns represent the total number of lots representing a particular tribal group and rows represent the types and frequencies of neighboring lots. Asterisks mark statistically significant frequencies as determined by p=values.

(21 percent) at the time with 121 Brothertown Indians in residence. Compared to the Brothertown populations of Long Prairie and Fond du Lac, this was the most diverse in terms of tribal ancestry. Family lines represented on the roll tie back to seven ancestral tribes. Just over a quarter of these individuals were of Narragansett descent, representing eight different family lines. Montaukett, Eastern Pequot, and Mohegan descendants constituted between 10 and 20 percent each, whereas all other groups represented less than 1 percent of the Brothertown Indian population of Brothertown, Wisconsin.

The early twentieth-century Brothertown population of Long Prairie, Minnesota, included individuals and families of six tribal ancestries. Brothertown Indians of Mohegan descent made up over half of the group, all of whom were members of the Johnson family line. Narragansett- and Montaukett-descended Brothertown Indians constituted just over 10 percent of the population each, whereas all other represented groups made up no more than 5 percent of the Brothertown Indian population in Long Prairie. A similar pattern existed in Fond du Lac, Wisconsin, where Brothertown Indians of four ancestral tribal groups lived as of 1901. Narragansett descendants composed nearly half of this population. Mashantucket Pequot descendants followed in relative frequency, representing over 30 percent. All other ancestral tribal groups represented approximately 5 percent or less of the Brothertown population of Fond du Lac in the early twentieth century.

The 1901 tribal roll also demonstrates that going back east to ancestral tribal lands was rarely a tenable option for Brothertown Indians moving away from Wisconsin in the latter half of the nineteenth century. Out of the 570 individuals listed on the roll, only 3 Brothertown Indians—Lester, Klisha, and Jerome Skeesucks—lived back in the ancestral homelands of the East Coast. The Skeesucks, who were of Narragansett ancestry, lived in Norwich, Connecticut—former Pequot Territory—as of 1901. Additionally, twenty-two Brothertown Indians lived in the general vicinity of Brothertown, New York, at the time. These relatively small numbers show that most Brothertown Indians chose to stay in the Midwest, where many still live today.

To summarize, this analysis identified several residential clusters of ancestral tribal groups in Brothertown settlement patterns, each of which changed through time. In the first few decades of the settlement's existence, Brothertown Indians of Narragansett, Mohegan, and Montaukett descent lived in loose residential clusters, or "neighborhoods" in Brothertown, New York. As time passed, these clusters generally dispersed and individuals and families of different tribal ancestries increasingly entangled themselves with one another in residential spaces across the landscape of Brothertown, New York (tables 7.2–7.4). In Wisconsin, Narragansett, Mohegan, Mashantucket Pequot, and Eastern Pequot maintained loose tribal neighborhoods in Brothertown. The Narragansett pattern is slightly skewed because Narragansett-descended Brothertown Indians owned nearly half of the lots in Brothertown, Wisconsin, as of 1840—more than double the amount of any other ancestral tribal group. Combined with other archival findings, the Pequot pattern suggests that there was a loose Pequot neighborhood in Brothertown, Wisconsin. The sharp increase in lots owned by Pequot-descended Brothertown Indians in Wisconsin also demonstrates that some Brothertown Indians joined the community later than others, potentially moving to Brothertown, New York, in the 1830s or moving directly from the East Coast to Wisconsin in the mid-nineteenth century. Love (1899:338, 349) notes that this was the case for at least a few Mashantucket and Eastern Pequot families, such as the Cocheats. Finally, in the late nineteenth century, Brothertown Indians began moving away from Brothertown. The final maps in the analyzed sequence illustrate this transformation. By the 1893, only a few Brothertown-owned lots remained, most in the northwest and southwest corners of the township, with a few located in the center of the town and others spread out on the eastern periphery.

With a few exceptions, tribal neighborhoods slowly dissolved within the larger Brothertown community (tables 7.2–7.6). Individuals and families of different tribal ancestry thus slowly came to see one another simply as Brothertown Indians and fellow community members. The reasons for this gradual shift were both genealogical and social in nature. As time passed, members of various ancestral tribal groups intermarried, creating new generations of mixed tribal ancestry, while the community as a whole came to share a history as Brothertown Indians. The 1901 tribal roll demonstrates that even when Brothertown Indians began selling their Wisconsin lands and moving away from the rest of the community, tribal ancestries were not very important in shaping decisions on where to go and with whom to live. The two largest Brothertown satellite communities to emerge at this time were both multitribal in composition. These individuals and families saw themselves as Brothertown Indians rather than as Narragansetts or Montauketts. Even when the structure of the community was challenged by land sales and departures, Brothertown Indians did not regroup according to their ancestral tribal affiliations. This fact is also evident in the relatively few Brothertown Indians who chose to return to their ancestral lands in New England or to the former Brothertown, New York, during the twentieth century.

Spaces of Life, Spaces of Death

The residential clusters identified here provide an interesting point of comparison for the cemetery patterns discussed in chapters 5 and 6. The similarities and differences between the two offer further insights into the internal dynamics of the Brothertown community while speaking to the differences that starting anew in Wisconsin made for the group as a whole. To begin, the numbers of Narragansett, Montaukett, Mohegan, and Pequot descendants depicted in the 1840 Wisconsin settlement map correlate with the respective frequencies of grave markers representing these groups in the cemeteries of Brothertown, Wisconsin. In other words, each group was well represented in Wisconsin settlement and cemetery patterns. However, the nature of the representations—residence versus death—contrasts markedly.

Settlement patterns reveal life at Brothertown as experienced, whereas cemetery patterns are representations of life and social relations constructed by the families and loved ones of the deceased. Each took shape within distinct networks of constraint, such as land availability and the consent of fellow community members in the case of the former, and larger trends in gravestone consumption and personal relationships between the deceased and the bereaved in the case of the latter. Building on the work of social theorist Henri Lefebvre (1991), archaeologist Stephen Mrozowski (2006:14–15) recognizes the differences between spatial perceptions, spatial conceptions, and spatial representations. In relation to this general typology, the settlement patterns analyzed here are perceived spaces in that they represent the ways Brothertown individuals and families experienced Brothertown, whereas the cemetery patterns analyzed previously are representational spaces in that they contained monuments marking the memories of individuals and their relations to one another.

In comparison to the settlement patterns, the cemeteries provide scant evidence for ancestral tribal neighborhoods, yet still speak of important communal changes between New York and Wisconsin. As depicted in the previous chapter (figure 6.7), Union Cemetery contains small clusters of ancestral tribal burials scattered throughout. These clusters only contain stones commemorating immediate family members. Lines of contiguous stones (i.e., aligned shoulder to shoulder in rows running north to south) usually represent child sibling or parent–child relationships, whereas stones placed in front of one another (i.e., aligned in a column running east to west) represent either adult sibling or parent–child relationships. The proximity of stones in the Brothertown half of Union Cemetery thus typically represents the nature of the genealogical connections between individuals in life. In fact, some stone clusters are organized in relation to the ages of the deceased. This general pattern speaks to the emphasis on immediate family connections in death as opposed to broader kinship ties and ancestral tribal identities.

Take, for example, three collections of stones commemorating members of the Mohegan-descended Johnson family in Union Cemetery. The first cluster sits in the southwest corner of the Indian section of Union Cemetery and consists of three stones commemorating Welthey Johnson, the wife of Orrin G. Johnson, and her children. The second cluster, located in the central part of the Indian section of Union Cemetery, consists of four stones commemorating a married couple, John W. and Rebecca Johnson, and their children, Rosetta Stevens and Wayland Johnson. The third cluster, located in the southeastern-central part of the Indian section, consists of three stones commemorating Almira Johnson, the wife of Rowland Johnson, and her sons, Henry and Hiram. The fathers and husbands in each of these family groups were first cousins (each of their fathers had the same father, John Johnson). In spite of the family ties between these groups (e.g., the children would have been second cousins), their respective clusters sit in distinct areas of the cemetery. This pattern also holds for a majority of the other stones in Union Cemetery, which explains the pattern of ancestral tribal clustering depicted in chapter 6.

Yet differences in grave distributions in the cemeteries of New York and Wisconsin show that this burial pattern was relatively new to the Brothertown community in the mid-nineteenth century. In contrast to Union Cemetery's clustered burial pattern, the graves of Niles Occom Cemetery of New York sit in tight, uniformly spaced rows and columns. Most stones sit in one of several long rows, each stone with approximately fifty-five to seventy centimeters separating it from the neighboring stones (chapter 5). A majority of the markers also sit within a small area, ten by fifteen meters in size. On average, a rectangle of the same area houses only fourteen grave markers in the Indian half of Union Cemetery. Furthermore, within the family clusters at Union Cemetery, sixty to one hundred centimeters separate individual markers, and even greater distances separate family clusters.

Although they loosely distributed their residences in Brothertown, New York, in relation to tribal ancestries, Brothertown Indians used very different organizational principles when burying their dead. This comparison suggests that the residential clusters identified here were perhaps based less on cultural distinctions within the Brothertown community—in the sense of unique sets of cultural practices, political organization, and oral tradition —and more on extended kinship networks. Furthermore, as Brothertown

Indians intermarried, new generations were born, broader communal experiences accrued, ancestral tribal distinctions diminished, and neighborhood loci began to intermesh and disperse. New senses of communal identity thus congealed within the group.

As discussed, the cemeteries of Wisconsin organized Brothertown society in terms of immediate family relations, demonstrating emergent emphases on individuality and small family units. During this time, Brothertown cemeteries transformed from spaces of communal remembrance to spaces of individual remembrance, not only because of their new spatial configurations but also because of their fairly rapid incorporation of purchased grave markers—nearly all of which bear texts and personalized inscriptions concerning the deceased. As opposed to the earliest Brothertown cemeteries, where the unique identities of the deceased were entangled with the larger community of ancestors, it was much easier to visit just one grave or a small set of family graves in Wisconsin. This emergent emphasis on individuality within the community likely shaped many Brothertown individuals' and families' decisions to eventually sell their Wisconsin lands and disperse across the Midwest rather than seek a new communal land base as they had in the past.

In this particular comparison, cemetery patterns predicted future shifts in settlement patterns and broader cultural changes within the Brothertown community. The communal emphasis of early Brothertown cemetery spaces preceded the gradual dispersal of tribal neighborhoods in settlement patterns, just as the emphasis on individuality in the Wisconsin cemeteries preceded the dispersal of Brothertown individuals and families across the Midwest and beyond. These patterns offer insights into the ways the seven ancestral tribes became one and subsequently transformed as they moved to a new landscape, became immersed in the world of consumer goods, and embraced new memory practices and conceptions of personhood.

Discussion and Conclusions

The spatial patterns analyzed in this chapter provide complementary (albeit somewhat distinct) perspectives of the ethnogenesis and endurance of the Brothertown community. The early settlement patterns exhibit several concentrations of ancestral tribal groups, and contemporaneous cemeteries offer no evidence of disparate tribal commemoration practices. This juxtaposition suggests that the residential clusters depicted in the settlement maps relate mostly to extended kinship networks rather than to the maintenance of distinct cultural and political entities (e.g., Pequots, Montauketts) within the Brothertown community.

These analyses also demonstrate the ways the Brothertown community transformed as it began anew in Wisconsin. Both settlement and cemetery patterns of Wisconsin speak to a decreased emphasis on extended kinship networks within the community through time. For example, the cemeteries contain no examples of extended kin buried in close proximity to one another. Instead, individuals were either buried on their own or with their siblings, parents, husbands, or wives.

Finally, this chapter demonstrates that cemeteries (representational spaces) signaled communal change before settlement patterns (perceived spaces). Likewise, communal change became manifest in Brothertown cemeteries before it was evident in the written discourses analyzed in chapter 4. The earliest Brothertown cemeteries provide evidence for the existence of a congealed Brothertown identity approximately two decades before the name "Brothertown" transformed into an ethnonym of a unified tribal entity (chapter 4) and several decades before the diminished emphasis on tribal ancestry or extended kinship networks in Brothertown settlements. The Wisconsin cemetery patterns also speak of an increased emphasis on the individuality of the deceased approximately four decades before the Brothertown Indians began dispersing across the Midwest.

8

Ethnogenesis and Endurance in the Modern World

TOWARD A DEEPER UNDERSTANDING OF COLONIAL CULTURE AND NATIVE AMERICAN IDENTITY POLITICS

NEARLY TWO AND A HALF CENTURIES have passed since Samson Occom began questioning his people's place in coastal New England, since members of several local tribes gathered at Mohegan to discuss their uncertainties about the future, and since Joseph Johnson went to Oneida in search of a new homeland. Although much has changed for the Brothertown community since the eighteenth century, the spirit of these ideas and actions lives on in the present. Like their ancestors, the Brothertown Indians continue to endure and resist the injustices of colonialism and its legacies. As reflected in a recent ruling by the Bureau of Indian Affairs (BIA) to deny the Brothertown Indian Nation federal acknowledgment as a tribe, the injustices remain, albeit in slightly new forms. The associated report on these findings, filed in 2009 by the BIA, dismisses tens of thousands of pages documenting the Brothertown community's autonomy, history, and genealogy. Perhaps more important than the physical body of evidence is the time—hours, days, weeks, months, years, and decades—that members of the Brothertown Indian Nation devoted to preparing the petition for tribal recognition, not considering the financial and emotional costs associated with such an endeavor.

Despite this major setback, the Brothertown Indians carry on as usual, organizing and attending monthly tribal council meetings, voting in tribal elections, taking part in community gatherings, and participating in the Brothertown Archaeology Project in various capacities. In addition to these everyday activities, some members also speak out against the colonial structures in which their community is enmeshed. For instance, Kathleen Brown-Pérez—Samson Occom's tenth great-granddaughter and chair of the Brothertown Indian Nation Federal Acknowledgement Committee—

recently evoked shades of the original Brothertown Indian movement by writing to Senator Byron Dorgan, the chair of the Senate Committee on Indian Affairs (see Toensing 2009). In her letter, Brown-Pérez critiqued the federal acknowledgment process, pointing out the "structural violence" inherent therein. Like the documents, cemeteries, and settlement patterns analyzed in the preceding chapters, these recent events demonstrate that change and continuity are forever entangled.

Confronting Colonialism in the Modern World

In this book, I adopted and developed a pragmatic approach to the archaeology of colonialism in Native North America, focusing specifically on the ethnogenesis and endurance of the Brothertown Indian community. For me, and hopefully for readers of this volume, pragmatism presents an avenue with which to further decolonize anthropological, archaeological, and historical perspectives on colonialism. With a gaze focused on the continuities and practicalities of social action, such a perspective offers deeper understandings of colonial culture in the past and a critical lens with which to consider the connections between archaeological practice, identity politics, and descendant communities in the present.

The documents, cemeteries, and settlement patterns discussed here speak to the internal dynamics of the Brothertown community as they articulated with its shifting relationship to other groups, particularly Euro-Americans. I focused on the interconnections of cultural continuity and change and on the multiple meanings and effects that material culture, practices, and ideas take on—or have—for different groups making their places within the shared milieu of colonialism. Because these identities still exist, it should come as no surprise that archaeological research means different things for different people (Atalay 2012). As seen in decades-long tensions between certain archaeological and Indigenous communities, the pragmatic impacts of archaeological research extend well beyond academic circles. Recognizing these effects, this book also examined the process by which I came to design and implement the research in collaboration with the Brothertown Indian Nation.

In confronting the complexities of modern colonialism in this final chapter, I must therefore address the nature of colonial culture in both the past and the present. Revisiting the patterns of written, material culture, and spatial discourses analyzed earlier, I attempt to break free from the dichotomous modes of thought that continue to haunt archaeologies of colonialism and, broadly speaking, contemporary understandings of Native American identities (Cipolla 2013b). In acknowledging the shared aspects of colonial culture, however, I also recognize the significance of establishing and maintaining communal boundaries and autonomous social identities within colonial contexts. In the spirit of pragmatism, I extend this discussion to consider the effects this book may have in the world today, specifically for the Brothertown Indian Nation's current political standing. I do so in hopes that other practitioners researching similar histories will ask the same questions of their own work.

The Negotiation of Brothertown History

As individuals and families of Narragansett, Niantic, Eastern Pequot, Mashantucket Pequot, Mohegan, Tunxis, and Montaukett ancestry negotiated their places in the modern world and became Brothertown, they simultaneously reproduced and transformed their identities and cultural repertoires. As they endured the hardships and violence of colonialism, they actively appropriated "foreign" practices and materials, such as the English language, Christianity, and, more specifically, Euro-American-style gravestones and monuments. Some of these changes clearly aided the Brothertown Indians in achieving communal goals and challenging dominant (colonial) schemes of social classification that attempted to divide colonial societies into discrete categories (i.e., Europeans versus others, colonists versus colonized). Other changes had unforeseen consequences for future generations. Rather than typifying these transformations as solely submissive or resistant, I explored Brothertown history in terms of its positioning between Indian and European cultural essences. I did so by tracking and analyzing shifts in writing, commemoration, and settlement at Brothertown and assessing their pragmatic effects both within the community and between it and the largely Euro-American world in which it existed. Indeed, at the heart of this book, I asked about the differences that changes in writing, commemoration, and settlement made for the Brothertown Indians, for their relationships with one another, for their connections with "outsiders," and for their future in general.

Analogous to Fredrik Barth's (1998a [1969]) approach to ethnic boundaries, Brothertown documents, cemeteries, and settlement patterns speak to the negotiated and shared nature of processes of social identification and colonial interaction. On the most basic level, the Brothertown movement resulted only from the meeting of "insiders" and "outsiders." The Brothertown community formed as a response (and a resistance) to colonialism and its legacies, yet took European introductions like Christianity and the English language as some of its central tenets. The shared nature of this history is particularly evident in the evolution of the name "Brothertown." Analysis of documents written by, to, and about the Brothertown Indians revealed disparate internal and external understandings of the name and the community to which it now refers. Furthermore, internal and external uses of the name changed in relation to one another as time passed. In written dialogue between Brothertown authors and their interlocutors, both Indian and Euro-American, "Brothertown" transformed from *a place* that housed segments of several refugee tribes from the East Coast to *a people*, a unified tribal entity known as the "Brothertown Indians" or the "Brothertown tribe."

Culturally ambiguous practices, materials, and names, like "Brothertown," played important roles in the unfolding of Brothertown history and the negotiation of colonial politics. Such phenomena were interpretable from multiple cultural perspectives, and thus often operated on *dual* registers. The "brother" in the name Brothertown denoted Christian brotherhood, Indian brotherhood, or both, depending on the reader or receiver, just as Brothertown cemeteries resembling those of their Euro-American neighbors likely held different meanings for Brothertown and Euro-American observers. Each of these qualities allowed the Brothertown community to situate itself in relation to a breadth of addressees, both literally and figuratively, at any point in time.

These patterns resemble what Barbara Voss (2008a, 2008c) refers to as the "limits of ethnogenesis." She uses this phrase to discuss the gives and takes of identity negotiation and the long-term pragmatic (though she does not use this term) outcomes of such processes. Given the diffuse nature of power, no single entity wields complete control in social interactions. Voss demonstrates that although it initially allowed a degree of freedom from the Spanish system of racial classification, Californio ethnogenesis ultimately offered no such escape from later forms of racialization and racism in California. Concurrently, the Brothertown Indians were never completely free from the "structuring structures" (Bourdieu 1977) of the larger colonial society situated around them. Rather, they drew on their knowledge of those structures to reflexively shape and navigate the system. For example, in the 1830s when the federal government began formulating plans to push them farther west into Indian Territory, the Brothertown Indians adopted a rhetoric of social evolution to hold on to their new Wisconsin lands. They did so by arguing that they occupied an interstitial space between Indian and white worlds. These arguments led to US citizenship, allotment, and associated land rights, allowing the Brothertown community to remain in Wisconsin. Despite this triumph, however, these changes eventually contributed to a major communal transformation in which individuals and families began selling their lots and dispersing across the Midwest. In fact, the repercussions of this decision to become citizens are still felt today. Most recently, it had negative impacts on the Brothertown Indian Nation's quest for federal acknowledgment, discussed next.

As with Michel de Certeau's (1984) assessment of walking in the city discussed in chapter 7, the decisions, actions, and processes examined in this book also had unintended consequences, particularly when considered in terms of multiple generations. Perhaps the most striking example of these is the gradual transformation in memory practices, conceptions of personhood, and social identity that coincided with shifts in the cemetery material culture analyzed in chapters 5 and 6. In addition to blurring the physical distinctions between Brothertown and Euro-American cemeteries at the time, purchased gravestones with text inscriptions also affected the ways future generations of Brothertown Indians re-membered their respective histories and related to one another.

During the mid-nineteenth century and between the landscapes of New York and Wisconsin, Brothertown cemeteries transformed from spaces of communal remembrance to spaces of individual remembrance. In the late eighteenth and early nineteenth centuries, the Brothertown Indians commemorated their loved ones using either handmade blank limestone grave markers or small burial mounds. The materiality of these cemeteries, including the types of markers and distribution of graves in tightly spaced rows and columns, emphasized communal histories and ancestries, downplaying distinctions between deceased individuals. Of note, these practices paralleled those of the seventeenth-century Narragansett and nineteenth-century Iroquois (chapter 5). In these societies, it was forbidden to speak the name of the deceased. The mystery surrounding the precise location of Samson Occom's grave also demonstrates the emphasis on communal remembrance at the time.

As the Brothertown Indians incorporated purchased stones bearing texts and started anew in Wisconsin, they increasingly emphasized the individuality of their deceased loved ones. Stone inscriptions from this period often include the deceased's name and biographical information, such as death date, age at death, and names of relatives. In contrast to the traditional forms of communal remembrance, as Brothertown Indians inscribed this information on grave markers, they embraced colonial forms of record keeping that emphasized a particular type of personhood and individuality. The spatial configurations of these later period cemeteries, laid out in small clusters of stones representing immediate family members, similarly emphasize individuality and immediate family relations over other communal ties. The materiality of these cemeteries allows Brothertown Indians to remember their personal genealogies and histories without reference to those of their fellow community members. Because the Brothertown Indians became US citizens with land rights at the time of these changes, these new representations of personhood and individual identity may relate to the emergent concerns over land inheritance that came with allotment. However, the cemetery analyses of chapters 5 and 6 suggest that this change was already underway within the Brothertown community before its members reached Wisconsin and well before they became landowners. In this light, landownership only augmented this new emphasis on individuality.

The emergent understandings of personhood and individual identity that influenced and took shape from these cemetery transformations also likely shaped the nature of the next Brothertown emigration. In contrast to previous moves, this time the Brothertown Indians left their lands as individuals and immediate family groups, dispersing across the Midwest. Although they drastically altered their geographical relationships with one another at this time, the Brothertown community endures to this day.

In *Archaeology and Colonialism: Culture Contact from 5000 BC to Present*, Chris Gosden (2004) defines colonialism in terms of the new relationships it forges between people and things. For Gosden, the concept of personhood is vital for understanding the nature of different colonial cultures. Constance Crosby's study of European-manufactured goods recovered from Native American graves in New England demonstrates just one of the ways that concepts of personhood were mediated through shifting networks of people and things in colonial North America. Crosby (2003 [1988]:199) asserted that "In the long run, the practice of including items belonging to the individual, and items representative of a person's wealth or status, helped to create a more personalized and personified link between the living and the dead." This book provides further perspective on these shifting relationships in Native North America, situating grave markers in terms of their places within these new networks and assessing their importance in terms of novel conceptions of individuality and personhood at Brothertown.

Identities, Landscapes, and the Dynamics of Social Life at Brothertown

This book also has implications for broader anthropological discourses and theories of social identity (see Cassella and Fowler 2005). In regard to the long-standing debates over ethnicity in the social sciences, these analyses demonstrate the mutual importance of both primordialist and instrumentalist perspectives (introduced in chapter 2). In terms of the former perspective, shared genealogies and extended kinship networks played central roles in the constitution of Brothertown "boundaries." Beginning with the mid-eighteenth-century marriage of Samson Occom (a Mohegan) to Mary Fowler (a Montaukett), and extending to the emphases on kinship networks and immediate family groups evident in settlement patterns and certain cemeteries, "blood ties" always weighed heavily in the Brothertown community. In terms of the latter perspective, becoming Brothertown also had advantages for Native peoples of the East Coast. It allowed them the chance to begin anew with increased access to higher quality farmland as well as a reprieve from colonial oppression. Kinship ties, common goals, and shared experiences complemented one another in this instance of ethnogenesis, thus revealing the benefits of integrating primordialist and instrumentalist theories of ethnicity rather than treating them as polar opposites.

The aspirations they held in common led future Brothertown Indians to share the landscape of Brothertown, New York, which in turn led to new kinship ties—both biological and fictive—between members of the seven ancestral tribal groups. Subtle patterns of ethnonymy in Brothertown documents speak to the centrality of the first settlement in the ethnogenesis of the Brothertown Indians. As individuals and families of various tribal ancestries shared this landscape, they became kin and eventually took the name of their new settlement as a collective ethnonym. With its members currently spread across the Midwest and beyond, however, the Brothertown Indian community no longer knows such boundaries. Although shared landscapes clearly shape the ways their inhabitants relate to one another and to other social entities, they are far from deterministic when it comes to defining communal boundaries (see also Canuto and Yaeger 2000a, 2000b).

After the Brothertown Indians relocated in the nineteenth century, beginning anew in Wisconsin Territory, outsider perspectives on the community shifted. As they changed landscapes in the 1830s and 1840s, the Brothertown Indians physically separated themselves from the material legacies of their settlement in New York. The ways they materialized their new settlement eventually aided them in their efforts to situate themselves socially between Indian and white worlds. For instance, their Wisconsin cemeteries closely resembled those of their Euro-American neighbors, and their New York cemeteries marked them as inherently non-Euro-American by virtue of the presence of "Indian" stones and mounds within.

Of course, communal boundaries were not the only vectors of identity negotiated at Brothertown. Categories of gender, race, religion, and class also played parts in shaping the textures of Brothertown social interactions. Similar to the findings of other studies of colonial encounters (Deagan 1983; Lucas 2004; Voss 2008b), gender and race politics structured the ways in which society classified future generations of Brothertown Indians. For example, in regard to a land dispute between Sarah Pendelton, a Brothertown woman who married and had children with a man of mixed African and Euro-American ancestry, the Brothertown Peacemakers (Brothertown Indians n.d.) ruled the following in 1796:

> We owe this Sarah to be one of the Naraganset Tribe, but according to our Brothertown agreement, and our ancient custom of our Nations that was made in the year 1789, and it being the tenth article of our Town Book; Thus agreed by the legal voters of the aforesaid Town that if any of our Indian woman or Girls shall marry Negro or any intermixt with Negro, shall forfeit all right and privilege to the Brothertown Lands and further agreed upon that she or they shall immediately be removed out of the said Town and never there after shall be suffered to reside therein anymore.

The confluence of sexual, gender, and racial politics at Brothertown thus repopulated the world with new generations of insiders and outsiders. As evinced by this excerpt, the Brothertown community attempted to enforce strict rules regulating communal (and ethnic) boundaries in the late eighteenth century. The receipt for William Peters' coffin (chapter 5) shows the challenges involved in regulating such boundaries. Although the Brothertown community classified Peters as black or of mixed ancestry (Silverman 2010:155) and took measures to push him out of the Brothertown settlement shortly after the Sarah Pendelton case concluded, he remained with the community for more than two decades. Upon his death in 1827, the Brothertown Peacemakers supplied payment for his coffin out of communal funds, demonstrating that Peters likely died as more of an insider than an outsider.

In addition to the politics of race (Silverman 2010), religious differences contributed to the internal dynamics of the Brothertown community. Although Christianity constituted a central tenet of the Brothertown movement, Brothertown cemeteries show a diversity of distinct Christian practices and beliefs within the community. This is apparent in the maintenance of distinct cemeteries and commemoration practices by a Baptist faction of Brothertown Indians in the settlements. Moreover, the stone inscriptions of

Brothertown, Wisconsin, display a wide range of understandings of death and the afterlife.

Communicating with Language, Material Culture, and Space

In any social interaction, actors communicate their social identities and situate themselves in relation to one another via discourses wrought from much more than words and phrases. As analyzed with the case of the Brothertown Indians, community leaders, individuals, and family groups sent messages about who they were in a variety of manners. These ranged from intentional acts of communication like writing a letter to a state representative to the quotidian practices of everyday life like living in a certain part of town.

Even the written discourse, however, said much more than the sum total of dictionary definitions of the words contained within. In addition to their conventional meanings, the language of the analyzed letters and documents also contained subtle, pragmatic messages that functioned to assist their authors in situating themselves in relation to their addressees and in achieving their goals. Brothertown authors aligned their community with a variety of addressees by carefully choosing their words. By using certain ethnonyms, modes of reference, or other allusions to cultural affiliation in one particular context and not another, the authors navigated the politics of colonialism (chapter 4). Here, again, I call attention to the negotiated nature of these texts. On the surface, they stand as testament to the Brothertown community's embrace of a set of European introductions, namely, written communication and the English language. In a deeper sense, they attest to the ways the Brothertown community appropriated these introduced ideas and practices and used them for their own ends—in most of the analyzed cases, to maintain their community.

This pragmatic approach to discourse also applies to material culture. In the case of this book, I examined cemetery discourse in New York and Wisconsin. With the introduction of text inscriptions in Brothertown, New York, the nature of Brothertown cemetery discourse was forever changed. As the Brothertown Indians began purchasing (rather than making) their loved ones' grave markers, text inscriptions became the primary means of marking relations between gravesites and defining connections between the living and the dead. It is possible that these relations were previously marked with stone shapes and sizes. With the incorporation of store-bought stones bearing texts came the homogenization of all other material dimensions of grave markers. In other words, the Brothertown Indians increasingly relied on text inscriptions to "speak louder" than other nontextual qualities of their markers while in New York. Later, in the Wisconsin cemeteries, stone forms took on importance once again, as Brothertown Indians began using them to mark age, gender, and religious distinctions. For instance, intentionally or otherwise, stone heights represent the relative ages of the deceased in many cases. In other instances, nontextual aspects of stones implicitly communicate information omitted in their text inscriptions. In most of these examples, stone imagery communicates religious or spiritual sentiments excluded from the stones' texts.

Decolonizing the Present

Throughout this book, I tried to further decolonize the archaeology of colonialism. In aspiring to engender new understandings of Brothertown history and its connections to broader colonial processes, I focused largely on people and events of the eighteenth, nineteenth, and early twentieth centuries. Though such a project clearly involves challenging epistemologies in the present, there is much left to accomplish in the way of decolonizing archaeology in the twenty-first century. Over the past few decades, a growing number of archaeologists and Native communities have begun to build strong relationships in hopes of moving in this direction. These interactions beget novel forms of archaeological practice, including Indigenous, collaborative, covenantal, and postcolonial archaeologies (Preucel and Cipolla 2008). In the first three chapters of this book, I discussed the development of the Brothertown Archaeology Project as the result of my interaction and collaboration with the Brothertown Indian Nation. Because a truly pragmatic archaeology must take into account the "work" that it does in the world, both within and beyond academic circles, it is now necessary to consider the practical outcomes of this collaboration.

Much like Brothertown history, the Brothertown Archaeology Project and this book resulted from the interaction of insiders and outsiders. The collaborative process informed everything from research design and data collection to analysis and interpretation. I only began thinking about research design after contacting the tribe, discussing the possibility of an archaeological research project, and receiving permission to move forward. Moreover, the project's focus on grave markers emerged through continued dialogue and interaction with tribal members. As discussed in chapter 3, several tribal elders first suggested that I focus on their historic cemeteries. We continued discussing this possibility over email in the months that followed, and I eventually flew to Wisconsin to present the idea to the tribal council during one of their monthly meetings. The council officially approved the cemetery research after we talked through our questions, concerns, and expectations. As we conducted the cemetery research, the Brothertown community shared information with me that I may not have uncovered on my own. I received emails, phone calls, and visits from members of the tribe seeking to contribute to the project by offering information on Brothertown history and their ancestors' grave markers. Likewise, the tribe allowed me special access to the Brothertown archival collection, housed in the tribal office.

The collaborative process also informed my interpretations in the sense of pragmatic weaving discussed in chapter 2 (Saitta 2007; see also Rorty 1991). My understandings of the contemporary Brothertown community influenced me to work toward a deeper understanding of colonial culture and Native American identity politics of the eighteenth, nineteenth, and early twentieth centuries. Like that of all communities making their places in the modern world, Brothertown culture is comprised of things, practices, and ideas that did not originate solely from within the Brothertown community. As the ethnonym "Brothertown Indian Nation" implies, however, the Brothertown Indians still make distinctions between insiders and outsiders. Within the shared cultural milieu of the modern world, the Brothertown Indian Nation has its own political organization and communal gatherings. Brothertown Indians recognize and celebrate their unique communal history and their ties to sacred sites. Members continue to work toward maintaining and preserving the community and its future, clearly demonstrated by their thirty-year quest for federal acknowledgment. Along with my interactions with members of the Brothertown community and the tribal council, these general observations emphasized the need to move beyond the dichotomous tropes often evoked in archaeologies of culture contact and colonialism. The Brothertown community—past and present—is much more complex than the differences between Native American and European, colonist and colonized, or accommodation and resistance. Rather than focusing solely on the origins of the practices and materials analyzed in the preceding chapters, I thus concentrated on the pragmatic effects they had on the community and on broader colonial society. This general pattern parallels Roland Barthes (1977) call for the "death of the author," discussed in chapter 2.

Reflexively, the Brothertown Archaeology Project also had practical effects within the Brothertown Indian Nation itself. The cemetery project collected information from a large portion of Brothertown grave markers, including their text inscriptions, imagery, and locations. This is particularly useful for those stones whose text inscriptions and imagery are beginning to fade. This information is now preserved in electronic and hard-copy catalogs of the stones. Furthermore, the ground-penetrating radar survey of Union Cemetery, Brothertown, Wisconsin (Cipolla 2010:528) revealed the locations of several unmarked Brothertown graves. The community can use this information to protect and recommemorate the once-lost graves of their ancestors. In certain instances, the archaeology project also served to connect younger members of the tribe with new dimensions of their cultural heritage. Participating in an archaeological survey of the historic settlement or cataloging the grave markers of their ancestors offered new points of reference with which to consider their community's history.

Non-Native landowners and residents of both Brothertown settlements were exposed to new perspectives on the places and spaces in which they currently live via the Brothertown Archaeology Project. The archaeology emphasized the Native presence in the landscapes of both Brothertown settlements. By interacting with archaeologists and members of the Brothertown Indian Nation in the context of the archaeology project, local landowners and residents were endowed with new senses of their everyday surroundings. More broadly, these experiences also help challenge widely accepted stereotypes of "Indian-ness" and myths of the vanishing Indian. By confronting contradictions of these tropes such as the stories of Brothertown Indians building the first Methodist Church in Wisconsin Territory or constructing the same roadways that the residents drive on daily, the current inhabitants of Brothertown renegotiated their understandings of Native communities, past and present.

The case of the Brothertown Indian Nation's petition for federal acknowledgment provides an important example with which to consider the future of collaborative archaeology and the connections between archaeological research and contemporary politics. In December 2009, Kathleen Brown-Pérez contacted me in regard to the comment period following the publication of the negative proposed findings against the Brothertown Indians' petition for federal acknowledgment. During this period, all interested and informed parties were invited to comment on the Office of Indian Affairs's findings, either supporting or refuting its claims. Brown-Pérez asked that I take a look at the report.

As I reviewed the proposed findings, I was surprised to learn that my work had been misconstrued and misappropriated by the authors. For example, the report (US Department of Interior—Indian Affairs 2009:12) states, "Scholarly archaeological excavations, even of sites in Wisconsin, do not provide evidence that any historical observer made a contemporaneous identification of an existing Indian entity (Cipolla 2007)." Although the bibliography of the report lists the source of this statement as "Cipolla 2007, Brothertown Indian Nation Archaeology Project," its origin remains unclear because the project had just begun in 2006 and no findings had been published by 2007.

Beyond the poor scholarship that went into the report, however, lies a much deeper issue concerning the relationship between archaeological data and the federal acknowledgment process. In direct contrast to the foregoing quotation, the Brothertown cemeteries analyzed in this volume do indeed provide evidence of outsiders identifying an "existing Indian entity" in Brothertown. The spatial distribution of Brothertown and non-Brothertown graves in Union Cemetery illustrates this point precisely. Nearly all Brothertown grave markers sit in the southern half of the cemetery, which is known locally as the "Indian half." In other words, the Brothertown Indians consistently chose to bury their loved ones in close proximity to other Brothertown Indians, and Euro-Americans consistently chose to bury their loved ones in close proximity to other Euro-Americans. The importance of this pattern should not be understated. Brothertown Indians and Euro-Americans alike recognized the disparities between their two groups. Other cemeteries surveyed as part of the Brothertown Archaeology Project provide similar examples of these historically recognized social and cultural distinctions. The fact that local Euro-American residents continue to refer to the southern half of the cemetery as the Indian half also suggests that it was known as such since the 1850s, when Euro-Americans and Brothertown Indians began sharing the landscape.

Although these facts do not change the Brothertown Indian Nation's current political standing, they do highlight an underexplored use of archaeological data (Mrozowski et al. 2009). One of the criteria that petitioning tribes must demonstrate to become federally recognized is that a large portion of its members lived as part of an identified Indian community, distinct from other groups (Office of Federal Acknowledgement 2011). Archaeological histories sometimes speak directly to these issues, particularly in cases where the communities in question did not speak and write in English, as the Brothertown Indians did. In these cases, archaeological remains may represent core pieces of evidence, but archaeologists have yet to fully apply their work in such instances. This is just one direction in which archaeologists can further decolonize archaeology and partially redress the injustices of colonialism in the spirit of pragmatism (Preucel and Mrozowski 2010; Saitta 2007).

Final Thoughts

> Fourteen years ago, you called upon me in Clinton and told me that the graves of your kindred in the Indian Cemetery in Deansville [formerly Brothertown, New York] had been desecrated by the whites.
>
> —North (1893)

So reads the first line of an 1893 letter written by Edward North, a professor in the Department of Greek Language and Literature at Hamilton College in Oneida County, New York, addressed to Symian Fowler, a Brothertown Indian. Fowler contacted North in 1879 seeking help in protecting his ancestors' graves in Brothertown, New York. The "whites" mentioned in the letter were likely Euro-American farmers encroaching on Brothertown burial grounds in efforts to increase their arable land. Although the precise outcome of Fowler's effort is unclear from the letter, it does speak indirectly to the Brothertown Indians' enduring ties to their ancestors and their former home in New York. Even half a century after the community had departed for a new home in Wisconsin Territory, Brothertown Indians maintained ties to these sacred sites.

Efforts, connections, and tensions such as those hinted at in North's letter are precisely what led to the ethnogenesis and endurance of the Brothertown community. In their edited volume on the archaeology of communities, Marcello Canuto and Jason Yaeger (2000b:5) define *community* broadly as "a dynamic socially constituted institution that is contingent upon human agency for its creation and continued existence." Throughout this book, I have attempted to demonstrate the complex nature of this agency, particularly within the contexts of colonialism. It is always diffuse, even in situations of extreme power differentials, and is thus rarely limited to either "insiders" or "outsiders." I tracked the ways in which a subaltern group actively created and shaped their places in the Euro-American world that surrounded them. These instances of Brothertown agency often took place in dialogue with the outside world. In contexts of culture contact, colonialism, and multiculturalism, communities—ethnic or otherwise—exist via continuous interaction between insiders and outsiders as they communicate their identities, classify those around them, and exchange ideas and materials. Though these negotiations are overt and intentional at times, in other instances they occur in the seemingly apolitical contexts of everyday life. As the Brothertown Indians wrote to one another and to outsiders, mourned and commemorated the losses of their loved ones, and chose lots on which to live, they also shaped who they were, forged a new type of Native community, and navigated the politics of colonialism, albeit in small, incremental steps.

Moreover, such agency is not limited to people alone. Instead, it flows through networks of humans and things. As pointed out by thinkers like Alfred Gell (1998), Chris Gosden (2005), Bruno Latour (2005), and recent studies in relational archaeology (e.g., Hodder 2012), material culture continually connects and influences the human agents that surround it, past, present, and future. Through these connections, the Brothertown Indians negotiated their places in the world, achieving certain goals and challenging dominant modes of social classification. Yet the nonhuman nodes within these networks exercised their own types of agency, contributing to future communal transformations unforeseen by their original creators, consumers, and users.

At their heart, these findings offer a harsh critique of the dichotomous modes of thought prevalent throughout the history of archaeological studies of culture contact and colonialism. Returning to Charles Peirce's concept of synechism, Brothertown history is best conceived as a series of negotiations and continuities between colonial domination and subaltern resistance, between insiders and outsiders, and between humans and material culture. To study colonialism in the modern world is not to focus solely on any one of these concepts but to scrutinize the interconnections between them. As the Brothertown community emerged and endured the legacies of colonialism, it did so in constant interaction with other peoples, landscapes, and materials. Such a history attests to the complexities of the past five centuries of colonial entanglement in North America, to the myriad responses that Native peoples had to various forms of European colonialism, and to the need to further decolonize archaeology.

References

Agha, Asif. 2005. Voice, Footing, Enregisterment. *Journal of Linguistic Anthropology* 15: 38–59.

———. 2007. *Language and Social Relations*. Cambridge: Cambridge University Press.

Ales, Marion Fisher. 1993. A History of the Indians on Montauk, Long Island. In *The History and Archaeology of the Montauk*, vol. 3, 2nd ed., ed. Gaynell Stone, 5–66. Stony Brook, NY: Suffolk County Archaeological Association and Nassau County Archaeological Committee.

Anderson, Benedict. 1983. *Imagined Communities*. London: Verso.

Ashcroft, Bill, Gareth Griffiths, and Helen Tifflin. 1989. *The Empire Writes Back*. London: Routledge.

Atalay, Sonya. 2006. Indigenous Archaeology as Decolonizing Practice. *American Indian Quarterly* 30:280–310.

———. 2012. *Community-Based Archaeology: Research with, by, and for Indigenous and Local Communities*. Berkeley: University of California Press.

Barth, Fredrik. 1994. Enduring and Emerging Issues in the Analysis of Ethnicity. In *The Anthropology of Ethnicity: Beyond "Ethnic Groups and Boundaries,"* ed. Hans Vermeulen and Cora Govers, 11–32. Amsterdam: Het Spinhuis.

———. 1998a [1969]. Introduction. In *Ethnic Groups and Boundaries: The Social Organization of Cultural Difference*, ed. Fredrik Barth, 9–38. Long Grove, IL: Waveland Press.

———, ed. 1998b [1969]. *Ethnic Groups and Boundaries: The Social Organization of Cultural Difference*. Long Grove, IL: Waveland Press.

Barthes, Roland. 1977. The Death of the Author. In *Image, Music, Text*, trans. Stephen Heath, 142–48. New York: Hill and Wang.

Basso, Keith H. 1996a. *Wisdom Sits in Places: Landscapes and Language among the Western Apache*. Albuquerque: University of New Mexico Press.

———. 1996b. Wisdom Sits in Places: Notes on a Western Apache Landscape. In *Senses of Place*, ed. Steven Feld and Keith H. Basso, 5–90. Santa Fe: School of American Research.

Beaudry, Mary C. 1988a. Introduction. In *Documentary Archaeology in the New World*, ed. Mary C. Beaudry, 1–4. Cambridge: Cambridge University Press.

———. 1988b. Words for Things: Linguistic Analysis of Probate Inventories. In *Documentary Archaeology in the New World*, ed. Mary C. Beaudry, 43–50. Cambridge: Cambridge University Press.

———, ed. 1988c. *Documentary Archaeology in the New World*. Cambridge: Cambridge University Press.

Belknap, Jeremy, and Jedidiah Morse. 1955 [1796]. Report on the Oneida, Stockbridge and Brotherton Indians, *Indian Notes and Monographs* 54. New York: Museum of the American Indian, Heye Foundation.

Bell, Edward L. 1994. *Vestiges of Mortality and Remembrance: A Bibliography on the Historical Archaeology of Cemeteries*. London: Scarecrow Press.

Bhabha, Homi K. 1994. *The Location of Culture*. London: Routledge.

Bourdieu, Pierre. 1977. *Outline of a Theory of Practice*, trans. Richard Nice. Cambridge: Cambridge University Press.

———. 1990. *The Logic of Practice*, trans. Richard Nice. Cambridge: Cambridge University Press.

Bragdon, Kathleen J. 1996. *Native People of Southern New England, 1500–1650*. Norman: University of Oklahoma Press.

———. 1997. Massachusett Kinship Terminology and Social Organization, 1620–1750. *Northeast Anthropology* 54:1–14.

Bragdon, Kathleen J., and William S. Simmons. 1998. Eastern Pequot Indians of Connecticut. Petition for federal acknowledgment as an American Indian tribe. Report submitted to the Branch of Acknowledgment and Research, Bureau of Indian Affairs, Department of Interior, Washington, DC (unpublished manuscript).

Bread, Daniel. 2006 [1820]. Forced from New York in the 1820s. In *Wisconsin Indian Literature: Anthology of Native Voices*, ed. Kathleen Tigerman, 222–23. Madison: University of Wisconsin Press.

Bromberg, Francine W., and Steven J. Shephard. 2006. The Quaker Burying Ground in Alexandria, Virginia: A Study of Burial Practices of the Religious Society of Friends. *Historical Archaeology* 40:57–88.

Brooks, Joanna, ed. 2006. *The Collected Writings of Samson Occom, Mohegan*. Oxford: Oxford University Press.

Brothertown Indian Nation. n.d. Brothertown Meetings at Little Falls, Minnesota, 1992–2005. Unpublished document. Fond du Lac, WI: Brothertown Indian Nation Archives.

Brothertown Indians. n.d. Brothertown Records, 1788–1810, 1901. Unpublished document (copy of original). Madison: Wisconsin Historical Society.

———. 1791. Letter to the New York State Assembly, January 1791. In *The Collected Writings of Samson Occom, Mohegan*, ed. Joanna Brooks, 157–58. Oxford: Oxford University Press.

———. 1811. Letter to "the tribes Composing the Confederation of the West," June 16, 1811. Unpublished document (copy of original). Fond du Lac, WI: Brothertown Indian Nation Archives.

———. 1825. Letter to President James Monroe, February 8, 1825. Unpublished document (copy of original). Fond du Lac, WI: Brothertown Indian Nation Archives.

———. 1827a. Letter to James Baker, Secretary of War of the United States, January 17, 1827. Unpublished document (copy of original). Fond du Lac, WI: Brothertown Indian Nation Archives.

———. 1827b. Letter to President John Quincy Adams, January 17, 1827. Unpublished document (copy of original). Fond du Lac, WI: Brothertown Indian Nation Archives.

———. 1827c. Coffin receipt dated May 17, 1827. Unpublished document. Albany: New York State Archives.

———. 1827d. Coffin receipt dated June 7, 1827. Unpublished document. Albany: New York State Archives.

———. 1838. Letter to President Martin Van Buren, February 6, 1838. Unpublished document (copy of original). Fond du Lac, WI: Brothertown Indian Nation Archives.

Brown, Ian. 1978. Historic Artifacts and Sociocultural Change: Some Warnings from the Lower Mississippi Valley. *Conference of Historic Sites Archaeology Papers* 13:109–22.

Brucker, Andrea R., and Caroline K. Andler. 2011. *Letters Home from the Brothertown "Boys."* Bloomington, IN: AuthorHouse.

Bushnell, David I., Jr. 1920. *Native Cemeteries and Forms of Burial East of the Mississippi*. Washington, DC: Smithsonian Institution, Bureau of American Ethnology.

Butler, Eva L. 1946. The Brush or Stone Memorial Heaps of Southern New England. *Bulletin of the Archaeological Society of Connecticut* 19:3–12.

Cannon, Aubrey. 1989. The Historical Dimension in Mortuary Expressions of Status and Sentiment. *Current Anthropology* 30:437–58.

Canuto, Marcello A., and Jason Yaeger. 2000a. Introducing an Archaeology of Communities. In *The Archaeology of Communities: A New World Perspective*, ed. Marcello A. Canuto and Jason Yaeger, 1–15. London: Routledge.

———, eds. 2000b. *The Archaeology of Communities: A New World Perspective*. London: Routledge.

Cassella, Eleanor Conlin, and Chris Fowler. 2005. Beyond Identification: An Introduction. In *The Archaeology of Plural and Changing Identities*, ed. Eleanor Conlin Cassella and Chris Fowler, 1–7. New York: Springer.

Cave, Alfred A. 1996. *The Pequot War*. Amherst: University of Massachusetts Press.

Certeau, Michel de. 1984. *The Practice of Everyday Life*. Berkeley: University of California Press.

Chilton, Elizabeth. 2005. Farming and Social Complexity in the Northeast. In *North American Archaeology*, ed. Timothy R. Pauketat and Diana DiPaolo Loren, 138–60. Malden, MA: Blackwell.

———. 2008. So Little Maize, So Much Time: Understanding Maize Adoption in New England. In *Current Northeast Paleoethnobotany II*, ed. John P. Hart, 53–59. Albany: University of the State of New York Press.

Cipolla, Craig N. 2008. Signs of Identity, Signs of Memory. *Archaeological Dialogues* 15:196–215.

———. 2010. The Dualities of Endurance: A Collaborative Historical Archaeology of Ethnogenesis at Brothertown, 1780–1910. PhD dissertation, University of Pennsylvania Department of Anthropology.

———. 2011. Commemoration, Community, and Colonial Politics at Brothertown. *Midcontinental Journal of Archaeology* 36:145–72.

———. 2012a. Peopling the Place, 'Placing' the People: An Archaeology of Brothertown Discourse. *Ethnohistory* 59:51–78.

———. 2012b. Practice Theory. In *Encyclopedia of Global Archaeology*, ed. Claire Smith. New York: Springer Reference.

———. 2012c. Social Archaeology. In *Encyclopedia of Global Archaeology*, ed. Claire Smith. New York: Springer Reference.

———. 2012d. Textual Artifacts, Artifactual Texts: An Historical Archaeology of Brothertown Writing. *Historical Archaeology* 46:91–109.

———. 2013a. Resituating Homeland: Motion, Movement, and Ehtnogenesis at Brothertown. In *Shifting People, Shifting Things: Archaeologies of Movement*, ed. Mary C. Beaudry and Travis G. Parno, 117–32. New York: Springer Press.

———. 2013b. Native American Historical Archaeology and the Trope of Authenticity. *Historical Archaeology*, in press.

Cipolla, Craig N., and Caroline Andler. 2007. A Brief Historical Overview of the Brothertown Indian Nation. Website, http://web.mac.com/craigcipolla/Brothertown_Archaeological_Project/History.html (accessed August 20, 2012).

Cipolla, Craig N., Stephen W. Silliman, and David B. Landon. 2007. "Making Do": Nineteenth-Century Subsistence Practices on the Eastern Pequot Reservation. *Northeast Anthropology* 74:40–63.

Colden, Cadwallader. 1904 [1750]. *The History of the Five Nations of Canada*. New York: A. S. Barnes.

Colwell-Chanthaphonh, Chip, and T. J. Ferguson, eds. 2008. *Collaboration in Archaeological Practice*. Lanham, MD: AltaMira.

Commuck, Thomas. 1851, Letter to I. A. Lapham Concerning Calumet County History. Unpublished manuscript. Madison: Wisconsin Historical Society.

———. 1855. Sketch of the Brothertown Indians. In *Wisconsin Historical Collections*, vol. 4, ed. L. C. Draper, 291–98. Madison: Wisconsin Historical Society.

Cordell, Linda S., and Vincent J. Yannie. 1991. Ethnicity, Ethnogenesis, and the Individual: A Processual Approach towards Dialogue. In *Processual and Postprocessual Archaeologies: Multiple Ways of Knowing the Past*, ed. Robert W. Preucel, 96–107. Carbondale: Center for Archaeological Investigations, Southern Illinois University at Carbondale.

Crosby, Constance A. 2003 [1988]. From Myth to History, or Why King Philip's Ghost Walks Abroad. In *The Recovery of Meaning: Historical Archaeology in the Eastern United States*, ed. Mark P. Leone and Parker B. Potter, Jr., 183–210. Clinton Corners, NY: Percheron Press.

Cunningham, Keith. 1989. Navajo, Mormon, Zuni Graves: Navajo, Mormon, Zuni Ways. In *Cemeteries and Gravemarkers: Voices of American Culture*, ed. Richard E. Meyer, 197–216. Ann Arbor, MI: UMI Research Press.

Curtis, S. 1785. Field Book of the Survey of the Indian Lands in Brothertown, Oneida Co., New York. Unpublished manuscript. Clinton, NY: Hamilton College Archives.

Cusick, James G. 1998a. Historiography of Acculturation: An Evaluation of Concepts and Their Application in Archaeology. In *Studies in Culture Contact: Interaction, Culture Change, and Archaeology*, ed. James G. Cusick, 126–45. Carbondale: Center for Archaeological Investigations, Southern Illinois University.

———, ed. 1998b. *Studies in Culture Contact: Interaction, Cultural Change, and Archaeology*. Carbondale: Center for Archaeological Investigations, Southern Illinois University.

Daniel, E. Valentine. 1984. *Fluid Signs: Being a Person the Tamil Way*. Berkeley: University of California Press.

Deagan, Kathleen. 1983. *Spanish St. Augustine: The Archaeology of a Colonial Creole Community*. Gainesville: University Press of Florida.

Decora, Waukon. 2006 [1829]. The Treaty of 1829. In *Wisconsin Indian Literature: Anthology of Native Voices*, ed. Kathleen Tigerman, 65. Madison: University of Wisconsin Press.

Deetz, James. 1978 [1963]. Archaeological Investigations at La Purisima Mission. In *Historical Archaeology: A Guide to Substantive and Theoretical Contributions*, ed. Robert L. Schuyler, 160–90. Farmingdale, NY: Baywood Publishing.

———. 1989. Foreword. In *Cemeteries and Gravemarkers: Voices of American Culture*, ed. Richard E. Meyer, ix–xiv. Ann Arbor, MI: UMI Research Press.

———. 1996 [1977]. *In Small Things Forgotten: An Archaeology of Early American Life*. New York: Anchor Books, Doubleday.

Deetz, James, and Edwin S. Dethlefsen. 1967. Death's Head, Cherub, Urn and Willow. *Natural History* 76:29–37.

———. 1971. Some Social Aspects of New England Colonial Mortuary Art. *Memoirs of the Society for American Archaeology* 25:30–38.

DeForest, John W. 1964 [1851]. *History of the Indians of Connecticut: From the Earliest Known Period to 1850*. Hamden, CT: Archon Books.

Den Ouden, Amy E. 2005. *Beyond Conquest: Native Peoples and the Struggle for History in New England*. Lincoln: University of Nebraska Press.

Dethlefsen, Edwin S., and James Deetz. 1966. Death's Heads, Cherubs, and Willow Trees: Experimental Archaeology in Colonial Cemeteries. *American Antiquity* 31: 502–10.

Díaz-Andreu, Margarita, and Sam Lucy. 2005. Introduction. In *The Archaeology of Identity: Approaches to Gender, Age, Status, Ethnicity and Religion*, ed. Margarita Díaz-Andreu, Sam Lucy, Stasa Babic, and David N. Edwards, 1–12. New York: Routledge.

Fairclough, Norman. 1992. *Discourse and Social Change*. Cambridge: Polity.

Fawcett, Melissa Jayne. 2000. *Medicine Trail: The Life and Lessons of Gladys Tantaquidgeon*. Tucson: University of Arizona Press.

Featherstonhaugh, George H. 1840. Map of Brothertown Township, Wisconsin. Unpublished manuscript. Madison: Wisconsin State Archives.

Feld, Steven, and Keith H. Basso. 1996. Introduction. In *Senses of Place*, ed. Steven Feld and Keith H. Basso, 3–12. Santa Fe, NM: School of American Research.

Ferguson, Kelly A. 2010. A Macrobotanical Analysis of Native American Maize Agriculture at the Smith's Point Site. M.A. thesis, University of Massachusetts, Boston, Department of Anthropology.

Ferguson, Leland. 1992. *Uncommon Ground: Archaeology and Early African America, 1650–1800*. Washington, DC: Smithsonian Institution Press.

Ferris, Neal. 2009. *The Archaeology of Native-Lived Colonialism: Challenging History in the Great Lakes*. Tucson: University of Arizona Press.

Fitts, Robert K. 1990. *Puritans, Yankees, and Gravestones: A Linguistic Analysis of New England Gravestone Inscriptions*. Columbia: South Carolina Institute of Archaeology and Anthropology.

Fitzgerald, Stephanie. 2008. Mohegan Wood-Splint Basket. In *Early Native Literacies in New England: A Documentary and Critical Anthology*, ed. Kristina Bross and Hilary E. Wyss, 52–56. Amherst: University of Massachusetts Press.

Flemming, George D. 2005. *Brotherton: New Jersey's First and Only Indian Reservation and the Communities of Shamong and Tabernacle That Followed*. Medford, NJ: Plexus Publishing.

Forbes, Harriette M. 1927. *Gravestones of Early New England and the Men Who Made Them, 1653–1800*. Boston: Houghton Mifflin.

Fortes, Meyer. 1936. Culture Contact as a Dynamic Process, an Investigation in the Northern Territories of the Gold Coast. *Africa* 28:24–55.

Foster, George M. 1960. *Culture and Conquest: America's Spanish Heritage*. Chicago: Quadrangle Books.

Foucault, Michel. 1990. *The History of Sexuality*, vol. 1, trans. Robert Hurley. New York: Vintage.

Frazier, Patrick. 1992. *The Mohicans of Stockbridge*. Lincoln: University of Nebraska Press.

Garman, James C. 1994. Viewing the Color Line through the Material Culture of Death. *Historical Archaeology* 28:74–93.

Geertz, Clifford. 1963. The Integrative Revolution: Primordial Sentiments and Civil Politics in the New States. In *Old Societies and New States*, ed. Clifford Geertz, 105–57. New York: Free Press.

Gell, Alfred. 1998. *Art and Agency: An Anthropological Theory*. Oxford: Oxford University Press.

Gibson, Susan G., ed. 1980. *Burr's Hill, a 17th Century Wampanoag Burial Ground in Warren, Rhode Island*. Providence, RI: Haffenreffer Museum of Anthropology, Brown University.

Giddens, Anthony. 1979. *Central Problems in Social Theory: Action, Structure and Contradiction in Social Analysis*. Berkeley: University of California Press.

———. 1984. *The Constitution of Society: Outline of the Theory of Structuration*. Berkeley: University of California Press.

Goldstein, Lynn. 1981. One-Dimensional Archaeology and Multi-Dimensional People: Spatial Organisation and Mortuary Analysis. In *The Archaeology of Death*, ed.

Robert Chapman, Ian Kinnes, and Klavs Randsborg, 53–69. Cambridge: Cambridge University Press.

Gosden, Chris. 2001. Postcolonial Archaeology: Issues of Culture, Identity, and Knowledge. In *Archaeological Theory Today*, ed. Ian Hodder, 241–61. London: Blackwell.

———. 2004. *Archaeology and Colonialism: Cultural Contact from 5000 BC to the Present.* Cambridge: Cambridge University Press.

———. 2005. What Do Objects Want? *Journal of Archaeological Method and Theory* 12:193–211.

Gupta, Akhil, and James Ferguson. 1992. Space, Identity, and the Politics of Difference. *Cultural Anthropology* 7:6–23.

———. 1997. Culture, Power, Place: Ethnography at the End of an Era. In *Culture, Power, Place: Explorations in Critical Anthropology*, ed. Akhil Gupta and James Ferguson, 1–32. Durham, NC: Duke University Press.

Hall, Martin. 1999. Subaltern Voices? Finding the Spaces between Things and Words. In *Historical Archaeology: Back from the Edge*, ed. Pedro Paulo A. Funari, Martin Hall, and Siân Jones, 193–203. London: World Archaeological Press.

Hanks, William F. 1987. Discourse Genres in a Theory of Practice. *American Ethnologist* 14:668–92.

Hart, John P. 2008. Evolving the Three Sisters: The Changing Histories of Maize, Bean, and Squash in New York and the Greater Northeast. In *Current Northeast Paleoethnobotany II*, ed. John P. Hart, 87–99. Albany: University of the State of New York Press.

Hayes, Katherine Howlett. 2011. Occulting the past. Conceptualizing Forgetting in the History and Archaeology of Sylvester Manor. *Archaeological Dialogues* 18: 197–221.

———. 2013. *Slavery Before Race: Europeans, Africans, and Indians on Long Island's Sylvester Manor Plantation, 1651–1884*. New York: New York University Press.

Heller, John Otto. n.d. Narrative of Lots of Brothertown Reserve. Unpublished manuscript (copy of original). Fond du Lac, WI: Brothertown Indian Nation Archives.

Hill, Jonathan D., ed. 1996. *History, Power, and Identity: Ethnogenesis in the Americas, 1492–1992*. Iowa City: University of Iowa Press.

Hodder, Ian. 1982. *Symbols in Action: Ethnoarchaeological Studies of Material Culture.* Cambridge: Cambridge University Press.

———. 2012. *Entangled: An Archaeology of the Relationships between Humans and Things.* Malden, MA: Wiley-Blackwell.

Hodge, Christina J. 2005. Faith and Practice at an Early-Eighteenth-Century Wampanoag Burial Ground: The Waldo Farm Site in Dartmouth, Massachusetts. *Historical Archaeology* 39:73–94.

Horning, Audrey. 2007. Cultures of Contact, Cultures of Conflict? Identity Construction, Colonialist Discourse, and the Ethics of Archaeological Practice in Northern Ireland. *Stanford Journal of Archaeology* 5:107–33.

Ingold, Tim. 1993. The Temporality of Landscape. *World Archaeology* 25:152–74.

James, William. 1907. *Pragmatism: A New Name for Some Old Ways of Thinking*. New York: Longmans, Green.

Jarvis, Brad. 2010. *The Brothertown Nation of Indians: Land Ownership and Nationalism in Early America, 1740–1840*. Lincoln: University of Nebraska.

Jett, Stephen C. 1994. Cairn and Brush Travel Shrines in the United States Northeast and Southwest. *Northeast Anthropology* 48:61–67.

Johnson, Joseph. 1998a [1772–73]. To all Enquiring Friends, 1772 or 1773. In *To Do Good to My Indian Brethren: The Writings of Joseph Johnson, 1751–1776*, ed. Laura J. Murray, 177–80. Amherst: University of Massachusetts Press.

———. 1998b [1773]. Letter to Samson Occom, October 1, 1773. In *To Do Good to My Indian Brethren: The Writings of Joseph Johnson, 1751–1776*, ed. Laura J. Murray, 192–93. Amherst: University of Massachusetts Press.

Johnson, Matthew H. 1999. Rethinking Historical Archaeology. In *Historical Archaeology: Back From the Edge*, ed. Pedro Paulo A. Funari, Martin Hall, and Siân Jones, 23–36. London: World Archaeological Press.

Jones, Siân. 1997. *The Archaeology of Ethnicity: Constructing Identities in the Past and Present*. London: Routledge.

Joyce, Rosemary A., and Jeanne Lopiparo. 2005. Postscript: Doing Agency in Archaeology. *Journal of Archaeological Method and Theory* 12:365–74.

Keane, Webb E. 2003. Semiotics and the Social Analysis of Material Things. *Language and Communication* 23:409–25.

Keister, Douglas. 2004. *Stories in Stone: A Field Guide to Cemetery Symbolism and Iconography*. Layton, UT: Gibbs Smith.

Larson, Pier M. 1996. Desperately Seeking "the Merina" (Central Madagascar): Reading Ethnonyms and Their Semantic Fields in African Identity Histories. *Journal of South African Studies* 22:541–60.

Latour, Bruno. 2005. *Reassembling the Social: An Introduction to Actor-Network-Theory*. Oxford: Oxford University Press.

Lefebvre, Henri. 1991. *The Production of Space*. Malden, MA: Blackwell.

Leone, Mark P. 2010. *Critical Historical Archaeology*. Walnut Creek, CA: Left Coast Press.

Leone, Mark P., and Parker B. Potter. 2003 [1988]. Introduction: Issues in Historical Archaeology. In *The Recovery of Meaning: Historical Archaeology in the Eastern United States*, ed. Mark P. Leone and Parker B. Potter, 1–22. Clinton Corners, NY: Percheron Press.

Leone, Mark P., Parker B. Potter, Jr., and Paul Shackel. 1987. Towards a Critical Archaeology. *Current Anthropology* 28(3):283–302.

Liebmann, Matthew. 2008a. The Innovative Materiality of Revitalization Movements: Lessons from the Pueblo Revolt of 1680. *American Anthropologist* 110:360–72.

———. 2008b. The Intersection of Archaeology and Postcolonial Studies. In *Archaeology and the Postcolonial Critique*, ed. Matthew Liebmann and Uzma Z. Rizvi, 1–20. Lanham, MD: AltaMira.

Liebmann, Matthew, and Melissa S. Murphy, eds. 2011. *Enduring Conquests: Rethinking the Archaeology of Resistance to Spanish Colonialism in the Americas*. Santa Fe, NM: School for Advanced Research.

Lightfoot, Kent G. 2004. *Indians, Missionaries, and Merchants: The Legacy of Colonial Encounters on the California Frontiers*. Berkeley: University of California Press.

Lightfoot, Kent G., Antoinette Martinez, and Ann M. Schiff. 1998. Daily Practice and Material Culture in Pluralistic Social Settings: An Archaeological Study of Culture Change and Persistence from Fort Ross, California. *American Antiquity* 63:199–222.

Linden, Blanche M. G. 1980. The Willow Tree and Urn Motif: Changing Ideas about Death and Nature. *Markers* 1:149–155.

Loew, Patty. 2001. *Indian Nations of Wisconsin: Histories of Endurance and Renewal*. Madison: Wisconsin Historical Society.

———. 2003. *Native People of Wisconsin*. Madison: Wisconsin Historical Society.

Loren, Diana DiPaolo. 2008. *In Contact: Bodies and Spaces in the Sixteenth- and Seventeenth-Century Eastern Woodlands*. Lanham, MD: AltaMira.

Love, William DeLoss. n.d. The Grave of Samson Occom. Unpublished manuscript. Kirkland, NY: Hamilton College Archives.

———. 1894. Samson Occom: The Founding of Brothertown by Christian Indians. *Utica Morning Herald*, February 4. Clinton, NY: Hamilton College Archives.

———. 1899. *Samson Occom and the Christian Indians of New England*. Syracuse, NY: Syracuse University Press.

Lucas, Gavin. 2004. *An Archaeology of Colonial Identity: Power and Material Culture in the Dwars Valley, South Africa*. New York: Kluwer Academic/Plenum Publishers.

Ludwig, Allen I. 1966. *Graven Images: New England Stonecarving and its Symbols, 1650–1815*. Middleton, CT: Wesleyan University Press.

Mandell, Daniel R. 2008. *Tribe, Race, History: Native Americans in Southern New England, 1780–1880*. Baltimore: Johns Hopkins University Press.

McBride, Kevin A. 1989. Phase I and II Archaeological Investigations, West Ferry Site (RI-84), Jamestown Elementary School, Jamestown, Rhode Island. Unpublished document.

———. 1990a. The Historical Archaeology of the Mashantucket Pequot. In *The Pequots: The Pequots: The Fall and Rise of an American Indian Nation*, ed. Laurence Hauptman and James Wherry, 96–116. Norman: University of Oklahoma Press.

———. 1990b. Phase I Archaeological Reconnaissance Survey, Northwestern Section, Jamestown Elementary School, West Ferry Site (RI-84), Jamestown, Rhode Island. Unpublished document.

———. 1993. "Ancient and Crazie": Pequot Lifeways during the Historic Period. In *Algonkians of New England: Past and Present*, ed. Peter Benes, 63–75. Boston: Boston University.

McGuire, Randall H. 2003 [1988]. Dialogues with the Dead: Ideology and the Cemetery. In *The Recovery of Meaning: Historical Archaeology in the Eastern United States*, ed.

Mark P. Leone and Parker B. Potter, 435–80. Clinton Corners, NY: Percheron Press.

McMullen, Ann. 1987. Looking for People in Woodsplint Basketry Decoration. In *A Key into the Language of Woodsplint Baskets*, ed. Ann McMullen and Russell G. Handsman, 102–23. Washington, CT: American Indian Archaeological Institute.

Merrell, James H. 1989. *The Indians' New World: Catawbas and Their Neighbors from European Contact through the Era of Removal*. Chapel Hill: University of North Carolina Press.

———. 1999. *Into the American Woods*. New York: Norton.

Miller, Guion. 1904. Brothertown Roll, 1901. Unpublished document (copy of original). Fond du Lac, WI: Brothertown Indian Nation Archives.

Moreland, John. 2001. *Archaeology and Text*. London: Duckworth.

Morgan, Lewis Henry. 1962 [1851]. *League of the Iroquois*. New York: Citadel Press.

Morson, Gary S. 1981. *The Boundaries of Genre: Dostoevsky's Diary of a Writer and the Traditions of Literary Utopia*. Austin: University of Texas Press.

Mosher, Belva. n.d. Diary, 1917–1923. Unpublished document. Fond du Lac, WI: Brothertown Indian Nation Archives.

Mrozowski, Stephen A. 2006. *The Archaeology of Class in Urban America*. Cambridge: Cambridge University Press.

Mrozowski, Stephen A., Holly Herbster, David Brown, and Katherine L. Priddy. 2009. Magunkaquog Materiality, Federal Recognition, and the Search for a Deeper History. *International Journal of Historical Archaeology* 13:430–63.

Murray, Laura J., ed. 1998a. *To Do Good to My Indian Brethren: The Writings of Joseph Johnson, 1751–1776*. Amherst: University of Massachusetts Press.

———. 1998b. The Brotherton Idea. In *To Do Good to My Indian Brethren: The Writings of Joseph Johnson, 1751–1776*, ed. Laura J. Murray, 168–173. Amherst: University of Massachusetts Press.

———. 1998c. Eleazar Wheelock's School. In *To Do Good to My Indian Brethren: The Writings of Joseph Johnson, 1751–1776*, ed. Laura J. Murray, 50–53. Amherst: University of Massachusetts Press.

———. 1998d. The Oneida Mission. In *To Do Good to My Indian Brethren: The Writings of Joseph Johnson, 1751–1776*, ed. Laura J. Murray, 54–58. Amherst: University of Massachusetts Press.

Mytum, Harold. 2002 [2001]. *Recording and Analysing Graveyards*. York: Council for British Archaeology in association with English Heritage.

Nassaney, Michael S. 1989. An Epistemological Enquiry into Some Archaeological and Historical Interpretations of 17th-Century Native American-European Relations. In *Archaeological Approaches to Cultural Identity*, ed. Stephen Shennan, 76–93. London: Unwin Hyman.

New York State. 1788. Treaty of Fort Schuyler. In *The Brothertown Indians Record Book, 1788–1901*. Unpublished manuscript. Madison: Wisconsin Historical Society.

———. 1791. An Act for the Relief of the Indians residing in Brothertown and New

Stockbridge, February 21. In *The Brothertown Indians Record Book, 1788–1901*. Unpublished manuscript. Madison: Wisconsin Historical Society.

———. 1795. An Act Relative to Lands in Brothertown, March 31. In *The Brothertown Indians Record Book, 1788–1901*. Unpublished manuscript. Madison: Wisconsin Historical Society.

———. 1796. An Act for the Relief of the Indians who are Intitled to Lands in Brothertown, March 4. In *The Brothertown Indians Record Book, 1788–1901*. Unpublished manuscript. Madison: Wisconsin Historical Society.

New York State Superintendents of the Brothertown and Stockbridge Indians. 1785. Brotherton Indian Records. Unpublished manuscript. Clinton, NY: Hamilton College Archives.

New York Surveyor General. 1795. Map of Brothertown. Unpublished manuscript. Albany: New York State Archives.

Nicholas, George P., and Thomas D. Andrews. 1997. Indigenous Archaeology in the Postmodern World. In *At a Crossroads: Archaeology and the First Peoples in Canada*, ed. George P. Nicholas and Thomas D. Andrews, 1–18. Burnaby, BC: Simon Fraser University Press.

North, Edward. 1893. Letter to Symian P. Fowler, October 13, 1893. Document on file, Clinton, NY: Hamilton College Archives.

Occom, Samson. 2006a [1752]. Letter to Solomon Williams, November 1, 1752. In *The Collected Writings of Samson Occom, Mohegan*, ed. Joanna Brooks, 64–65. Oxford: Oxford University Press.

———. 2006b [1761]. Journal 4, May 30, 1761–July 7, 1761. In *The Collected Writings of Samson Occom, Mohegan*, ed. Joanna Brooks, 259–62. Oxford: Oxford University Press.

———. 2006c [1761]. Journal 5, September 15, 1761–October 22, 1761. In *The Collected Writings of Samson Occom, Mohegan*, ed. Joanna Brooks, 263–64. Oxford: Oxford University Press.

———. 2006d [1765]. Autobiographical Narrative, First Draft, November 28, 1765. In *The Collected Writings of Samson Occom, Mohegan*, ed. Joanna Brooks, 51–52. Oxford: Oxford University Press.

———. 2006e [1768]. Autobiographical Narrative, Second Draft, September 17, 1768. In *The Collected Writings of Samson Occom, Mohegan*, ed. Joanna Brooks, 52–58. Oxford: Oxford University Press.

———. 2006f [1768]. Letter to Robert Keen, September 27, 1768. In *The Collected Writings of Samson Occom, Mohegan*, ed. Joanna Brooks, 83–84. Oxford: Oxford University Press.

———. 2006g [1771]. Letter to Eleazar Wheelock, July 24, 1771. In *The Collected Writings of Samson Occom, Mohegan*, ed. Joanna Brooks, 98–100. Oxford: Oxford University Press.

———. 2006h [1774]. Letter to Eleazar Wheelock, January 6, 1774. In *The Collected Writings of Samson Occom, Mohegan*, ed. Joanna Brooks, 109–10. Oxford: Oxford University Press.

———. 2006i [1784]. Letter to Solomon Welles, September 26, 1784. In *The Collected Writings of Samson Occom, Mohegan*, ed. Joanna Brooks, 124–26. Oxford: Oxford University Press.

———. 2006j [1785]. Journal 12, October 4, 1785–December 4, 1785. In *The Collected Writings of Samson Occom, Mohegan*, ed. Joanna Brooks, 301–13. Oxford: Oxford University Press.

———. 2006k [1786]. Journal 16, June 26, 1786–December 10, 1786. In *The Collected Writings of Samson Occom, Mohegan*, ed. Joanna Brooks, 336–52. Oxford: Oxford University Press.

———. 2006l [1791]. Sorrow Fills Our Hearts. In *The Collected Writings of Samson Occom, Mohegan*, ed. Joanna Brooks, 132. Oxford: Oxford University Press.

———. 2006m [1791]. Letter to the New Stockbridge Community, December 1791. In *The Collected Writings of Samson Occom, Mohegan*, ed. Joanna Brooks, 135. Oxford: Oxford University Press.

———. 2006n [1792]. Letter to New York Governor George Clinton, 1792. In *The Collected Writings of Samson Occom, Mohegan*, ed. Joanna Brooks, 137–39. Oxford: Oxford University Press.

Office of Federal Acknowledgement. 2011. Office of Federal Acknowledgement Guidelines and Precedent Manual. Electronic document, http://www.bia.gov/WhoWeAre/AS-IA/OFA/OFAGuidelines/index.htm (accessed February 17, 2011).

Oneida Headmen. 2006 [1775]. Oneida Counsel Peace between Two Brothers. In *Wisconsin Indian Literature: Anthology of Native Voices*, ed. Kathleen Tigerman, 217–18. Madison: University of Wisconsin Press.

Orser, Charles E., Jr. 1996. *A Historical Archaeology of the Modern World*. New York: Plenum.

———. 2006. On Finding Focus. *Archaeological Dialogues* 13:202–5.

Ortner, Sherry B. 1984. Theory in Anthropology since the Sixties. *Comparative Studies in Society and History* 26:126–66.

Ottery, Rudi. n.d. The Rudi Ottery Papers. Boston: New England Historic Genealogy Society.

Ottery, Will, and Rudi Ottery. 1989. *A Man Called Sampson, 1580–1989*. Weare, NH: Penobscot Press.

Parker Pearson, Michael. 1982. Mortuary Practices, Society and Ideology: An Ethnoarchaeological Study. In *Symbolic and Structural Archaeology*, ed. Ian Hodder, 99–113. Cambridge: Cambridge University Press.

———. 1999. The Archaeology of Death and Burial. College Station: Texas A&M University Press.

Parmentier, Richard J. 1994. *Signs in Society*. Bloomington: Indiana University Press.

Peirce Edition Project, ed. 1998. *The Essential Peirce: Volume 2 (1893–1913)*. Bloomington: Indiana University Press.

Pickering, Deborah. 1999. Brothertown Trip—June 11–20, 1999. Unpublished document. Fond du Lac, WI: Brothertown Indian Nation Archives.

Potawatomi. 2006 [1836]. Chief Menominee's Petition. In *Wisconsin Indian Literature: Anthology of Native Voices*, ed. Kathleen Tigerman, 166. Madison: University of Wisconsin Press.

Preucel, Robert W. 2006. *Archaeological Semiotics*. Malden, MA: Blackwell.

Preucel, Robert W., and Alexander A. Bauer. 2001. Archaeological Pragmatics. *Norwegian Archaeological Review* 34:85–96.

Preucel, Robert W., and Craig N. Cipolla. 2008. Indigenous and Postcolonial Archaeologies. In *Archaeology and the Postcolonial Critique*, ed. Matthew Liebmann and Uzma Z. Rizvi, 129–40. Lanham, MD: AltaMira.

Preucel, Robert W., and Stephen A. Mrozowski. 2010. The New Pragmatism. In *Contemporary Archaeological in Theory: The New Pragmatism*, ed. Robert W. Preucel and Stephen A. Mrozowski, 1–50. Malden, MA: Wiley-Blackwell.

Quimby, George, and Alexander Spoehr. 1951. Acculturation and Material Culture. *Fieldiana* 36:107–47.

Rainville, Lynn. 1999. Hanover Deathscapes: Mortuary Variability in New Hampshire, 1770–1920. *Ethnohistory* 46:541–97.

Redfield, Robert, Ralph Linton, and Melville J. Herskovits. 1936. Memorandum for the Study of Acculturation. *American Anthropologist* 38:149–52.

Roosens, Eugene. 1994. The Primordial Nature of Origins in Migrant Ethnicity. In *The Anthropology of Ethnicity: Beyond "Ethnic Groups and Boundaries,"* ed. Hans Vermeulen and Cora Govers, 81–104. Amsterdam: Het Spinhuis.

Rorty, Richard. 1991. *Objectivity, Relativism, and Truth: Philosophical Papers*, vol. 1. Cambridge: Cambridge University Press.

Rubertone, Patricia E. 2000. The Historical Archaeology of Native Americans. *Annual Review of Anthropology* 29:425–46.

———. 2001. *Grave Undertakings: An Archaeology of Roger Williams and the Narragansett Indians*. Washington, DC: Smithsonian Institution Press.

———. 2012. Monuments and Sexual Politics in New England Indian Country. In *The Archaeology of Colonialism: Intimate Encounters and Sexual Effects*, ed. Barbara L. Voss and Eleanor Conlin Casella, 232–51. Cambridge: Cambridge University Press.

Sahlins, Marshall. 1985. *Islands of History*. Chicago: University of Chicago Press.

Saitta, Dean J. 2003. Archaeology and the Problems of Men. In *Essential Tensions in Archaeological Method and Theory*, ed. Todd L. VanPool and Christine S. VanPool, 11–16. Salt Lake City: University of Utah Press.

———. 2007. *The Archaeology of Collective Action*. Gainesville: University Press of Florida.

Saussure, Ferdinand de. 2005 [1972]. *Course in General Linguistics*. Chicago: Open Court.

Schneider, Tammy. 2003. "This Once Savage Heart of Mine": Joseph Johnson, Wheelock's "Indians," and the Construction of Christian/Indian Identity, 1764–1776. In *Reinterpreting New England Indians and the Colonial Experience*, ed. Colin G. Calloway and Neal Salisbury, 232–63. Boston: Colonial Society of Massachusetts.

Schoolcraft, Henry R. 1853. Information Respecting the History, Condition, and Prospects of the Indian Tribes of the United States: Collection Prepared under the Direction of the Bureau of Indian Affairs Per Act of Congress of March 3, 1847. Philadelphia: Lippincott, Grambo.

Schuyler, Robert L. 1978 [1977]. The Spoken Word, the Written Word, Observed Behavior and Preserved Behavior. In *Historical Archaeology: A Guide to Substantive and Theoretical Contributions*, ed. Robert L. Schuyler, 269–77. Farmingdale, NY: Baywood.

Sheets, John H., A. H. Henderickson, and O. B. DeLaurier. 1935. Todd County Histories: Reynolds, Thursday May 16, 1935, Compiled by Evelyn Perkins. Fond du Lac, WI: Brothertown Indian Nation Archives.

———. 1936. Todd County Histories: Villard, Thursday May 7, 1936, Compiled by Evelyn Perkins. Fond du Lac, WI: Brothertown Indian Nation Archives.

Shennan, Stephen J., ed. 1989. *Archaeological Approaches to Cultural Identity*. London: Unwin Hyman.

Sider, Gerald. 1994. Identity as History: Ethnohistory, Ethnogenesis and Ethnocide in Southeastern United States. *Identities* 1:109–22.

Silliman, Stephen W. 2001. Agency, Practical Politics and the Archaeology of Culture Contact. *Journal of Social Archaeology* 1:190–209.

———. 2004. *Lost Laborers in Colonial California: Native Americans and the Archaeology of Rancho Petaluma*. Tucson: University of Arizona Press.

———. 2005. Culture Contact or Colonialism? Challenges in the Archaeology of Native North America. *American Antiquity* 70:55–74.

———, ed. 2008. *Collaborating at the Trowel's Edge: Teaching and Learning in Indigenous Archaeology*. Tucson: University of Arizona Press.

———. 2009. Change and Continuity, Practice and Memory: Native American Persistence in Colonial New England. *American Antiquity* 74:211–30.

———. 2010. Indigenous Traces in Colonial Spaces: Archaeologies of Ambiguity, Origin, and Practice. *Journal of Social Archaeology* 10:28–58.

Silliman, Stephen W., and Thomas A. Witt. 2010. The Complexities of Consumption: Eastern Pequot Cultural Economics in 18th-Century Colonial New England. *Historical Archaeology* 44(4):46–68.

Silverman, David J. 2001. The Impact of Servitude on the Society and Culture of Southern New England Indians, 1680–1810. *New England Quarterly* 74:622–66.

———. 2010. *Red Brethren: The Brothertown and Stockbridge Indians and the Problem of Race in Early America*. Ithaca, NY: Cornell University Press.

Silverstein, Michael. 1976. Shifters, Linguistic Categories, and Cultural Descriptions. In *Meaning in Anthropology*, ed. Keith Basso and H. Selby, 11–55. Albuquerque: University of New Mexico Press.

———. 1996. The Secret Life of Texts. In *Natural Histories of Discourse*, ed. Michael Silverstein and Greg Urban, 81–105. Chicago: University of Chicago Press.

Silverstein, Michael, and Greg Urban, eds. 1996. *Natural Histories of Discourse*. Chicago: University of Chicago Press.

Singer, Milton. 1978. For a Semiotic Anthropology. In *Sight, Sound, and Sense*, ed. Thomas A. Sebeok, 202–32. Bloomington: Indiana University Press.

Simmons, William S. 1970. *Cautantowwit's House: An Indian Burial Ground on the Island of Conanicut in Narragansett Bay*. Providence, RI: Brown University Press.

———. 1986. *Spirit of the New England Tribes: Indian History and Folklore*. Hanover, NH: University Press of New England.

Smith, Linda Tuhiwai. 1999. *Decolonizing Methodologies: Research and Indigenous Peoples*. London: Zed Books.

Smoak, Gregory E. 2007. *Ghost Dances and Identity: Prophetic Religion and American Indian Ethnogenesis in the Nineteenth Century*. Berkeley: University of California Press.

Spicer, Edward H. 1961. *Perspectives in American Indian Culture Change*. Chicago: University of Chicago Press.

———. 1962. *Cycles of Conquest: The Impact of Spain, Mexico, and the United States on the Indians of the Southwest*. Tucson: University of Arizona Press.

Stone, Gaynell. 1987. Spatial and Material Aspects of Culture: Ethnicity and Ideology in Long Island Gravestones, 1670–1820. PhD dissertation, State University of New York at Stony Brook, Department of Anthropology.

Strathern, Marilyn. 1988. *The Gender of the Gift: Problems with Women and Problems with Society in Melanesia*. Berkeley: University of California Press.

Sturtevant, William C. 1971. Creek into Seminole. In *North American Indians in Historical Perspective*, ed. Eleanor Burke Leacock and Nancy Oestreich Lurie, 92–128. New York: Random House.

Tantaquidgeon, Gladys, and Jayne G. Fawcett. 1987. Symbolic Motifs on Painted Baskets of the Mohegan-Pequot. In *A Key into the Language of Woodsplint Baskets*, ed. Ann McMullen and Russell G. Handsman, 94–101. Washington, CT: American Indian Archaeological Institute.

Tarlow, Sarah. 1999. *Bereavement and Commemoration: An Archaeology of Mortality*. Malden, MA: Blackwell.

Thomas, David Hurst, ed. 2000. *Skull Wars: Kennewick Man, Archaeology, and the Battle for Native American Identity*. New York: Basic.

Thomas, Nicholas. 1991. *Entangled Objects: Exchange, Material Culture, and Colonialism in the Pacific*. Cambridge, MA: Harvard University Press.

Titus, W. A. 1938. Brothertown: A Wisconsin Story with a New England Background. *Quarterly of the Wisconsin Historical Society* 21:293–300.

Toensing, G. C. 2009. Brothertown Member to Dorgan: 'Structural Violence' underlies federal Indian policies. Indian Country Today Media Network. Electronic Document, http://indiancountrytodaymedianetwork.com/ictarchives/2009/12/26/brothertown-member-to-dorgan-%25e2%2580%2598structural-violence%25e2%2580%2599-underlies-federal-indian-policies-82805 (accessed April 15, 2013).

Trigger, Bruce G. 2006. *A History of Archaeological Thought,* 2nd ed. Cambridge: Cambridge University Press.

United States. 1832a. Wisconsin Land Negotiations between Federal Government, Wisconsin Indians, Stockbridge-Munsee, and Brothertown, August 29, 1832. Unpublished manuscript (copy of original). Fond du Lac, WI: Brothertown Indian Nation Archives.

———. 1832b. Stambaugh Treaty, October 27, 1832. Unpublished manuscript (copy of original). Fond du Lac, WI: Brothertown Indian Nation Archives.

———. 1839. Report on Brothertown Petition for United States Citizenship, 1839. Unpublished manuscript (copy of original). Fond du Lac, WI: Brothertown Indian Nation Archives.

US Department of Interior, Indian Affairs. 2009. Proposed Findings against Acknowledgment of the Brothertown Indian Nation, August 17, 2009. Electronic document, http://www.bia.gov/WhoWeAre/AS-IA/OFA/RecentCases/index.htm (accessed August 10, 2010).

Veit, Richard F., and Mark Nonestied. 2008. *New Jersey Cemeteries and Tombstones: History in the Landscape*. New Brunswick, NJ: Rutgers University Press.

Venables, Robert. 1993. A Chronology of Brothertown History to 1850. In *The History and Archaeology of the Montauk*, vol. 3, 2nd ed., ed. Gaynell Stone, 515–34. Stony Brook, NY: Suffolk County Archaeological Association and Nassau County Archaeological Committee.

Vermeulen, Hans, and Cora Govers. 1994. Introduction. In *The Anthropology of Ethnicity: Beyond "Ethnic Groups and Boundaries*," ed. Hans Vermeulen and Cora Govers, 1–10. Amsterdam: Het Spinhuis.

Voss, Barbara L. 2007. Image, Text, Object: Interpreting Documents and Artifacts as "Labors of Representation." *Historical Archaeology* 41:147–71.

———. 2008a. "Poor People in Silk Shirts": Dress and Ethnogenesis in Spanish-Colonial San Francisco. *Journal of Social Archaeology* 8:404–32.

———. 2008b. Domesticating Imperialism: Sexual Politics and the Archaeology of Empire. *American Anthropologist* 110:191–203.

———. 2008c. *The Archaeology of Ethnogenesis: Race and Sexuality in Colonial San Francisco*. Berkeley: University of California Press.

Wallace, Anthony F. C. 1956. Revitalization Movements. *American Anthropologist* 58:264–81.

Watkins, Joe. 2000. *Indigenous Archaeology: American Indian Values and Scientific Practice*. Lanham, MD: AltaMira.

White, John R. 1974. Historic Contact Sites as Laboratories for the Study of Culture Change. *Conference of Historic Sites Archaeology Papers* 9:153–63.

White, Marian E. 1967. *An Early Historic Niagra Frontier Iroquois Cemetery in Erie County, New York: Archaeology and Physical Anthropology of the Kleis Site*. Rochester: New York State Archaeological Association.

White, Richard. 1991. *The Middle Ground: Indians, Empires, and Republics in the Great Lakes Region, 1650–1815*. Cambridge: Cambridge University Press.

Wilkie, Laurie A. 2006. Documentary Archaeology. In *The Cambridge Companion to Historical Archaeology*, ed. Dan Hicks and Mary C. Beaudry, 13–33. Cambridge: Cambridge University Press.

Williams, Howard. 2006. *Death and Memory in Early Medieval Britain*. Cambridge: Cambridge University Press.

Williams, Roger. 1973 [1643]. *A Key into the Language of America*, ed. John J. Teunissen and Evelyn J. Hinz. Detroit: Wayne State University Press.

Witt, Thomas A. 2007. Negotiating Colonial Markets: The Navigation of 18th-Century Colonial Economies by the Eastern Pequot. MA thesis, University of Massachusetts, Boston, Department of Anthropology.

Wonderley, Anthony. 1997. Montauketts among the Brothertons, in the Land of the Oneidas. Conference paper given in organized session at the New York State History Conference, Saratoga, NY. Clinton, NY: Hamilton College Archives.

———. 1999. Brothertown, New York, 1785–1796. Conference paper given in organized session at the Annual Meeting of the American Society for Ethnohistory, Mashantucket, CT. Clinton, NY: Hamilton College Archives.

Index

About the Author

CRAIG CIPOLLA RECEIVED HIS PHD in anthropology from the University of Pennsylvania in 2010 and is currently a lecturer at the University of Leicester, where he holds a Marie Curie Research Fellowship and directs both the Centre for Historical Archaeology and the Master's Program in Historical Archaeology. His research interests include Native North America, colonialism, historical archaeology and anthropology, collaborative archaeology, and archaeological method and theory. His work has appeared in such publications as *Historical Archaeology*, *Ethnohistory*, *Archaeological Dialogues*, and *Archaeology and the Postcolonial Critique*. Cipolla received research grants for his work at Brothertown from the National Science Foundation, the European Commission, the University of Pennsylvania Museum of Archaeology and Anthropology, and the Penn Center for Native American Studies.